PRAYER, POWER, AND THE PROBLEM OF SUFFERING:
Mark 11:22–25 in the Context of Markan Theology

SOCIETY
OF BIBLICAL
LITERATURE

DISSERTATION SERIES
J. J. M. Roberts, Old Testament Editor
Charles Talbert, New Testament Editor

Number 105

PRAYER, POWER, AND THE PROBLEM OF SUFFERING:
Mark 11:22-25 in the Context of Markan Theology

by
Sharyn Echols Dowd

Sharyn Echols Dowd

PRAYER, POWER, AND THE PROBLEM OF SUFFERING:

Mark 11:22-25 in the Context of Markan Theology

Scholars Press
Atlanta, Georgia

PRAYER, POWER, AND THE PROBLEM OF SUFFERING:
Mark 11:22-25 in the Context of Markan Theology

Sharyn Echols Dowd

Ph.D., 1986
Emory University

Advisor:
Carl R. Holladay

Library of Congress Cataloging-in-Publication Data

Dowd, Sharyn Echols.
  Prayer, power, and the problem of suffering: Mark 11:22–25 in the
context of Markan theology / Sharyn Echols Dowd.
    p.   cm. – (Dissertation series / Society of Biblical
literature ; v. 105)
  Thesis (Ph.D.) – Emory University, 1986.
  Bibliography: p.
  ISBN 1-555-40251-8.   ISBN 1-555-40252-6 (pbk.)
  1. Bible. N.T. Mark XI, 22 – 25 – Criticism, interpretation, etc.
2. Jesus Christ – Teachings. 3. Prayer – Biblical teaching.
4. Power – Biblical teaching. 5. Suffering – Biblical teaching.
I. Title. II. Series: Dissertation series (Society of Biblical Literature): v. 105
BS2585.2.D69 1988
226'.306 – dc 19   88-19898

Contents

PART III: PRAYER AND THEODICY IN MARK

Abbreviations

Abbreviations for classical sources are those of the *Oxford Latin Dictionary* (1982) and Liddell-Scott-Jones, *Greek-English Lexicon* (9th ed., 1968). Except for the additions on the list which follows, all other abbreviations follow the "Instructions for Contributors" published by the Society of Biblical Literature in the 1980 *Member's Handbook*, pages 83–97.

AJP	*American Journal of Philology*
ANRW	*Aufstieg und Niedergang der römischen Welt*
FS	Festschrift
LS	*Louvain Studies*
OCD	*Oxford Classical Dictionary*
PRS	*Perspectives on Religious Studies*
SVF	*Stoicorum veterum fragmenta,* ed. H. von Arnim

Acknowledgments

I am indebted to my dissertation adviser, Professor Carl R. Holladay, for incisive critique and instruction at every stage of the preparation of this study, always given with an eye to strengthening, but not to controlling, the process and the outcome. The other members of my committee, Professors Hendrikus W. Boers, Vernon K. Robbins, Fred B. Craddock and Don E. Saliers, also provided careful reading and criticism, for which I am grateful.

Much of the research and writing of this study has been done at Wake Forest University, where I have taught part-time from 1984–87. During this period my former teacher, Professor Charles H. Talbert of the Department of Religion has been my mentor, critic, and sounding-board with respect to the issues addressed in the study. The other members of the Department of Religion, and especially the chairman, Professor Carlton Mitchell, have provided a supportive environment in which to write and to learn how to teach.

I would also like to express appreciation for the persons who read and commented on portions of the study at various stages in its preparation. They are Professor Elizabeth Struthers Malbon of Virginia Polytechnic Institute and State University, Professor William A. Beardslee of the Center for Process Studies, and Professor Reginald H. Fuller of the Protestant Episcopal Seminary in Virginia. I am indebted to Dr. Theodore J. Weeden of the Asbury First United Methodist Church of Rochester, New York for valuable historical information on the development of Markan studies in this country. For the strengths of the study, I owe much to those who have read and commented on it; the weaknesses that remain are my responsibility.

I received assistance in the translation of a Spanish study from Professor Susan Linker of Wake Forest University and Ms. Judi Dean of Mt. Tabor High School, and in the translation of a Latin primary source from Professor Robert Ulery of Wake Forest. Mrs. Carrie Thomas, assistant reference librarian at Wake Forest, provided efficient assistance with inter-library loans. Ms. Marie Soyars has been an accurate, efficient, and patient typist.

My formation as a Christian, a minister and a scholar during the years of my seminary and graduate training has been greatly influenced by my spiritual director, Dr. Betty W. Talbert, of Trinity Center in Winston-Salem, North Carolina. Her instruction, guidance, support, and prayers are integral to the person I am and to the work I do. Betty, Charles, Caroline, and Richard Talbert have been a faithful support community throughout the past ten years. To them and for them I am especially thankful.

Finally, I would like to express profound appreciation to my parents, Mr. and Mrs. Edward J. Dowd, who have loved me, prayed for me, and given me generous financial assistance through the years. To them, and to all the members of the community of faith who have been channels of God's grace to me, I am grateful.

1
Prayer in Mark:
The Problems and a Proposal

The purpose of this study is the investigation of the theological function of prayer in the Gospel of Mark. As the title suggests, an attempt will be made to show that the function of prayer is closely related to the problem of theodicy, or the problem of the tension between divine power and human suffering. This problem is posed by the text of the gospel itself in the way that the central character, Jesus, is portrayed. There is a sharp contrast between what the Markan Jesus teaches about prayer (11:22-25), and what happens when he puts his own teaching into practice (14:32-42).

The logia collection in 11:22-25 constitutes the gospel's longest explicit teaching about prayer. Here the Markan Jesus promises the unlimited power of God in response to believing prayer. Whatever the community of faith requests in prayer will be done for it (11:24). These promises of powerful assistance in response to requests accompanied by faith are entirely consistent with the way in which the author of Mark portrays the ministry of Jesus in the first part of the gospel. Jesus is empowered by God to render powerful assistance to human need, and the evangelist makes it clear that there can be no question about Jesus' willingness (1:40-41) or ability (9:22-23) to help. Jesus' power is available to those who ask for help. No one who asks fails to receive. The incident of the withering of the fig tree, with which the prayer teaching is connected, is proof that what the Markan Jesus says, happens (11:23).

In the Gethsemane prayer scene, however, Jesus cries out to his Father for deliverance from his impending suffering and death (14:36) and nevertheless dies in agony on a cross. Moreover, before his death, Jesus predicts that the disciples will also be persecuted (13:9) and martyred (10:30). The problem of the failure of Jesus' prayer in Gethsemane is solved for the reader by the evangelist's interpretation of Jesus' death as willed by God. This is made clear in the passion predictions and is implied in the prayer itself. The problem then becomes how the teaching on prayer in 11:22-25 is to be understood in the light of the gospel as a whole. Does Jesus' modeling of prayer in Gethsemane simply cancel his teaching on prayer in chapter 11?[1] How is prayer understood to function in the Markan narrative and in the community for which it was written?

[1] Some scholars think so. See chapter 9.

THE NEGLECT OF 11:22–25 BY MARKAN SCHOLARSHIP

Although the theological function of prayer in Luke-Acts has received considerable attention,[2] the Markan treatment of prayer has been neglected by scholars. In comparison with Luke, Mark has less material about prayer, and the author is therefore thought to have had little interest in prayer.[3] Perhaps as a consequence of the emphasis of the Markan hypothesis on Mark as a source of information about the life of Jesus, studies of prayer that have focused on Mark have done so primarily as a way of getting behind the gospel to the prayer life of the historical Jesus.[4]

It is true that the amount of material on prayer in the Gospel of Mark is not extensive. The Markan Jesus teaches about prayer in 9:29, 11:17, 11:22–25, 12:40, 13:18 and 14:38. In the Gethsemane pericope, 14:32–42, and in 1:35, 6:46 and 15:34 the Markan Jesus models prayer.[5] It should not be overlooked that the scene in Gethsemane, which comes at a pivotal point in the passion narrative,[6] is, after all, a prayer scene. Since the Fourth Gospel

---

[2] Studies of prayer in Luke-Acts include: Wilhelm Ott, *Gebet und Heil* (SANT 12; Munich: Kösel-Verlag, 1965); O. G. Harris, "Prayer in Luke-Acts" (Ph.D. dissertation, Vanderbilt University, 1966); A. A. Trites, "The Prayer Motif in Luke-Acts," *Perspectives on Luke-Acts* (ed. C. H. Talbert; Danville, VA: Baptist Professors of Religion, 1968) 168–86; P. T. O'Brien, "Prayer in Luke-Acts," *TynBul* 24 (1973) 111–27.

[3] O'Brien, "Prayer," 116.

[4] This is the purpose of the study by Malachy Marrion, "Petitionary Prayer in Mark and in the Q Material" (S.T.D. dissertation, Catholic University of America, 1974). Jose Caba (*La oración de petición: Estudio exegético sobre los evangelios sinópticos y los escritos joaneos* [AnBib 62; Rome: Biblical Institute, 1974]) treats isolated logia from the synoptics according to their contents, with the intent of getting back to the teaching of the historical Jesus. Caba devotes three pages to a very generalized sketch of what he takes to be the effect of Markan redaction (323–26). The unpublished dissertation by Armin Dietzel, "Die Gründe der Erhörungsgewissheit nach den Schriften des Neuen Testamentes" (Inaugural dissertation, Johannes Gutenberg Universität, Mainz, 1955), does not investigate the prayer theology of Mark. Dietzel includes Markan references in a discussion of the prayer practice of Jesus and his disciples in the synoptic gospels. His work is valuable primarily as a source of primary references to prayer in Greek and Latin materials. For these he seems to rely mostly on the two Latin discussions of prayer in the classical sources: Carolus Ausfeld, *De Graecorum Precationibus Quaestiones* (Leipzig: Teubner, 1903) and Georg Appel, *De Romanorum Precationibus* (Giessen: Töpelmann, 1909; reprinted New York: Arno Press, 1975).

[5] Jesus blesses food in 6:41, 8:6, and 14:22. See chapter 5 for a discussion of the Markan Jesus as a model for prayer.

[6] H. W. Boers ('Where Christology Is Real," *Int* 26 (1972) 316–17) writes, ". . . Mark 14:41 evidently performs a crucial function in the transition which combines Christ's resolute intention to go up to Jerusalem to die (8:27 - 14:41) with his passiveness in the actual passion narrative." Jesus himself announces the beginning of his suffering by his statement, "The hour has come" (14:41), as Boers points out in "Four Times the Gospel of Mark," (Mimeographed) 6. A similar point is made by W. H. Kelber, "The Hour of the Son of Man and the Temptation of the Disciples (Mark 14:32–42)," *The Passion in Mark* (ed. W. H. Kelber; Philadelphia: Fortress, 1976) 45. About the announcement of Judas' arrival in 14:42, Kelber writes, "Judas 'comes' to set into motion the passion proper."

is evidence that it was quite possible to write a life of Jesus without the prayer in Gethsemane, our evangelist's decision to include the prayer scene is important. It suggests that prayer may have been more important to the author of Mark than scholars have thought, and that it would be worthwhile to examine the logia collection in 11:22-25 to see what view of prayer is advocated there.

When one turns to the commentaries and studies on the Gospel of Mark, one discovers that 11:22-25 has not been regarded as worthy of serious exegesis. In some studies, such as those by Marxsen[7] and Weeden,[8] the prayer logia are not discussed at all. One of the objections raised by scholars who do discuss the logia collection is that it is awkwardly located in Mark 11, where it follows the observation that the fig tree, which failed to provide Jesus with figs on the previous day, has withered. To Peter's observation, "Master, look! The fig tree which you cursed has withered," the Markan Jesus responds, "Have faith in God." The sayings about faith, prayer, and forgiveness follow.

Josef Schmid objects that "the sayings recorded here, which appear to be in answer to Peter's remark (v 21), have not a logical context with the cursing of the fig tree. The latter was not an act of faith, or of prayer."[9] The placement of the sayings after the second half of the fig tree pericope does intrude into what would otherwise have been a neat double intercalation: cursing of the fig tree (11:12-14), temple "cleansing" episode (11:15-19), reaction to the withered tree (11:20-21), reaction to the temple episode (11:27-33).[10] This kind of Markan "carelessness" was overlooked in earlier times when scholars influenced by form criticism regarded the gospel as a scissors-and-paste collage of materials. More recently, scholars have tended to take the evangelist seriously as a writer and theologian, and this kind of organizational anomaly has, accordingly, become more difficult to explain.[11]

The studies of J. R. Donahue and Donald Juel have demonstrated that the author of Mark used the fig tree pericope to signify the destruction of the temple. By using the intercalation technique, the evangelist makes the intercalated stories mutually interpretative. The barren temple will suffer the same fate as the barren fig tree.[12] This makes the location of the prayer logia even more problematic,

[7] Willi Marxsen, *Mark the Evangelist* (trans. J. Boyce, D. Juel, W. Poehlmann, R. A. Harrisville; Nashville/New York: Abingdon, 1969).

[8] T. J. Weeden, *Mark—Traditions in Conflict* (Philadelphia: Fortress, 1971).

[9] Josef Schmid, *The Gospel According to Mark* (RNT; ed. A. Wikenhauser and O. Kuss; trans. K. Condon; Staten Island, NY: Mercier Press, 1968) 211. See also P. J. Achtemeier, *Mark* (Proclamation; Philadelphia: Fortress, 1975) 24.

[10] W. R. Telford (*The Barren Temple and the Withered Tree* [Sheffield: JSOT, 1980] 39-49) believes that the early tradition connected the triumphal entry, the cleansing of the temple and the question of Jesus' authority. On his reading these three parts of the original story have been separated by the insertion of the fig tree episode.

[11] Dissenting from the view that the author of Mark was a competent writer is J. C. Meagher, *Clumsy Construction in Mark's Gospel* (New York: Edwin Mellen, 1979).

[12] J. R. Donahue, *Are You the Christ? The Trial Narrative in the Gospel of Mark*

because their placement after Peter's recognition that the cursed fig tree has withered (11:21) seems to interpret the fig tree pericope as a straightforward example of the kind of power promised to believing prayer. The evangelist has either created *two* interpretations of the fig tree pericope, or, if the prayer logia were already attached to the fig tree pericope in the tradition, the author has allowed one interpretation to stand and created a second one by inserting the temple "cleansing" story between the cursing of the tree and the observation that it has withered. In this case, the author of Mark either failed to notice the conflict in interpretations or saw the two interpretations as complementary.

W. R. Telford does not believe the two interpretations can be reconciled, so he concludes that 11:24-25 comes from the hand of a later readactor and that 11:23 originally referred not to the power of faith but to the destruction of the temple ("this mountain" is the temple mount).[13] Therefore, verses 24 and 25 need not be interpreted as part of the text of Mark. Of course, this position is completely lacking in textual evidence.

The need for a study of Mark 11:22-25 in its context within the gospel is demonstrated by the confusion over whether the present arrangement inhibits or enhances the interpretation of the component parts. Does the chapter make sense in its present form, and if so, what sense does it make?

The usual procedure adopted by commentators on Mark is to deal with the logia collection by paraphrasing it, and then, in some cases, adding a warning that the promises made by the Markan Jesus about the power available to believing prayer are not to be taken seriously. Vincent Taylor writes, ". . . it is not true to say prayers are answered because we believe we have received our request."[14] B. W. Bacon thinks that the passage is "an encouragement to fanaticism. Prayer [is regarded as] a spell which, if properly applied, can override the divinely appointed order of things."[15] Schmid is afraid that such teaching could "give rise to an excessively forward and irreverent form of piety."[16] Ernst Haenchen agrees. Commenting on 11:23, he writes, "Ein Glaube solcher Art is noch nichts Religiöses." The idea that faith is a condition for answered prayer is, according to Haenchen, "sehr gefährlich." He warns, "Von hier geht der Weg zur 'Christian Science,' einer christlich gekleideten Lehre von der Autosuggestion

(SBLDS 10; Missoula: Scholars, 1973) 114 and passim; Donald Juel, *Messiah and Temple. The Trial of Jesus in the Gospel of Mark* (SBLDS 31; Missoula: Scholars, 1977) 127-39 and passim. John Cook ("A Text Linguistic Approach to the Gospel of Mark" [Ph.D. dissertation, Emory University, 1985] 279-83) objects to the identification of the fig tree with Israel. On this issue see chapter 2 of this study.

[13] Telford, *Barren*, 49-59.

[14] Vincent Taylor, *The Gospel According to St. Mark* (London: Macmillan, 1953) 467.

[15] B. W. Bacon, *The Beginnings of Gospel Story* (New Haven: Yale University, 1904) 163.

[16] Schmid, *Mark*, 212.

und Suggestion."[17] C. F. D. Moule is especially offended by the implication that prayer can be used destructively:

> Still more difficult is the use of this destructive miracle as an example of splendid faith, to reinforce the lesson that there is nothing too difficult for prayer to achieve. Perhaps we may guess that the evangelist, or the tradition on which he drew, has here put together bits and pieces of scattered incidents and sayings into a shape which does not correspond either with the mind of Jesus or with the actual facts![18]

Often the exhortation to forgiveness in 11:25 is the only part of the passage in which the commentator can find any real value.[19]

Phillip Carrington deals with the passage by allegorizing. For him, "this mountain" is a symbol for the temple, which is a symbol for the "corrupt clericalism and vested interests" that will "vanish before the faith of the gospel movement."[20] Swete and Schweizer interpret Mark 11:22-25 by 1 Cor 13:2; what is important is not faith that moves mountains, but faith manifested in love.[21]

The Markan prayer teaching has been ignored, written out of the text entirely, contradicted and allegorized. It has not yet been analyzed and interpreted in terms of its function within Mark 11, or within the gospel as a whole.

---

[17] Ernst Haenchen, *Der Weg Jesu* (Berlin: Töpelmann, 1966) 391. It is not entirely clear what the sources for all this scholarly hysteria may be. Haenchen, clearly, objects to Christian Science. One can only speculate about the kinds of abuses that motivate the comments of others.
In 1981, Charles Farah, professor of theology and historical studies at Oral Roberts University in Oklahoma, published an article in which he criticized a "burgeoning heresy" within pentecostal and charismatic circles that Farah called "faith-formula theology" (Charles Farah, "A Critical Analysis: The 'Roots and Fruits' of Faith-Formula Theology," *Pneuma* 3 [1981] 3-21). Exponents of the position that Farah criticizes teach that medical treatment for illness is inconsistent with faith, and that a sick Christian should not admit to being sick, but should, instead, "confess" that she or he is healed (6-7). In other words, proper faith will eliminate all suffering in a person's life (10). The pastoral problems resulting from this teaching have been enormous (18-19). See also Gordon Fee, "The Gospel of Prosperity—An Alien Gospel," *The Pentecostal Evangel,* June 24, 1979, 4-8. On faith as a condition for effective prayer, see chapter 5 of this study.

[18] C. F. D. Moule, *The Gospel According to Mark* (Cambridge: Cambridge University Press, 1965) 91. Moule has a relatively lengthy discussion of the fig tree story, but the two sentences quoted are his entire commentary on 11:22-25.

[19] See, for example, Haenchen, *Weg,* 392.

[20] P. Carrington, *According to Mark* (Cambridge: Cambridge University Press, 1960) 243.

[21] H. B. Swete, *The Gospel According to St. Mark* (Grand Rapids: Eerdmans, 1956) 260; Eduard Schweizer, *The Good News According to Mark* (trans. D. Madvig; Atlanta: John Knox, 1970) 235.

THE MARKAN ATTITUDE TOWARD MIRACLES:
A HISTORY OF THE DEBATE

Because the Markan Jesus promises his disciples in 11:22-25 that they can expect to receive "everything" in response to believing prayer, illustrating this promise with the example of a mountain being uprooted and thrown into the sea, it would seem fair to say that the results promised to prayer exceed the bounds of the ordinary. In other words, the prayer advocated in 11:22-25 is prayer for God to act; the disciples are taught to pray for miracles. This brings us into an aspect of Markan scholarship that has *not* been neglected in recent years. In fact, one of the most frequently discussed issues in the interpretation of the Gospel of Mark has been the question of the evangelist's attitude toward that part of the Jesus tradition that emphasizes the availability of divine power to the Christian community. These materials, which include stories about Jesus' power over demons, over diseases, and over nature, are referred to in this study as miracle stories.[22]

During the last twenty years, Markan scholars, particularly those in the United States, have tended to read the gospel as an attempt to counter or correct the theology of the miracle traditions by subordinating the miracles to the passion. Since the disciples in Mark are promised what can only be regarded as miraculous results in response to believing prayer, and are given power to perform the same mighty works that Jesus performed (3:15, 6:7-13), failing only when they neglect prayer (9:28-29), the question arises as to whether the evangelist, like the commentators surveyed above, may have wanted to correct the theology of the prayer logia. What is the evangelist's attitude toward the teaching about prayer that he received from his tradition and incorporated in his gospel?

This study presupposes that, as Norman Perrin once wrote, traditional materials "will tell us something of the Marcan purpose because he must agree with their emphases to have allowed them to stand."[23] Specifically, with reference to the miracle traditions and to the faith/prayer logia that are similar in their emphasis on the availability of divine power to the community of faith, this study will take the position that the Markan attitude toward the theological assumptions of these traditions is not "No!" but rather, "Yes, but . . ." This study will demonstrate that while the gospel narrative does exercise control over the

---

[22] Miracle stories are found in abundance in the first seven chapters of Mark, and less frequently in the central discipleship section (chapters 8-10). In the Jerusalem prologue to the passion narrative (chapters 11-13), the withering of the fig tree is the only miracle performed by Jesus. In the passion narrative (chapters 14-16) Jesus performs no miracles in the sense that the term miracle story is usually employed. The passion narrative does, however, contain references to Jesus' foreknowledge (14:13-16, 14:18, cf. 11:1-6), portents accompanying the crucifixion (14:33-38) and the resurrection, which is not narrated, but is reported (16:1-8).

[23] N. Perrin, "The Creative Use of the Son of Man Traditions by Mark," *USQR* 23 (1967-68) 358.

way in which these traditions are understood, it nevertheless encourages, rather than discourages, the basic assumptions of the miracle and prayer traditions.

The following history of research into Mark's theological stance with respect to the miracle traditions is presented in an attempt to trace the development of the interpretation of the gospel as anti-miracle polemic and to locate the stance of the present study in the context of a growing dissatisfaction with that view.

Mark as Anti-Miracle Polemic

Since the Markan miracle stories are stories about *Jesus'* miracles, their interpretation is closely tied to the debate about Markan christology, and specifically to the debate over "divine man" christology. In his 1981 article, "The 'Divine Man' as the Key to Mark's Christology—The End of an Era?"[24] and more extensively in his book *The Christology of Mark's Gospel*,[25] Jack Kingsbury describes the rise and fall of the divine man hypothesis as a key to the Markan christological program. One of the most interesting aspects of this survey is the change in the way the miracle tradition with its alleged "divine man" christology was evaluated theologically by the scholars who discussed it. Kingsbury writes:

. . . what is noteworthy about the first period of the divine-man approach to Mark's christology is that the concept of divine man was clearly being used in a positive sense in order to claim that, except for the idea of preexistence, Mark's understanding of Jesus as the Messiah . . . is fundamentally the same as that of Paul. The second period of this approach began in the late 1950s and runs to the present. This period, however, has been marked by a striking change: theologically, the Hellenistic concept of divine man, as it finds expression in the Gospel of Mark, has no longer been adjudged to be a positive factor but a negative one.[26]

Kingsbury describes this shift in the evaluation of divine man christology and of the miracle stories that were connected with it, but he does not attempt to discover the factors that caused the shift. Such an attempt is the purpose of this discussion.

Until the recent development of literary criticism, it had been an unquestioned assumption of New Testament scholarship that the gospels could not be understood apart from their context in the historical development of primitive Christianity. The problem has been the construction of that developmental context from limited sources. An important feature of the constructed context for the understanding of the gospels has been the dynamic that is understood to motivate the development of early Christianity—the catalyst that keeps the process in motion. Since F. C. Baur, the catalyst that has been suggested again and again in New Testament studies is theological conflict. Competition between

---

[24] *Int* 35 (1981) 243-57.
[25] Philadelphia: Fortress, 1983.
[26] Ibid., 28.

theological emphases (christology, eschatology, pneumatology) is thought to explain the diversity within Christian literature of the first 150 years. This is not, of course, the only solution to the problem of development that has been appealed to, but it is an important one, and its durability may be attributed to the fact that the earliest New Testament documents, the letters of Paul, are indeed polemical literature.

Thus, the interpretation of the Pauline corpus and the scenarios of theological conflict that emerge from that interpretation provide the setting in which later New Testament documents, including the gospels, are read and interpreted. This has been especially true of Mark, since it has been thought to be the earliest gospel and therefore the one closest in time to the problems that gave rise to Paul's letters. The following account of the shift in the interpretation of the attitude of the author of Mark toward the traditions about Jesus as miracleworker will demonstrate the extent to which the interpretation of Mark followed a change in the understanding of Paul's attitude toward the miraculous. For a variety of reasons, scholars have generally been unwilling to hold for long to a reading of Mark that diverged significantly from what was thought to be the theology of Paul.

The portrayal of Jesus as a Hellenistic miracle-worker was first noted in modern times by F. C. Baur (*Appolonios von Tyana und Christos,* 1832),[27] and the emphasis on the continuity between Christianity and its Hellenistic environment was the special concern of the *religionsgeschichtliche Schule* in the twentieth century. Reitzenstein, Bousset, and Wetter before World War I, and Windisch and Bieler between the wars, accumulated the evidence from the environment that connected divine power with the working of miracles, and they made a strong case for the Hellenistic divine man as the model for the formation of the miracle traditions about Jesus and for Paul's self-understanding.[28]

In his study of primitive Christian attitudes toward miracle, Anton Fridrichsen (1925) held that for both Paul and Mark, miracle had an apodictic function; the miracles legitimate the message and the messenger.[29] Windisch developed a similar position in *Paulus und Christos* (1934). He thought that Jesus the wonder-worker would have been understood as a divine man by the Hellenistic world, and that Paul's own self-concept as an apostle was shaped in direct imitation of the God-sent bearer of power and wisdom.[30] There was a significant difference, however, between the two positions. Fridrichsen thought

---

[27] Morton Smith, "Prolegomena to a Discussion of Aretalogies, Divine Men, The Gospels and Jesus," *JBL* 90 (1971) 188.

[28] This research is summarized by Gail P. Corrington in "The Divine Man in Hellenistic Popular Religion" (Ph.D. dissertation, Drew University, 1983) 8–25.

[29] *Le probleme du miracle dans Le Christianisme primitif* (Strasbourg: Faculty of Protestant Theology, 1925), ET: *The Problem of Miracle in Primitive Christianity* (trans. R. A. Harrisville and J. S. Hanson; Minneapolis: Augsburg, 1972) 60–61, 67.

[30] Corrington, "Divine Man," 18–22.

that the eschatological emphasis of the New Testament concept of miracle distinguished it sharply from Jewish and pagan thaumaturgy,[31] whereas Windisch and Bieler (*Theios Aner,* 1935-36) emphasized the similarity between the Christian conceptions and those of the Hellenistic environment.[32]

In the history-of-religion studies, as well as in the work of the form critics like Dibelius and Bultmann, the legitimacy of this positive use of miracle by the author of Mark was not called into question. Under the influence of Wrede, these critics argued that the miracle and exorcism stories were invented by the community in order to supply the manifestations of divine power that were lacking in the oldest Jesus traditions. Such stories were needed to support the church's claims. During the period of form criticism, the "messianic secret" was still understood as a restriction on the *knowledge* of Jesus' identity as the bearer of divine power. Not until later did the secrecy motif come to be regarded as a restriction on the *interpretation* of Jesus' identity.

The view that the author of Mark agreed with his miracle tradition and with Paul about the positive value of miracle for understanding christology and discipleship persisted until the early 1960s. Thus, in 1959 T. A. Burkill could write:

> He [the evangelist] shares the apostolic conviction that the Messiahship is made manifest in the wonders which Jesus performs; in St. Mark's estimation, as in that of the church generally, Jesus' miraculous deeds are proof of his divine origin and evidence of his supernatural power. This conception was an essential factor in the exposition of the apostolic gospel of the crucified Messiah.[33]

As late as 1962, P. J. Achtemeier was interpreting the Markan treatment of the miracle tradition as part and parcel of the author's passion theology:

> Thus, the miracle of the stilling of the storm indicates in part what the cross, with the resurrection, indicates supremely: in Jesus, the power of God can and does conquer the powers of darkness arrayed against him.[34]

---

[31] Fridrichsen, *Problem,* 58-59.

[32] Scholars who still insist on the eschatological character of the Markan miracles include D.-A. Koch, *Die Bedeutung der Wundererzählungen für die Christologie des Markusevangeliums* (Berlin/New York: Walter de Gruyter, 1975); Gerd Theissen, *The Miracle Stories of the Early Christian Tradition* (trans. F. McDonagh; ed. J. Riches; Philadelphia: Fortress, 1983); B. Patten, "The Thaumaturgical Element in the Gospel of Mark" (Ph.D. dissertation, Drew University, 1976); and H. C. Kee, *Miracle in the Early Christian World* (New Haven: Yale University Press, 1983) 159-70. Paul Achtemeier denies to Mark the eschatological emphasis which is obvious in the miracle interpretation of Q. See Achtemeier's review of Koch, *JBL* 95 (1976) 666 and of Theissen, *Semeia* 11 (1978) 65.

[33] T. A. Burkill, "The Notion of Miracle with Special Reference to St. Mark's Gospel," *ZNW* 50 (1959) 33.

[34] P. J. Achtemeier, "Person and Deed: Jesus and the Storm-Tossed Sea," *Int* 16 (1962) 176.

Meanwhile, however, Pauline scholarship was moving in a direction that would profoundly alter the interpretation of the Gospel of Mark.

In 1919, Karl Barth published *Der Romerbrief,* inaugurating an interpretation of Paul which revived Luther's emphasis on the centrality of the *theologia crucis* over against any triumphalist *theologia gloriae.* With the rise of neo-orthodoxy and the emphasis on the cross in the interpretation of Paul, the emphases of the history-of-religion school fell increasingly into the background.[35] Interpreters of Paul became embarrassed by the charismatic or pneumatic aspects of his ministry.[36] Scholars like Käsemann, Schmithals, and Wilckens began to argue that not only was Paul's theology of the cross incompatible with Windisch's understanding of Paul as a miracle-worker, but that, in fact, Paul's opponents accuse him of a distinctly un-apostolic lack of spiritual power.[37] In addition, it was held that Paul himself did not claim to be a miracle-worker. 2 Corinthians 12 was reinterpreted paradoxically to mean that Paul identified divine power exclusively with suffering and weakness.[38] Paul was thus recruited into the service of the ongoing Lutheran/Kantian battle against *Schwärmerei.*[39] The study of Paul that was to have the greatest impact on Markan scholarship was Dieter Georgi's 1958 Heidelberg dissertation, "Die Gegner des Paulus im 2. K. 2,14 - 7,4 und 10–13," published as *Die Gegner des Paulus im 2. Korintherbrief* in 1964.[40]

Like Windisch, Georgi made the connection between a christology that saw the manifestation of the divine at work in Jesus through his miracles and a view of apostleship that expected similar phenomena to be displayed in the ministry of the Christian missionary. Unlike Windisch, however, Georgi attributed that view of christology and discipleship not to Paul but to his opponents.[41] Those opponents were, according to Georgi, neither Baur's "Judaizers" nor Bultmann's and Schmithals' "gnostics" but Hellenistic Jewish-Christian missionaries who held to a divine man christology, practiced pneumatic speech, boasted of visionary experiences, and performed "signs and wonders" to legitimate their status as apostles.[42] This kind of triumphalism not only challenged Paul's authority on

---

[35] See "The New Emphasis on Theological Interpretation," in W. G. Kümmel, *The New Testament: The History of the Investigation of Its Problems* (trans. S. M. Gilmour and H. C. Kee; Nashville/New York: Abingdon, 1972) 363–404.

[36] J. Jervell, "Der schwache Charismatiker," *Rechtfertigung: Festschrift für Ernst Käsemann zum 70. Geburtstag* (ed. J. Friedrich, W. Pöhlmann and P. Stuhlmacher; Tübingen: Mohr, 1976) 185–87.

[37] Ibid., 185–86.

[38] Ibid., 187, 197.

[39] E.g., E. Schweizer, "Die Kirche als Leib Christi in den paulinischen Antilegomena," *Neotestamentica* (Zurich/Stuttgart: Zwingli Verlag, 1963) 310–12.

[40] WMANT 11; Neukirchen-Vluyn: Neukirchener, 1964.

[41] Ibid., 234–41.

[42] Ibid., 296ff.

the basis of his alleged weakness, it also effectively denied the theological significance of the cross.[43] Georgi argued that the christology and self-understanding of Paul's opponents was by no means limited to Corinth. He believed that the divine man christology and the view of missions as a competition with pagan and Jewish miracle-workers was widespread in Hellenistic Christianity; and he argued that it is this christology and view of apostleship that is reflected in the miracle traditions behind the synoptic gospels and Acts.[44] According to Georgi, Mark and Luke-Acts preserved this theological tendency of their sources, whereas Matthew reverted to the earlier view of the miracles as eschatological signs of the coming Kingdom of God.[45] It was Georgi's view of the Markan theological position with respect to miracle that was to undergo thorough revision at the hands of Markan scholars.

The identification of the theological views of the author of Mark with those of the opponents of Paul was not to stand for long. Redaction criticism, introduced by Marxsen's study of Mark[46] was methodologically geared to look for ways in which the evangelist *differed* with the sources he received.[47] The tide of scholarly interest was going against a position like Georgi's, which held that the author of Mark had adopted the same stance as that of his tradition, let alone a view that set Mark over against Paul. On the contrary, it was much easier for redaction criticism to imagine the evangelists struggling against theological opponents with heretical views. Paul had been faced with such battles; was it not likely that the gospel writers had been struggling against heretics as well? Since redaction criticism focused on changes made by the evangelists in the interpretation of traditions, those changes must have reflected problems caused by theological opponents against whom the evangelists were then seen as polemicizing. This posture was particularly characteristic of redaction critics in this country.[48]

The idea of theological conflict as the occasion for the writing of Mark began in earnest in 1961 with the publication of two very different articles, one in German and one in English.[49] Johannes Schreiber, developing suggestions of

[43] Ibid., 289.

[44] Ibid., 210–18.

[45] Ibid., 214. In other words, Matthew preserves the tendency of Q.

[46] W. Marxsen, *Der Evangelist Markus* (FRLANT 67; Göttingen: Vandenhoeck & Ruprecht, 1956).

[47] N. Perrin, *What Is Redaction Criticism?* (Philadelphia: Fortress, 1969) 38–39; R. H. Stein, "What is *Redaktionsgeschichte?*" *JBL* 88 (1969) 45–56.

[48] In 1963, for example, C. H. Talbert ("Luke-Acts: A Defense Against Gnosticism" [Ph.D. dissertation, Vanderbilt University, 1963]) read Luke as a polemic against a gnostic christological heresy similar to that opposed by Paul in Colossae and Corinth (according to Schmithals).

[49] T. E. Boomershine ('Mark 16:8 and the Apostolic Commission," *JBL* 100 [1981] 230 n. 17) traces the view of Mark as a reflection of intra-Christian polemic back as far as A. Kuby, "Zur Konzeption des Markus-Evangeliums," *ZNW* 49 (1958) 52–64.

Conzelmann,[50] argued in "Die Christologie des Markusevangeliums" that there are two competing christologies in Mark: the divine man christology of the miracle traditions and the kenosis myth of the gnostic savior.[51] He also thought that the criticism of the disciples in Mark was aimed at the Palestinian Christian community.[52] Meanwhile, Joseph Tyson had come independently to the conclusion that Mark's disciples stood for the Jerusalem church, which, Tyson thought, had no theological use for the cross and had an authoritarian view of church leadership.[53]

The interpretation of Mark as a polemic against theological opponents did not catch on immediately. Eduard Schweizer, for example, continued to read the theological tensions in the gospel as the evangelist's own struggle to make sense of the reality of divine power and of the necessity of suffering.[54] Although he himself found the portrayal of Jesus in the miracle stories somewhat "crass,"[55] in most of his work Schweizer refrained from projecting his own distaste for the miraculous onto the author of Mark.

The distinction of being the first scholar to work out a full-blown reconstruction of the heretical opponents opposed by the author of the Gospel of Mark belongs to T. J. Weeden, whose dissertation, "The Heresy that Necessitated Mark's Gospel," was accepted by the faculty of the Claremont Graduate School in 1964. His reconstruction was fundamentally dependent on Georgi's unpublished dissertation on 2 Corinthians, which had been called to his attention by J. M. Robinson.[56]

---

[50] Sean P. Kealy, *Mark's Gospel: A History of its Interpretation* (New York: Paulist, 1982) 170.

[51] J. Schreiber, "Die Christologie des Markusevangeliums," *ZTK* 58 (1961) 154– 83; see especially 158.

[52] Kealy, *History,* 170.

[53] J. B. Tyson, "The Blindness of the Disciples in Mark," *JBL* 80 (1961) 261-68.

[54] "Anmerken zur Theologie des Markus," *Neotestamentica* (Stuttgart: Zwingli Verlag, 1963) 93-104.

[55] E. Schweizer, "Die theologische Leistung des Markus," *EvT* 24 (1964) 343.

[56] Even before Georgi's dissertation was published in 1964, his reconstruction of the Hellenistic Christian mission and its use of miracle had come to the attention of Helmut Koester at Harvard and James Robinson at Claremont. In their studies of diversity among early Christian communities Koester and Robinson found that Georgi's work provided an important point on the trajectory of the early interpretation and use of miracle traditions. Koester knew about Georgi's research because he had been an important influence on Georgi as Assistant Professor of New Testament at Heidelberg during the period when Georgi was a student there (*Directory of American Scholars* [8th ed.; 4 vols; New York: Bowker, 1982] 4:290. In the "Vorwart" to *Die Gegner,* Georgi writes of Koester, "Er is mit dem werden dieser Arbeit aufs engste verbunden."). In his RGG[3] article of 1959, "Häretiker im Urchristentum," Koester followed Georgi's suggestion that the theology of Paul's opponents in 2 Corinthians was the same as that of the miracle traditions behind Mark and, Koester thought, of the "signs-source" behind John (18-19). Koester's bibliography for this article included only published works; thus, no reference to Georgi

Weeden began with the German presupposition that early Christianity was so preoccupied with eschatology that it had no interest in the past and no interest in narrating the life of Jesus.[57] Since he assumed that not only was "gospel" a literary form without precedent in the ancient world, but also that the writing of a narrative about the past would have run counter to the eschatological focus of early Christianity, Weeden regarded the creation of the gospel form by the author of Mark as an "astonishing phenomenon,"[58] requiring an explanation. The explanation was that the gospel form was created out of the necessity for discrediting a group of heretics who were threatening the Markan community.

A study of Mark 13 convinced Weeden that the messianic impostors of 13:6 and 13:21-23 were the opponents whose activities had prompted the writing of the gospel.[59] These opponents say "*ego eimi*" in the name of Jesus and are "false Christs and false prophets" (13:22). According to Weeden, the false prophets are false because they show "signs and wonders."[60] Thus, the evangelist's opponents are miracle-workers who have pneumatic experiences in which they identify with Christ.

It had been customary up to this point to label enthusiastic spiritualists as "gnostics," and Weeden had read that literature.[61] But two factors in Markan studies militated against hypothesizing gnostic opponents behind the gospel. In the first place, Eduard Schweizer had already demonstrated that *ego eimi* was not a gnostic formula.[62] In the second place, there was no evidence that Mark's opponents held to a docetic christology, which would have been characteristic of gnostics.[63] This is the point at which Georgi's work came to Weeden's rescue. Georgi's Jewish-Christian missionaries with their divine man christology and

---

appeared. This created an embarrassing situation for Koester when James Robinson attributed Georgi's insight to Koester (See Koester, "One Jesus and Four Primitive Gospels," *HTR* 61 (1968) 233 n. 106).

Robinson cited Georgi's *Die Gegner* in the published version of his address to the SBL in 1964 ("Kerygma and History in the New Testament," *The Bible in Modern Scholarship* [ed. J. P. Hyatt; Nashville: Abingdon, 1965] 114-50), but he must have known about Georgi's work much earlier, because in the fall of 1962, as part of a course at Claremont on the Corinthian correspondence, he suggested that T. J. Weeden read the microfilm copy of "Die Gegner" to see whether there was a connection between the divine man heresy in Corinth and the miracle traditions behind Mark (According to a letter to me from T. J. Weeden, December 6, 1984, used with his permission).

[57] T. J. Weeden, "The Heresy That Necessitated Mark's Gospel" (Ph.D. dissertation, Claremont, 1964) 6.

[58] Ibid., 7.

[59] Weeden, letter.

[60] Weeden, "Heresy," 79-82.

[61] Ibid., 71.

[62] Ibid., 74.

[63] Ibid., 88.

self-understanding and their pneumatic experiences had all the needed characteristics for Weeden's hypothetical opponents and none of the liabilities. Weeden
concluded that the author of Mark created the gospel form under pressure to
combat the christology and view of discipleship brought into his community by
divine man interlopers like those in Corinth.[64]

Schreiber and Tyson had already suggested that the author of Mark
deliberately portrays the disciples in a bad light. Weeden found in the gospel a
pattern in which the evangelist portrays the disciples' relation to Jesus as
degenerating from unperceptiveness to misconception to rejection and flight.[65]
The author "is assiduously involved in a vendetta against the disciples. He is
intent on totally discrediting them."[66] By discrediting the disciples in the course
of the narrative, the evangelist also discredits his opponents, whose theological
views are placed on the lips of the disciples, while the correct views are placed
on the lips of Jesus.[67] The author of Mark portrays Jesus as a divine man who
works miracles in the first part of the gospel only to show that this is a false
christology after Jesus' rebuke of Peter's confession in 8:27-33. Peter confesses
to a divine man christology and Jesus repudiates this view.[68] Given this picture
of the Markan intent and technique, one can see why Weeden chose not to
discuss the prayer logia in 11:22-25, since here extravagant promises about power
for disciples are found on the lips of Jesus after the emphasis on suffering in
chapters 8-10.

How did such a radically new reading of Mark come to have so great an
impact on Markan scholarship? The answer is that Weeden's work came to the
attention of the leading American redaction critic of Mark, the late Norman
Perrin. Perrin happened to hear Weeden read a paper based on his dissertation
at the 1966 meeting of the Society of Biblical Literature.[69] Although Robinson
had cited Die Gegner in the published version of his 1964 address to the Society
("Kerygma and History in the New Testament"),[70] and although Helmut Koester
had also begun to cite Georgi's study by 1965,[71] it appears to have been primarily
through Perrin's use of Weeden's work that the thesis of Die Gegner came to the
attention of American Markan scholars. This was important, because even those
scholars who found Weeden's thesis too speculative were influenced by Perrin's
version of it or by Georgi's identification of miracle stories with groups of Christians whose views were opposed by Paul. The miracle tradition, suspect since the

---

[64] Weeden, *Traditions*, 95-98.

[65] Ibid., 26-51.

[66] Ibid., 50.

[67] Ibid., 54-69.

[68] Ibid., 58-66.

[69] Weeden, letter.

[70] As far as I have been able to determine, Robinson does not cite Weeden's dissertation
in his studies of early Christian trajectories.

[71] "GNOMAI DIAPHOROI: The Origin and Nature of Diversification in the History
of Early Christianity," *HTR* 58 (1965) 279-318.

Enlightenment as "unhistorical," had now become the carrier of an infectious heresy as well.

In the late 1960s Perrin was in the process of shifting the focus of his research from the historical Jesus to the christology of the early church.[72] In "The Son of Man in the Synoptic Tradition," Perrin had begun to move toward a consideration of the christology of Mark, having learned from Schreiber and Tyson that christology was to be regarded as "a major purpose in the writing of the Markan gospel."[73] Weeden's work was a catalyst for Perrin[74] in the sense that Weeden, relying on Georgi, provided specific heretical opponents for Mark and set the christology of those opponents in a plausible context within the early Christian mission. Perrin also seems to have picked up from Weeden the idea that Mark constructed his narrative so that "the false Christology is put on the lips of the disciples and the true Christology on the lips of Jesus."[75] Mark's theological program was corrective christology.

Perrin began to cite Weeden's unpublished dissertation immediately in his own research on the Markan use of the Son of Man traditions,[76] and later in his widely read *What Is Redaction Criticism?*[77] Perrin never went as far as Weeden with the corrective christology hypothesis. Whereas Weeden had argued that the author of Mark completely rejected "Son of God" as a title for Jesus,[78] the most

[72] Norman Perrin, *A Modern Pilgrimage in New Testament Christology* (Philadelphia: Fortress, 1974) 7.

[73] N. Perrin, "The Son of Man in the Synoptic Tradition," *BR* 13 (1968) 21.

[74] N. Perrin, "The Christology of Mark: A Study in Methodology," *JR* 51 (1971) 178.

[75] Perrin, "Synoptic Tradition," 21. This was an extension of the idea that the disciples represent Mark's opponents, which goes back at least as far as Tyson.

[76] "Creative Use" (1967-68) 357-65.

[77] *Redaction Criticism* (1969), 54-56.

[78] Weeden, *Traditions,* 58-59. Weeden consistently relies on the notion that the title Son of God designated a *theios anēr* and that the principal identifying characteristic of a *theios anēr* or *huios theou* was the performance of miracles. In *Traditions in Conflict,* he makes this connection between the title Son of God and a divine man christology and refers to Koester's "One Jesus and Four Primitive Gospels" (*HTR* 61 (1968) 203-47 = *Trajectories through Early Christianity* (Philadelphia: Fortress, 1971) 158-204). In his note, Weeden says that Koester argues for the connection between "divine man" and "Son of God" (*Traditions,* 58 n. 9). Koester does not, however, argue for the connection; he merely asserts it (*Trajectories,* 188 n. 103).

Traditions in Conflict and *Trajectories* were published in the same year: 1971. In addition to "One Jesus and Four Primitive Gospels," Weeden's source for the connection between the "divine man" and "Son of God," *Trajectories* included another, previously unpublished, article by Koester, "The Structure and Criteria of Early Christian Beliefs" (*Trajectories,* 205-31). In this article, Koester conceded that, "It is not possible to prove that Son of God was a common designation for the miracle worker in the Hellenistic and Roman world" (217 n. 22, citing A. D. Nock, *Early Gentile Christianity and Its Hellenistic Background* [1964] 45).

that Perrin ever said was that "Son of Man" was used to "interpret" or "reinterpret" and "give content to" the title "Son of God."[79] With Perrin's encouragement, Weeden published the essence of his argument in ZNW in 1968.[80] In the same year Koester, relying on Georgi, expressed the opinion that the author of Mark was criticizing the "inherent tendency of the tradition of the miracle stories" by means of "the creed of Jesus crucified."[81]

In the 1960s Markan redaction critics were still defining redactional activity primarily in terms of alterations that the evangelist had made in the interpretation of received traditions.[82] The whole procedure was dependent on being able to identify the pre-Markan tradition. The confidence with which this task was undertaken remained high for some time, despite the widely divergent results that were achieved. The attempts to isolate the pre-Markan miracle traditions were a case in point. If the evangelist's opponents had been divine man missionaries, it was thought that they might have used written collections of miracle stories (called "aretalogies" by some scholars) to legitimate their status. This, it was thought, was the content of the "letters of recommendation" of which Paul's opponents in Corinth boasted.

L. E. Keck found a "double cluster" of previously collected miracle stories in Mark 3-6.[83] His study was published in 1965, before the studies of Georgi and Weeden had been widely read. Keck used an adaptation of Schreiber's view of the christology of Mark, suggesting that the "Hellenistic" portion of the miracle tradition represented a divine man christology that the evangelist wanted to "check and counterbalance" with his theology of the cross.[84] Keck's contribution to the developing picture of Mark's theological polemic was so timely that its

---

[79] Perrin, "Synoptic Tradition," 21. Eduard Schweizer had said practically the same thing in 1964: ". . . 14,62, wo ähnlich wie 8,27–32 der Christustitel zwar positiv aufgenommen, aber sogleich durch den Menschensohntitel interpretiert wird" ("Leistung," 351).

[80] T. J. Weeden, "The Heresy That Necessitated Mark's Gospel," ZNW 59 (1968) 145–58. Weeden says in his letter that Morton Enslin, when he was editor of JBL, had rejected the article as "speculative thinking."

[81] Koester, "One Jesus," Trajectories, 189. Koester refers to Conzelmann in n. 105 as "the first to call attention to the fact that Mark's tradition was thoroughly 'messianic' and that Mark criticized his tradition by the theory of the 'messianic secret'." The reference is to Conzelmann's "Gegenwart und Zukunft in der synoptischen Tradition," ZTK 54 (1957) 293ff. Hendrikus Boers points out to me that one can see the "criticism"-of-the-"messianic"-tradition theory as early as Dibelius. I think, however, that both Dibelius and Conzelmann think of Mark's "criticism" in terms of the withholding of full knowledge about Jesus' identity until after the resurrection. In the work of Weeden and Koester, however, Mark is seen as denying the theological legitimacy of miracle. This reading reflects the influence of Georgi's reading of Paul.

[82] See, for example, Stein, "Redaktionsgeschichte."

[83] L. E. Keck, "Mark 3,17–12 and Mark's Christology," JBL 84 (1965) 341–58.

[84] Ibid., 357–58.

influence was not blunted by Burkill's point-for-point refutation three years later.[85] The attempt to define the limits and contents of the pre-Markan miracle tradition was carried on by P. J. Achtemeier and H.-W. Kuhn.[86] Their reconstructions of the traditional materials differed from each other's and from Keck's. In fact, Kuhn does not even refer to Keck. Both Achtemeier and Kuhn depend heavily on Georgi's study to provide a *Sitz im Leben* for the pre-Markan collections.[87] Both believe that Mark corrects the christology of his miracle traditions, though neither accepts Weeden's entire thesis.[88]

This reading of Mark as anti-miracle polemic was never unanimously accepted. Siegfried Schulz maintained that the gospel adopted the theological emphasis of the miracle traditions, rather than opposing it. This had been Georgi's position. In 1958, the same year that Georgi's dissertation was completed, Schulz had published an article in which he stated opinions about the theology of Paul's opponents that were very similar to Georgi's, though apparently independent of his work.[89] In 1967, Schulz published *Die Stunde der Botschaft,* in which he asserted that the pre-Markan miracle tradition encouraged participation in the miracles of the divine man Jesus.[90] The gospel perpetuated this *theologia gloriae.*[91] This, however, meant that the author of Mark took a theological position almost identical with the one that Pauline scholarship was attributing to Paul's opponents. As a result, Schulz's reading of Mark was less attractive to many scholars than Weeden's reading.

Weeden's dissertation was published in 1971, as *Mark—Traditions in Conflict.* By this time, Weeden had become identified with the so-called "Chicago school" made up of students and associates of Perrin.[92] Much of the redaction-critical work on Mark in this country has been done by this group of scholars, most of whom were influenced, at least initially, by the emphases of Weeden, as Perrin had been. As a result, a loose consensus emerged in the 1970s

[85] T. A. Burkill, "Mark 3:7–12 and the Alleged Dualism in the Evangelist's Miracle Material," *JBL* 87 (1968) 409–17.

[86] P. J. Achtemeier, "Toward the Isolation of Pre-Markan Miracle Catenae," *JBL* 89 (1970) 265–91 and "The Origin and Function of the Pre-Marcan Miracle Catenae," *JBL* 91 (1972) 198–221. H.-W. Kuhn, *Ältere Sammlungen im Markusevangelium* (SUNT 8; Göttingen: Vandenhoeck & Ruprecht, 1971). W. Schmithals (*Wunder und Glaube* [Neukirchen-Vluyn: Neukirchener, 1970] 7) thinks that 4:35–6:6a was received by the evangelist in its present form and has undergone only minor alterations at his hand.

[87] Achtemeier, "Origin and Function," 210–11; Kuhn, *Sammlungen,* 211–13.

[88] Achtemeier, "Origin and Function," 198, 218, 221; Kuhn, *Sammlungen,* 225.

[89] "Die Decke des Moses," *ZNW* 49 (1958) 1–30.

[90] S. Schulz, *Die Stunde der Botschaft* (Hamburg: Furche, 1967) 77.

[91] Ibid., 54–59, 64–79.

[92] Weeden became so identified with Perrin's group that when a translation of his *ZNW* article appeared in a collection edited by Rudolph Pesch, Pesch referred to "Weedens Lehrer Norman Perrin . . ." (*Das Markus-Evangelium* [Darmstadt: Wissenschaftliche Buchgesellschaft, 1979] 10).

around Weeden's basic themes: the Markan purpose as corrective christology, the disciples as surrogates for Mark's opponents, and Mark's insistence on the superiority of suffering to manifestations of power as the authentic mode of Christian existence. Both Donahue[93] and Kelber[94] initially adopted the corrective christology thesis, although Kelber thought that "Son of Man" was the title preferred by Mark's opponents, which Mark corrected with "Son of God." Kelber also agreed with Weeden and Perrin that the disciples stood for Mark's opponents, although Kelber followed Tyson, Trocmé, Tagawa, and Crossan in maintaining that the opponents were not exponents of a divine man christology, but rather the leaders of the Jerusalem church.[95] Vernon Robbins agreed with Achtemeier that Mark's opponents held to a triumphalist view of the Lord's Supper that was associated with the miracle traditions and that Mark corrected this emphasis with his passion theology.[96]

If the power of a consensus is indicated by the selection of authors for popular or preaching commentaries, then the publication of Achtemeier's *Mark* in the Proclamation series in 1975 and Kelber's *Mark's Story of Jesus* (1979)[97] are significant. When a conservative scholar out of the British tradition can give assent to a non-traditional position, as Ralph Martin affirmed the essential core of Weeden's argument in *Mark: Evangelist and Theologian* (1972), then "consensus" is not too strong a characterization of the influence of that position.[98]

Re-Evaluation of Markan Theology

At the same time that the interpretation of Mark which was derived from Georgi's position on miracle was gaining adherents, there was an undercurrent of resistance, which grew stronger at the end of the 1970s and the beginning of the 1980s. While most scholars were in agreement with the thesis that the author of Mark sought to control the interpretation of the miracle tradition by his use of it, many were unwilling to concede that the gospel was a polemic against opponents. Others doubted that the evangelist was negatively disposed toward

---

[93] *Trial*, 180.

[94] W. H. Kelber, *The Kingdom in Mark* (Philadelphia: Fortress, 1974) 22, 80 and passim.

[95] Ibid., 64.

[96] V. K. Robbins, "Last Meal: Preparation, Betrayal, and Absence (Mark 14:12-25)" *The Passion in Mark* (ed. W. Kelber; Philadelphia: Fortress, 1976) 27, 38-40.

[97] Philadelphia: Fortress, 1979.

[98] "We conclude that Weeden has correctly identified Mark's theological interest in contrasting two rival christologies—one of power, the other of suffering—but his further endeavour to place the disciples and their successors in Mark's church . . . rests on a fragile base." What I regard as significant here is Martin's consent to the thesis that the author of Mark is "a controversialist, opposing a dangerous trend in christological belief and practice in his own church situation . . ." (*Mark: Evangelist and Theologian* [Exeter: Paternoster, 1972] 153). See further, 150-53, 175, 216-17.

the miracle tradition at all. Of course, Georgi and Schulz had thought that the evangelist's theology was in continuity with that of his sources, but they also aligned him with Paul's triumphalist opponents. In 1965, M. E. Glasswell published a study entitled "The Use of Miracles in the Markan Gospel."[99] Glasswell sensed the tension in the gospel between Jesus' miraculous power and his suffering and death, but he did not attribute the tension to a polemic against opponents. He thought that the author of Mark viewed the miracles as illustrations of Jesus' identity but not as proofs, either of christology or of the truth of the gospel proclamation.[100] Karl Kertelge agreed. In his *Die Wunder Jesu im Markusevangelium* (1970), Kertelge argued that although the pre-Markan tradition represented a divine man christology,[101] the evangelist himself viewed the miracles as an anticipation of the full revelation in the cross and resurrection.[102] The ambiguity which the author displays toward the tradition has to do with his desire to resist the tendency to view *dunameis* as *sēmeia,* that is, as self-evident proof of the credentials of the wonder-worker.[103] A thorough analysis of the miracle terminology in Mark led Vernon Robbins to a similar conclusion: the author is opposed to *sēmeia,* but not to *dunameis.*[104] Robbins concluded that "healing tradition and performance of exorcisms are an integral part of Marcan christology and discipleship."[105]

A similar distinction between Jesus' powerful acts and the signs that legitimate a prophet was made by A. B. Kolenkow, who thought that the Markan community included healers who were being opposed by the community's leadership.[106] More recently, M. J. Selvidge Schierling has suggested that the evangelist may have had an interest in "legitimating the role of faith healer within the community."[107]

Some scholars who agreed with Weeden that the Gospel of Mark was a polemic against opponents disagreed with the view that those opponents were miracle-workers. Tagawa argued that the author of Mark did not regard the

[99] M. E. Glasswell, "The Use of Miracles in the Markan Gospel" *Miracles* (ed. C. F. D. Moule; London: Mowbray, 1965) 151–62.

[100] Ibid., 154, 161.

[101] (Munich: Kösel, 1970) 89, 209.

[102] Ibid., 202.

[103] Ibid., 23–29.

[104] V. K. Robbins, "*Dynamis* and *Sēmeia* in Mark," *BR* 18 (1973) 16.

[105] Ibid., 20. Robbins calls attention to the view of Ulrich Luz ('Das Geheimnismotiv und die markinische Christologie," *ZNW* 56 (1965) 28–30) that Mark tried to combine a divine man christology with a theology of the cross without destroying the force of either. On this issue see also M. E. McVann, "Dwelling Among the Tombs: Discourse, Discipleship, and the Gospel of Mark 4:35 - 5:43" (Ph.D. dissertation, Emory University, 1984) 174.

[106] A. B. Kolenkow, "Beyond Miracles, Suffering and Eschatology," *SBL 1973 Seminar Papers* (2 vols.; ed. G. MacRae; Cambridge, MA: SBL, 1973) 2:169–70, 189.

[107] "Woman, Cult and Miracle Recital: Mark 5:24–34" (Ph.D. dissertation, St. Louis University, 1980) 172.

miracles as a lower form of revelation but put them on an equal footing with Jesus' teaching.[108] In *The Kingdom in Mark,* Kelber argued that in his polemic against the Jerusalem church the evangelist had used the miracle tradition as a positive part of his theological program: the Markan Jesus performs these signs of the kingdom among both Jews and Gentiles, thus uniting the disparate elements of the author's own church.[109]

H. C. Kee used a different approach in his work on Mark. His sociological reading of the gospel, *Community of the New Age* (1977), portrayed the evangelist's community as an apocalyptic sect that viewed the miracles of Jesus as the defeat of the evil powers and the sign of the imminent eschatological victory of God.[110] According to Kee, the author of Mark makes it clear that "the prophetic-charismatic ministry" of Jesus is to be reproduced in the ministry of the Markan community.[111]

The 1970s saw increasing attacks on one of the principal features of the interpretation of Mark that was based on Georgi's work: the postulation of written collections of miracle stories prior to Mark, which could have been used by the evangelist's opponents. It was the identification of this miracles collection that Keck, Achtemeier, and Kuhn had taken as their task, unfortunately with divergent results. In fact, Kuhn admitted having some doubt as to whether the cycles he identified behind the Gospel of Mark ever actually existed in the form he described.[112] In his detailed study of the Markan miracles, Ludgar Schenke pointed out that the literary criteria that point to the existence of a written "signs source" behind John are completely lacking in Mark.[113] Even if there had been an oral collection of miracle stories prior to Mark, Schenke argued, there is no justification for the assumption that such a collection had its *Sitz im Leben* in a Jewish-Christian mission like the one described by Georgi. Furthermore, a christology that is closely connected with miracle is not thereby automatically anti-Pauline, according to Schenke.[114]

The work of D.-A. Koch further eroded confidence in the existence of pre-Markan miracle collections. Koch conceded that some individual stories may have been found by the evangelist in written form, but insisted that the evidence is insufficient to establish the collections posited by Keck, Achtemeier and Kuhn.[115] Without denying the tension in the gospel between power and suffering,

---

[108] Kenzo Tagawa, *Miracles et Evangile* (EHPR 62; Paris: Presses Universitaires de France, 1966) 87–92. See also F. J. Matera, "Interpreting Mark — Some recent theories of Redaction Criticism," *LS* 2 (1968) 117–28.

[109] Kelber, *Kingdom,* 63 n. 52.

[110] H. C. Kee, *Community of the New Age* (Philadelphia: Westminster, 1977) 27, 38.

[111] Ibid., 88. See also Kee, *Miracle,* 167.

[112] Kuhn, *Sammlungen,* 203, 209, 214.

[113] Ludgar Schenke, *Die Wundererzählungen des Markusevangeliums* (Stuttgart: Katholisches Bibelwerk, 1974) 386.

[114] Ibid., 386–87.

[115] Koch, *Bedeutung,* 39.

Koch asserted that the evangelist himself restricted the interpretation of the miracle tradition while retaining a positive evaluation of it. According to Koch, both divine power and the reality of the cross were important to the author of the gospel.[116] Koch's doubts about the existence of a pre-Markan miracle collection and his belief that the evangelist placed positive value on the miracle stories were seconded by the French scholars who contributed to *Les Miracles de Jésus selon le Nouveau Testament* (1977).[117] Simon Legasse questions the existence of such fixed collections and suggests that the stories circulated independently.[118] Paul Lamarche attacks the view that the scarcity of miracle stories after Peter's confession indicates that "Mark has set out to disdain miraculous signs and invites his reader to base his faith not on the powers of Jesus but instead on his powerlessness."[119] On the contrary, Lamarche believes that "the power of Jesus and his weakness are inseparable and correlative" in the gospel.[120]

Ernest Best also insists that the miracle traditions have positive value in Mark, pointing out that "even the passion itself is interpreted through miracles: the noonday darkness (15:33), the rent veil (15:38), the empty tomb (16:1-8)."[121] On the misunderstanding of the miracles by the disciples in Mark, Best writes:

> The way of the cross is misunderstood (8:32; 9:30–37; 10:32–45); that does not mean Mark does not have a positive place for it. The miracles are misunderstood (6:52; 8:14–21); that should not mean they are to be rejected. They were a part of the life of the early church (2 Cor. 12:12; Heb. 2:4; Acts *passim*); what is required is their understanding and repetition. Mark does not then simply replace a divine man christology with a passion christology.[122]

---

[116] Ibid., 189. The extent of Georgi's influence on Markan studies in this country is illustrated by the review of Koch's work by Achtemeier (*JBL* 95 (1976) 666–67). Achtemeier takes Koch severely to task for failing to take into account Georgi's thesis on the *Sitz im Leben* of the miracle traditions. The conjecture that was a bold innovation in 1964 when Weeden first made it had become by 1976 so much a part of critical orthodoxy that a Markan scholar's failure to follow suit could be characterized as "impossible to justify" (667).

[117] Ed. Xavier Léon-Dufour; Paris: Editions du Seuil, 1977.

[118] "L'Historien en quête de l'événement," *Miracles de Jésus*, 115–16.

[119] "Les Miracles de Jésus selon Marc," *Miracles de Jésus*, 224.

[120] Ibid.

[121] "The Miracles in Mark," *RevExp* 75 (1978) 543. The references cited by Best are usually eliminated from discussions of the Markan miracles, probably because they are not performed by Jesus. From a form-critical point of view, this is legitimate, but when one comes to evaluate the Markan attitude toward miracle from a theological point of view, Best's observation is appropriate. If the evangelist is opposed to the idea that miracle may be revelatory, why the rending of the veil?

[122] Ibid. Note that Best reads 2 Cor 12:12 as a reference to miracle rather than "paradoxically" as a reference to suffering. See his arguments against Weeden's position in *Following Jesus. Discipleship in the Gospel of Mark* (JSNTSup 4; Sheffield: JSOT, 1981) 237–42.

Taking the position that the evangelist's purpose in writing the gospel was not polemical but pastoral,[123] Best points out that both the miracles *and* the passion are ambiguous. If the cross displays Jesus' vulnerability, the miracles show him as able to come to the help of the community. But if some are attracted to the Markan community by the charismatic activity which goes on there, they must learn the significance of the cross.[124] Thus, for Best, the author of Mark struggles not against "opponents," but against the dynamics resulting from the ambiguities of Christian existence itself. On the one hand, there is the tendency of Christians to "regard Jesus as someone who achieves things for them" and to "water down the cross."[125] On the other hand, Christians may become discouraged as they face persecution and temptation. This discouragement has to be dealt with as well.[126] The Markan community experiences both power and vulnerability and the gospel reflects that paradoxical experience.

Tagawa had emphasized the unity of Jesus' miracles with his teaching in Mark. This feature was stressed again by Koch and by A. M. Ambrozic.[127] It was this Markan focus on the dual nature of Jesus' authority—to teach and to heal and exorcise—that was partly responsible for these scholars' denial that Mark intended to discredit the miracle stories. In 1980, Achtemeier lent further support to this position in his article, " 'He Taught Them Many Things': Reflections on Marcan Christology."[128] In this study Achtemeier is also impressed with the positive function of miracle in Mark. He now thinks that the author wanted to emphasize that the Jesus who is already known by his community as a miracle-worker is also a teacher.[129] In this light, the Markan attitude toward miracle takes on a new shape:

> Yet a glance at the evidence shows clearly that Mark was not so negatively disposed toward the stories of Jesus' miraculous power as has often been implied, if not openly maintained.[130]

While the re-evaluation of Mark's attitude toward the miracle tradition was going on, the other pillars of the consensus on Mark were also beginning to

---

[123] Best, "Miracles," 539. More recently in *Mark: The Gospel as Story* (Edinburgh: T&T Clark, 1983) 51.

[124] Best, "Miracles," 542, 551 and passim.

[125] Ibid., 543.

[126] Ibid., 544.

[127] A. M. Ambrozic, "New Teaching with Power (Mk 1:27)," *Word and Spirit: Essays in Honor of David Michael Stanley, S.J. on his 60th Birthday* (ed. J. Plevnik; Willowdale, ON: Regis College, 1975) 113–49.

[128] *CBQ* 42 (1980) 465–81.

[129] Ibid., 480.

[130] Ibid., 476. But William Countryman, still following Achtemeier's earlier work, argues that the conversation about the two feedings in 8:14–21 devalues miracles. See L. Wm. Countryman, "How Many Baskets Full? Mark 8:14–21 and the Value of Miracles in Mark," *CBQ* 47 (1985) 643–55.

crack. The demise of the divine man hypothesis and the re-evaluation of Mark's attitude toward the disciples have been summarized by others, so a brief sketch will suffice for each.

Jack Kingsbury has documented the erosion of the view that Mark was written to combat a divine man christology.[131] W. von Martitz argued that *theios anēr* was a rare term in ancient Greek literature which was not a fixed expression in the pre-Christian era.[132] David Tiede demonstrated that the conception of what made a hero divine was extremely fluid in Greek thought and did not have to involve the working of miracles.[133] Carl Holladay's study of the term *theios anēr* in Hellenistic Judaism showed that the term had too many varied uses to be limited to the kind of missionary propaganda that Georgi had portrayed in *Die Gegner,* and that, in the places where the term was used, miracle-working did not always play a crucial role.[134] The demise of the divine man hypothesis has been accompanied by the rehabilitation of "Son of God" as a christological title. Eduard Schweizer, Otto Betz, John Donahue, and a number of others now tend to connect the title with a royal messianism that Mark has modified for his own purposes.[135]

Recent critiques of the disciples-as-opponents hypothesis have been discussed by Gregory Waybright in his 1984 dissertation, "Discipleship and Possessions in the Gospel of Mark: A Narrative Study."[136] The list of scholars who deny that Mark's attitude toward the disciples is wholly negative includes Ernest Best, Gunter Schmahl, Norman Peterson, R. C. Tannehill, H.-J. Klauck, Joanna Dewey, Klemens Stock and Elizabeth Struthers Malbon.[137] The new consensus on the disciples that is emerging is that they are portrayed by Mark not merely negatively, but with both positive and negative characteristics. The evangelist's purpose is to influence the readers/hearers of the gospel to be followers of Jesus while remaining alert to the pitfalls into which disciples sometimes stumble. Malbon writes:

---

[131] See notes 24 and 25 above. In Kingsbury's *Christology of Mark's Gospel,* see 33–45.

[132] W. von Martitz, "υἱός," *TDNT* 8 (1972) 334–40.

[133] D. Tiede, *The Charismatic Figure as Miracle Worker* (SBLDS 1; Missoula: Scholars, 1972) 4–13, 98–99, 289, 291.

[134] Carl R. Holladay, *Theios Anēr in Hellenistic Judaism* (SBLDS 40; Missoula: Scholars, 1977) 236–39, 241. Eugene Gallagher (*Divine Man or Magician?* [SBLDS 64; Chico: Scholars, 1982]) attempts to rehabilitate Bieler's theory, but he has so generalized the category of "divine man" as to render it practically useless. See W. R. Schoedel and B. J. Malina, "Miracle or Magic?" *RelSRev* 12 (1986) 31–39.

[135] J. R. Donahue, "Temple, Trial, and Royal Christology (Mark 14:53–65)," *The Passion in Mark* (ed. W. Kelber; Philadelphia: Fortress, 1976) 72–79. Kingsbury, *Christology,* 36–37.

[136] (Ph.D. dissertation, Marquette University, 1984) 16–21.

[137] Ibid. See also Elizabeth Struthers Malbon, "Fallible Followers: Women and Men in the Gospel of Mark," *Semeia* 28 (1983) 29–48 and her "Disciples/Crowds/Whoever: Markan Characters and Readers," *NovT* 28 (1986) 104–30.

The disciples of Jesus are portrayed in the Gospel of Mark with both strong points and weak points in order to serve as realistic and encouraging models for hearers/readers who experience both strength and weakness in their Christian discipleship.[138]

If the gospel of Mark is not an anti-miracle polemic which is designed to discredit a divine man christology held by a Christian group represented in the narrative by the disciples, then what kind of literature is the gospel, and what is its purpose? The following discussion will present an alternative to the now defunct consensus.

MARK AS DIDACTIC BIOGRAPHY

The gospel is presented as a narrative about the life of Jesus. It includes stories about Jesus' activities, about his relationship to his disciples, to others whom he helps or with whom he converses, to his opponents, and about his arrest, trial, death, and resurrection. It is clear, however, as Wrede pointed out in 1901, that the gospel is not a chronicle of historical events.[139] In 1969, K.-G. Reploh argued that the disciples in Mark represent Mark's community, and that the narrative is written to instruct and form the self-understanding of the Markan community.[140] This view of the purpose of Mark as formative literature has been reaffirmed by H. C. Kee, who points to the library at Qumran as evidence that even groups that expected an imminent end to the age preserved documents designed to regulate the life of an ongoing community.[141] Similarly, Ernest Best argues that the purpose of the author of Mark was neither historical nor polemical, but pastoral. Best writes:

> The Gospel was not written in order to expose and defeat those holding heretical views and forming a distinct group threatening Mark's community either from outside or from within it. By implication a second possible purpose has been rejected: the Gospel was not written to provide historical information about Jesus . . . Mark's purpose was pastoral. He wrote to build up his readers in faith.[142]

[138] Malbon, "Disciples," 104.

[139] W. Wrede, *Das Messiasgeheimnis in den Evangelien* (3rd ed.; Göttingen: Vandenhoeck & Ruprecht, 1963).

[140] K.-G. Reploh, *Markus—Lehrer der Gemeinde* (SBM 9: Stuttgart: Katholische Bibelwerk, 1969) 228–31. A similar position has recently been outlined by H.-J. Klauck using a different method: "Die Erzählerische Rolle der Jünger im Markusevangelium," *NovT* 24 (1982) 1–26. Attempts to describe the community from the text of the gospel must proceed with caution, of course. On this problem, see Achtemeier (" 'He Taught Them,' " 466–72) Best (*Mark*, 53–54) and Eugene E. Lemcio ("The Intention of the Evangelist, Mark," *NTS* 32 [1986] 187–206).

[141] Kee, *Miracle*, 166–67.

[142] Best, *Mark*, 51.

If Mark was written "to build up readers in faith," does that mean that the gospel is a sermon?[143] When Mark is compared with the sermons in the New Testament canon (e.g., Hebrews; Acts 2:14-40, 3:12-16, 7:2-53) it is apparent that however much or little narrative material may be included in a sermon, the sermons of the New Testament usually end with direct address in the imperative mood, unlike Mark![144]

According to Vernon Robbins, there was a type of didactic narrative in existence in the Hellenistic period that recounted the lives of disciple-gathering teachers like the Markan Jesus. These narratives existed in circles that "perpetuated their patterns of belief through biographical accounts of people who taught and enacted a particular system of thought and action."[145] The Gospel of Mark is a narrative of this type. It recounts the story of Jesus in order to shape the beliefs and actions of the community which takes its identity from him![146]

---

[143] Best (*Mark*, 141-45) wants to insist that Mark is not biography, but his discussion of genre is vague throughout. For example, he writes: "Mark has similarities with a number of other kinds of writings. It is narrative though the narrative is not put forward as fiction. It is consequently closer to biography. Unlike biography it is concerned to advance an ideological position and move its readers to practice more zealously the faith to which they are committed. In that respect it is more like a sermon" (141).

[144] Even Mark 13 is indirect discourse.

[145] V. Robbins, *Jesus the Teacher* (Philadelphia: Fortress, 1984) 10.

[146] Ibid. On Mark as biography, see also Schuyler Brown (*The Origins of Christianity* [Oxford: Oxford University Press, 1984] 41-44) and Martin Hengel (*Studies in the Gospel of Mark* [Philadelphia: Fortress, 1985] 32-37, 139-40). These scholars are building on the foundation laid by Charles Talbert in *What Is a Gospel?* (Philadelphia: Fortress, 1977).
Talbert classifies Mark as a Type B biography, or one which "aims to dispel a false image of the teacher and to provide a true model to follow" (98-99, 134). I don't find evidence of a false image of Jesus that Mark needs to counteract, except in 3:20-35. Here Mark does make it clear that Jesus' power to exorcise comes from the Holy Spirit and not from Beelzebul, as the scribes allege. This may have been a charge brought against the exorcists in Mark's own community by outsiders; it is, in my judgment, unlikely to have represented an alternative *Christian* interpretation of Jesus. See the discussion of this passage in chapter 7 of this study. The evangelists' technique of "balancing and controlling" the interpretation of problematic material is called "inclusive reinterpretation" by Talbert (122). Inclusive reinterpretation involves combining "different types of material with varying points of view into new wholes with perspectives different from their parts" (119). It is my view that this is an appropriate way to talk about what Mark has done in his gospel, but that it is not necessary to speak of a "false image" of Jesus.
If, as J. R. Donahue ('A Neglected Factor in the Theology of Mark," *JBL* 101 [1982] 587) suggests, Mark's treatment of suffering is not an attempt to deal with opponents but an attempt to deal with the problem of theodicy, then Talbert's observation that Mark has included "different types of material with varying points of view" is accounted for. The miracle traditions preserve the view that God has power to help God's people in their difficulties and the passion tradition and Mark's use of it to extend suffering into the life of discipleship preserve the view that God's people suffer despite their relationship with

During the first and second centuries of the Common Era, Christian communities held in common with pagan philosophical schools and with rabbinic schools the notion that the formation of disciples took place in two essential ways: through instruction and through example![47] During this period, any teacher was subject to scrutiny to determine whether his life was consistent with his teaching, and it was believed that disciples received as much benefit from observing the actions of their teacher as from listening to his instruction![48] Given these expectations about the formation of disciples, it is not surprising to discover that the gospel of Mark portrays Jesus as a disciple-gathering teacher who uses both words and actions to shape the attitudes and behavior of his disciple-companions![49] In other words, "Jesus' proclamation about God is paralleled by his obedience to God."[150] Consequently, we should expect to find issues of importance to the author presented to the audience of the gospel both in the form of teaching and in the form of example. This is in fact what we find in Mark's treatment of prayer![51]

The Markan Jesus teaches about prayer in 11:22-25 and, to a more limited extent, in 9:29, 11:17, 12:40, 13:18, and 14:38. In the Gethsemane pericope, 14:32-42, and in 1:35, 6:46, and 15:34 the Markan Jesus models prayer![52] That the formation of the community is a primary concern of the evangelist is evident from the fact that some of the most significant modeling of prayer in the gospel takes place when Jesus is alone, as far as the story is concerned. In Gethsemane, for example, the praying Jesus is observed only by the narrator and the audience.

This study will regard the Gospel of Mark as a didactic biographical narrative whose purpose is to shape the community that takes its identity from the central figure, "Jesus Christ [the Son of God]" (1:1). Although the formation of the Markan community has many aspects, we will be considering only one, that is, the function of prayer. We will be asking how prayer fits into the theology of Mark as a whole, and that will tell us something about how prayer functions in the life of the community for which this particular biographical narrative is the formative document.

---

the God who has power to help. Mark writes a narrative which controls the interpretation of the miracles and of the cross.

Talbert's most recent analysis of the features of ancient biography and their relevance for gospel genre will appear in an article, "Ancient biography," in the *Anchor Bible Dictionary* (ed. D. N. Freedman; Garden City, NY: Doubleday, forthcoming).

[147] C. H. Talbert, *Literary Patterns, Theological Themes and the Genre of Luke-Acts* (SBLMS 20; Missoula: Scholars, 1974) 90-95.

[148] Talbert, *What Is a Gospel?* 103.

[149] Robbins, *Teacher,* 126-28 and passim.

[150] Lemcio, "Intention," 201.

[151] This feature of Mark's treatment of prayer was pointed out to me by Charles Talbert.

[152] And perhaps also in 7:34, 10:16 and 11:14, which will be discussed as possible oblique references to prayer in the course of the study.

PROPOSAL FOR A STUDY OF THE THEOLOGICAL FUNCTION OF PRAYER IN MARK

Since the document before us is a didactic biographical narrative, probably from the first century of the Common Era, that was written for a Christian community, we will take seriously the concerns of ancient discipleship communities and focus our study on what the subject of this biography (Jesus) teaches about prayer and how he models prayer. We will devote the most space to the longest and apparently most important passages. The longest and most strategically located teaching on prayer is 11:22-25; the longest and most strategically located modeling of prayer is 14:32-42. Since we have already observed that the emphases of the two passages appear to be in theological tension with one another, and since we know that an ancient teacher was expected to display consistency between his teaching and his actions, it is clear that the apparent tension between the two focal passages will have to be given special attention.

Since the form and content of an ancient didactic biography was shaped in such a way as to provide for the formation of the community, when we inquire about the function of the teaching and modeling of prayer in Mark we will be especially interested in the effect that the narrative has on its audience. The term "audience" is used in recognition of the growing conviction among Markan scholars that the gospel was written to be read aloud to a group.[153] The audience of the gospel is the group that the author hopes to form into disciples through the teaching and example of Jesus. These early Christians did not hear the gospel in a vacuum, nor did the author write in a vacuum. "Any religious movement is inextricably caught up in the course of its culture."[154] An investigation of the cultural context of the gospel in the Hellenistic-Roman world of the imperial period will help us to understand what effect the literary devices and allusions in the gospel would have had on its audience and how the audience would have understood the claims made in the Markan prayer teaching and the portrayal of the Markan Jesus as an example to be followed. Those claims and that portrayal contribute to the tasks that sociologists of religion call "world-construction" and "world-maintenance" — the creation and continuation of the "plausibility structures" by means of which individuals are formed into religious communities.[155]

---

[153] Boomershine ("Mark, The Storyteller" [Ph.D. dissertation, Union Theological Seminary, New York, 1974] 332) is among those who think that Mark was written to be read publicly. Scholars have recently begun to refer to Mark's "readers/hearers" in order to take this possibility into account. Finding "readers/hearers" awkward, I have decided to refer to Mark's "audience" in subsequent discussion.

[154] J. M. Robinson, "Introduction: The Dismantling and Reassembling of the Categories of New Testament Scholarship," *Trajectories through Early Christianity* (by J. M. Robinson and H. Koester; Philadelphia: Fortress, 1971) 15.

[155] Peter L. Berger, *The Sacred Canopy* (Garden City, NY: Doubleday, Anchor, 1969) 3-51.

Method

A careful examination of the Markan narrative itself will be the essential core of this study. Since we are interested in the gospel as a document of formation, we will be examining the focal texts in their present form, once we have established the texts by dealing with the significant text-critical questions that may arise. Therefore, this study will not seek to determine to what extent the Markan theology of prayer is derived from the historical Jesus. Nor will the discussion in this study seek to establish which parts of the text are pre-Markan tradition and which are redactional.[156] The method employed here is an approach to redaction criticism that has become known as "composition criticism."

Redaction criticism was fundamentally dependent on the identification of the sources of a gospel. Once the sources had been identified, the redaction critic proceeded by attempting to determine how the evangelist had interpreted the sources by arranging the units of tradition, altering the emphases, and composing summary and transitional sections.[157] As attempts to isolate pre-Markan traditions consistently produced contradictory results, scholars turned more and more in the direction of methods that did not require the precise delineation of sources. As Kelber puts it, "with redaction and composition criticism . . . the hermeneutical focus is shifting from pre-Mkan traditions to the given entity of the Mkan text."[158]

This was a necessary step for discovering the theology of the evangelist. R. H. Stein had recognized in 1969 that redaction criticism could not claim to be able to describe the theology of the evangelists because "*Redaktionsgeschichte* seeks not the total theology of the evangelists but primarily their uniqueness in relation to their sources."[159] For this reason, redaction-critical

---

[156] On the methodological bankruptcy of Markan redaction criticism, see U. Luz, "Markusforschung in der Sackgasse," *TLZ* 105 (1980) 641–55. An illustration of the level of confusion that was already present in the mid-70s is the following footnote from Kelber's *Kingdom,* 22 n. 73. Kelber is citing Kuhn in support of the theory that the struggle in Mark is not between Jews and Christians, but between opposing groups of Christians: "This is also argued by Kuhn, *Sammlungen,* pp. 84–98, on behalf of the pre-Markan tradition. But as so often, what Kuhn claims for the tradition, we would claim for the redaction." When a method degenerates to the level of opposing assertions, it is time to re-examine the method, to say nothing of the positions that have resulted from its use.

[157] Stein, *"Redactionsgeschichte,"* 48–56; Perrin, *Redaction Criticism,* 1–2.

[158] Kelber, "Hour," 42. The term "composition criticism" is a translation of Ernst Haenchen's *Kompositionsgeschichte* (*Weg,* 24). Haenchen preferred this term for the discipline, but Marxsen's *Redaktionsgeschichte* (1956) was too firmly entrenched. Haenchen's terminology has been adopted by those students of Perrin who, as Kelber indicates in the quote noted above, attempt to take seriously the text as it stands. See also Donahue's comments on composition criticism in "Introduction: From Passion Traditions to Passion Narrative," *The Passion in Mark* (ed. W. H. Kelber; Philadelphia: Fortress, 1976) 16–17.

[159] Stein, *"Redactionsgeschichte,"* 53.

studies of the gospels tended to see the evangelists as standing in opposition to their sources. The theology of a gospel writer could then be reconstructed on the basis of only a small percentage of the total material in the gospel —that which could be traced to the hand of the evangelist.

Perrin had recognized that the traditional materials had to be included in any study of Mark's theology, since Mark "must have agreed with their emphases to have allowed them to stand." But he still placed the greatest weight on the ways in which the gospel writer had altered the tradition.[160] Since Perrin, Markan redaction critics have moved increasingly in the direction of examining the text as a whole in order to determine what concerns motivated its composition and what compositional procedures were used by the evangelist.

Composition criticism has not yet achieved the status of a precisely defined discipline within New Testament studies. Perhaps the most successful attempt at definition is found in John Donahue's dissertation, *Are You the Christ?*[161] According to Donahue, composition criticism "concentrates on modes of composition, literary devices, and the discovery of patterns and structures, all of which serve as an index to Mark's thought."[162] Donahue identifies two sets of categories used by composition criticism: "one, taken from an analysis of the gospel itself to discover compositional techniques which the evangelist uses; the other consists in the application of modes of interpretation taken from classical and contemporary literary criticism to the text of Mark."[163]

Donahue's own work is an excellent example of how Markan compositional technique may be discovered by careful analysis of the gospel text itself. If the method can be judged by its results, Donahue's discovery of the Markan "insertion technique" must be considered a significant contribution to the study of the gospel.[164] If one asks how Donahue arrived at this discovery or what method he used, the answer is not explicit. What is clear, however, is that the method depends on a close reading of the Markan narrative as it stands, which takes into account the observations about Markan style that have gained wide acceptance among scholars.[165] Donald Juel's *Messiah and Temple* followed up on Donahue's suggestions, refining, and in some instances correcting, his results.

Besides the discovery of Markan compositional techniques through analysis of the gospel text, Donahue refers to the "application of modes of interpretation taken from classical and contemporary literary criticism."[166] He cites the work of W. A. Beardslee and A. N. Wilder as examples of the application of modern

[160] Perrin, "Creative Use," 358.
[161] Donahue, *Trial*, 41–51.
[162] Ibid., 41.
[163] Ibid., 41–42.
[164] Ibid., 78–84, 241–43.
[165] Ibid., 78–79.
[166] Ibid., 41.

literary criticism to the gospels.[167] This is the direction in which Werner Kelber has moved, as evidenced by his *Mark's Story of Jesus, The Oral and the Written Gospel*[168] and by an article in which he redefines redaction criticism:

> From the standpoint of current American redaction criticism, each gospel represents an intricately designed religious universe, with plot and character development, retrospective and prospective devices, linear and concentric patternings and a continuous line of thematic cross-references and narrative interlockings. The art of interpretation consists in analyzing the complexities of the narrative construction and to comprehend individual parts in connection with the total architecture.[169]

This general shift of emphasis is also reflected in recent studies by Robert Tannehill,[170] Elizabeth Struthers Malbon,[171] and Hendrikus Boers.[172] David Rhoads and Donald Michie have carried the literary approach to the extent of reading the gospel as though it were a modern fictional narrative.[173] This latter approach, while fascinating, leaves itself open to the charge of anachronism. What is to prevent literary criticism of the type engaged in by Rhoads and Michie from losing its moorings in history? Mark is, after all, not a modern novel.

Some control on composition criticism is provided by the use of the categories of ancient Greek rhetoric rather than those of modern literary criticism. Although this kind of analysis has been applied primarily to the epistolary literature of the New Testament,[174] scholars are now working on the application of the categories to narrative texts. This is the approach of Standaert in *L'Evangile selon Mark: composition et genre litteraire*,[175] but Standaert's focus on the conventions of Greek drama results in a disregard for the biographical aspects of Mark's narrative. These aspects are better appreciated by Vernon Robbins' recent study, *Jesus the Teacher.* Robbins combines an awareness of techniques of narrative rhetoric in Greco-Roman literature with attention to social, cultural and religious conventions characteristic of Mediterranean antiquity.[176] These concerns provide historical anchors for composition criticism, but

---

[167] W. A. Beardslee, *Literary Criticism of the New Testament* (Philadelphia: Fortress, 1970); A. N. Wilder, *The Language of the Gospel* (New York: Harper and Row, 1964).

[168] Philadelphia: Fortress, 1983.

[169] "Redaction Criticism: On the Nature and Exposition of the Gospels," *PRS* 6 (1979) 14.

[170] "The Disciples in Mark: The Function of a Narrative Role," *JR* 57 (1977) 386–405; "The Gospel of Mark as Narrative Christology," *Semeia* 16 (1980) 57–95.

[171] "Fallible Followers," (1983); *Narrative Space and Mythic Meaning in Mark* (New York: Harper and Row, 1986).

[172] "Four Times Mark."

[173] D. Rhoads and D. Michie, *Mark as Story* (Philadelphia: Fortress, 1982). See also D. Rhoads, "Narrative Criticism and the Gospel of Mark," *JAAR* 50 (1982) 411–34.

[174] See the bibliography in George A. Kennedy, *New Testament Interpretation Through Rhetorical Criticism* (Chapel Hill: UNC Press, 1984).

[175] Nijmegen, 1978. Discussed by Best (*Mark,* 101–4) and by Hengel (*Studies,* 34–37).

[176] Robbins, *Jesus,* 6, 29 and passim.

this type of rhetorical criticism of gospel narrative is still in its infancy.
Thomas Boomershine has applied the method of rhetorical criticism developed by Muilenburg for use on Old Testament texts to the passion narrative of Mark.[177] This is appropriate because, while the gospel partakes of the form of didactic biography, as observed above, it is also influenced by the narrative texts of the Old Testament.[178] A study of Mark's compositional technique will necessarily combine insights gained through the analysis both of Greco-Roman biographical narrative and of Old Testament narrative. While there is a sense in which, as George Kennedy points out, "rhetoric is a universal phenomenon which is conditioned by basic workings of the human mind and heart and by the nature of all human society,"[179] the study of an ancient text such as a gospel must be careful to avoid anachronism—attributing to the evangelist techniques that were in fact developed much later. Boomershine gives as an example the device of the unreliable narrator, a narrative technique that came into existence only in the sixteenth century and cannot therefore be read into a gospel text.[180]

This study does not intend to break new ground methodologically. It is, in a sense, a test of composition criticism. In assuming that Mark includes in his narrative only material that has some positive value for him in the formation of his community, this study parts company with the redaction-critical studies of Mark that have read the gospel as a critique of received traditions. It locates itself among those studies of Mark that look for Markan compositional techniques in the gospel text as it stands and seek to determine how the evangelist has shaped the narrative and how the narrative seeks to shape the thought and action of the audience by teaching and example. The study of Mark is in a period of methodological transition. This study, like others, will be judged on the basis of its results.[181]

Arrangement

This study has three major parts. The first part, "The Prayer Logia in Mark 11," has two chapters. Chapter 2, "The Barren Temple and the New House of Prayer," deals with the problem of the arrangement of Mark 11, that is, whether the prayer logia collection really belongs in its present location, and if so, why the evangelist would have located it where he did. We will see that the relationship between temples and the efficacy of prayer in antiquity made it necessary for the author of Mark to reaffirm the importance and efficacy of prayer to

[177] Boomershine, "Storyteller."
[178] Robbins, *Jesus*, 55–60, 128–36; Best, *Mark*, 127.
[179] Kennedy, *Rhetorical Criticism*, 10.
[180] Boomershine, "Storyteller," 4 n. 7. See also 26 n. 35.
[181] While I am not persuaded by the objections raised to this approach by Lemcio ("Intention," 188, 195–97, 201–2), I hope to demonstrate that my view of the evangelist as a theologian is neither "too generous" nor "uncritical" (202).

compensate for his strong anti-temple stance in chapter 11 and in the gospel as a whole. In chapter 3 of this study, the surface structure of the logia collection will be analyzed and the problems of text and translation discussed in preparation for an examination of the theology of this teaching on prayer. The theological significance of the Markan prayer teaching is the subject of the second major part of this study. Chapter 4, "Prayer to the God Who Moves Mountains," focuses on the view of the God-world relationship that lies behind the logia collection. In the Stählin festschrift, *Verborum Veritas,* W. C. van Unnik has an article in which he addresses a simple question: Why, in the prayer scene in Gethsemane, does the Markan Jesus say to God, "Everything is possible for you"?[182] The answer to that question contributes to a discussion of the debate over divine omnipotence in the Hellenistic-Roman world and the significance of that debate for the understanding of Mark 11:23-24.

Chapter 5, "Prayer, Faith, and Power," deals with the subject of how faith is understood in the Markan prayer teaching and in the miracle stories. An important theological issue in the logia collection is the sense in which faith is to be understood as a condition for answered prayers (that is, for miracles). Chapter 6, "Prayer and Forgiveness," explores the sense in which forgiveness is a condition for effective prayer in Mark.

The third and final section of the study is an attempt to understand the tension in the gospel between the promise in Mark 11 of God's powerful response to believing prayer and the suffering that is also a part of the commission of the Markan Jesus and of his followers. In chapter 7, "The Will of God in Mark," the concept "will of God" is examined and found to be broader than the interpretation usually given to it by Markan scholars. For the author of Mark, both Jesus' miracles and his suffering were the will of God, and the evangelist uses this category in the formation of his community in ways that have analogies in the Hellenistic-Roman context.

Chapter 8, "Gethsemane and the Problem of Theodicy," presents a narrative analysis of the composition of the Gethsemane prayer scene as the place in the Markan narrative where the theme of the accessibility of divine power, represented by the miracle traditions, the prayer logia, and the previous modeling of prayer by Jesus in the gospel, runs head-on into the theme of the divine willing of Jesus' suffering and death, represented by the passion predictions. J. R. Donahue has argued that the Markan treatment of suffering does not "canonize suffering in itself as an absolute good or as the unique form of Christian discipleship," but rather deals with suffering as a part of the problem of theodicy: "the cross becomes the stumbling block because it cannot be reconciled with the way one thinks of God."[183] Thus, an important function of the Gethsemane

182 W. C. van Unnik, " 'Alles ist dir Möglich' (Mk 14,36)," *Verborum Veritas* (FS G. Stählin; ed. O. Böcher and K. Haacker; Wuppertal; Theologischer Verlag Rolf Brockhaus, 1970) 27.

183 Donahue, "Neglected Factor," 587.

pericope in the Markan narrative is that it serves as a focal point for the problem of theodicy in the gospel. Here the evangelist reconciles the theme of divine power with the necessity of suffering. The reconciliation of these two competing emphases takes place in a prayer scene. Prayer, which previously in the narrative had been associated with the accessibility of power, now becomes the activity in which suffering is faced and accepted. A careful study of this pericope reveals, however, that the Markan Jesus does not choose suffering instead of powerful rescue. Indeed, he asks to be spared the cross, appealing to God's omnipotence: "Everything is possible for you!" (14:36). What the Markan Jesus finally chooses in prayer is not power *or* suffering, but the will of God. Jesus is the one character in the gospel who does the will of God when it involves participating in the divine power and also when it involves suffering and death![184] His followers in the Markan community are to be formed by his teaching and example. What makes both power and suffering redemptive is their character as "will of God."

The final chapter of the study summarizes the findings and draws conclusions about the function of prayer in the gospel. The author of the Gospel of Mark does not solve the problem of theodicy with a theological formula, but with a narrative that shapes the praying of the community of faith. The Markan community experiences healing and exorcism as a part of its life. It experiences the divine power as accessible. At the same time, it is not immune to persecution (13:9) and martyrdom (10:39). Prayer functions in the gospel to remind the community that the power they experience comes from God and is accessible only through prayer (9:29) and that in losing their lives for Jesus' sake and for the sake of the gospel they are the faithful who "do the will of God." The community is influenced to pray, expecting power and accepting suffering.

[184] Ibid.

PART I

THE PRAYER LOGIA IN MARK 11

2

The Barren Temple
and the New House of Prayer

The instruction about faith, prayer, and forgiveness in Mark 11:22-25 is found in the section of the gospel which introduces the passion narrative. This section, consisting of chapters 11-13, is a literary unit framed by references to the Mount of Olives. At the beginning of this section, Jesus leaves the Mount of Olives and enters Jerusalem and the temple (11:1-11). At the end of the section, Jesus leaves the temple (13:1), predicts its destruction (13:2), returns to the Mount of Olives (13:3) and delivers a series of apocalyptic warnings while seated "opposite the temple" (13:3). The material within these bracketing references is unified by a focus on the temple; Jesus drives out the merchants, teaches the people and the disciples, and argues with his opponents in the temple.[1]

The prayer teaching follows immediately after the observation that the fig tree has withered (11:20-21). This would seem to indicate that the prayer of the community will have powerful effects analogous to the effect that Jesus' word has on the barren fig tree. In other words, the evangelist interprets the withering of the tree as an example of miraculous power. However, since the sixth century students of the gospel have understood the withering of the fig tree as a sign of the destruction that is about to overtake the temple establishment, and Jesus' disruptive actions as a prophetic condemnation of the temple. In this chapter we will examine the structure of Mark 11 and ask whether these two interpretations of the fig tree pericope can be reconciled, or whether one of them must be discarded. Why should the prayer logia be placed in their present position in chapter 11? Should they be there at all?

---

[1] Telford, *Barren*, 39. In support of the redactional unity of 11-13 Telford cites Trocmé, Perrin, and Barrett (*Barren*, 60 n. 2).

Much of the material in this chapter, as well as portions of chapters 3-6, was originally part of an unpublished paper, "Mark's Teaching on Prayer: The Influence of the Temple on the Structure of Mark 11," which I presented in Professor William A. Beardslee's graduate seminar on the Gospel of Mark in the spring quarter of 1982 at Emory University. Stephen Hre Kio, a member of that seminar, relied heavily on my paper in his article, "A Prayer Framework in Mark 11," *The Bible Translator* 37 (1986) 323-28. Unfortunately, acknowledgment of my work was accidentally omitted (see *TBT* 39 [1988] 148).

THE PROBLEM POSED BY THE STRUCTURE OF MARK 11

The problem of interpretation arises from the way in which the contents of Mark 11 are arranged:

11:1–10	Triumphal entry
11:11a	Visit to temple
11:11b	Return to Bethany
11:12–14	Cursing of fig tree
11:15a	Entry into Jerusalem
11:15b–18	Temple "cleansing" episode
11:19	Return to Bethany
11:20–21	Observation that the fig tree is withered
11:22–25	Prayer teaching
11:27a	Entry into Jerusalem
11:27b–33	Question about Jesus' authority

This arrangement is a result of the Markan compositional technique of intercalation; the evangelist often inserts one narrative into another.[2] In fact, chapter 11 contains a double intercalation, since the question about Jesus' authority should logically follow the temple cleansing. The fig tree narrative and the temple episode with the controversy it evoked have been interwoven: fig tree is cursed, temple episode, fig tree is withered, reaction to temple episode.[3] The Markan intercalations were regarded by von Dobschütz as a device to increase suspense in the narrative or to create the illusion of passing time.[4]

More recently, however, scholars following Nineham's lead have sought theological motivations behind this compositional technique.[5] Donahue's analysis of the intercalations demonstrated that the evangelist employed the technique to focus attention on two of his major theological concerns: the suffering and death of Jesus and the relationship between suffering and discipleship.[6] Many Markan scholars now regard the intercalations as attributable to the evangelist, and they tend to see the intercalated narratives as mutually interpretive.[7]

---

[2] The first discussion of Markan intercalation is usually attributed to E. von Dobschütz, "Zur Erzählungskunst des Markus," *ZNW* 27 (1928) 193–98. See the literature in Telford, *Barren*, 35 n. 102, and Donahue, *Trial*, 42, 58–63.

[3] The case for Markan literary activity is argued carefully by Telford (*Barren*, 39–49), who believes that the early tradition connected the triumphal entry, the cleansing of the temple, and the *Vollmachtsfrage*. On his reading these three parts of the original story have been separated by the insertion of the fig tree episode.

[4] von Dobschütz, "Erzählungskunst," 193–98.

[5] D. E. Nineham, *The Gospel of Saint Mark* (Baltimore: Penguin Books, 1963) 112.

[6] Donahue, *Trial*, 60–62.

[7] Telford, *Barren*, 48, and the literature cited on 63 n. 49.

This view of Markan narrative technique extends to all of the "sandwiched' stories an interpretation that had been applied to the fig tree/temple intercalation from the beginning. The earliest commentator on Mark, Victor of Antioch (6th century), asserted that Jesus "used the fig tree to set forth the judgment that was about to fall on Jerusalem."[8] When the Markan version of the "cleansing" episode is compared with those of the other evangelists, it is clear that the author of Mark does not portray Jesus as acting to eliminate abuses or to reform temple worship. Rather, the Markan version is narrated in such a way that Jesus is understood as putting an end to temple worship altogether.[9]

The justification given by the Markan Jesus for his action is that he rejects the temple because of its failure to be "a house of prayer for all nations." The temple is rejected for its failure to fulfill its mission. It is worth noting that from the evangelist's point of view, the temple cult was cancelled before the temple was destroyed by the Romans. We will return to this point later.

It is also important to make a distinction between the temple and Israel. By intercalating the fig tree and temple narrative, the author of Mark identifies the fate of the temple with the fate of the tree. The symbolic association of trees with temples is not unique to Mark, but is a religious universal, found not only in ancient Israelite religion and later in Judaism, but in numerous other ancient religious traditions.[10] However, to equate the fig tree with Israel, as some interpreters do, is probably to read more into the text than is there.[11] To observe that the evangelist rejects the Jerusalem temple is not to claim that he rejects Israel,[12] but it does seem clear that the fate of the fig tree foreshadows the fate of the temple in Mark 11.

But this view of the interpretation of the fig tree/temple narrative appears to be weakened by the presence of the prayer teaching in 11:22–25. These logia appear to interpret the fig tree incident as an example of the power of believing

[8] Quoted by C. E. B. Cranfield, *The Gospel According to Saint Mark* (Cambridge: Cambridge University Press, 1959) 356.

[9] Donahue, *Trial,* 114; Juel, *Messiah,* 127–39; Gerhard Münderlein, "Die Verfluchung des Feigenbaumes," *NTS* 10 (1963–64) 89–104; Schweizer, *Mark,* 233; Kelber, *Kingdom,* 100–102.

[10] Mircea Eliade, *Patterns in Comparative Religion* (Cleveland/New York: World, Meridian Books, 1963) 283–300, 367–87; E. A. S. Butterworth, *The Tree at the Navel of the Earth* (Berlin: Walter de Gruyter, 1970) 18–52; Samuel Terrien, "The Omphalos Myth and Hebrew Religion," *VT* 20 (1970) 315–38; E. O. James, *The Tree of Life* (Leiden: Brill, 1966) 143–44.

[11] The objections to the fig tree = Israel interpretation are discussed by Cook, "Text Linguistic Approach," 279–83. See also on this issue Telford, *Barren,* 128–204; Rudolf Pesch, *Das Markusevangelium* (2 vols.; HTKNT 2; Freiburg: Herder, 1976–77) 2:193–99; T. A. Burkill, "Anti-Semitism in St. Mark's Gospel," *NovT* 3 (1959) 34–53.

[12] To reject the Jerusalem temple is not to be guilty of anti-Semitism. The two groups that were the most critical of the temple at Jerusalem were the Samaritans and the Qumran community. It hardly seems appropriate to label either of these groups "anti-Semitic."

prayer that is promised to the disciples.[13] If the evangelist assembled and arranged the materials in chapter 11, then it would seem that he has deliberately created two interpretations of the fig tree pericope. Even if he found the prayer logia already attached to the fig tree story,[14] he has allowed that connection to stand while creating another interpretation by intercalating the fig tree story and appended sayings with the temple episode and its aftermath. At this point the interpreter of Mark has two options. She can assume that the text makes sense as it stands and attempt to reconcile the two Markan interpretations of the fig tree story, or she can conclude that one of the interpretations is non-Markan and therefore due to later interpolation. Telford chooses the latter option.

W. R. TELFORD: MARK 11:24-25 AS INTERPOLATION

That the author of Mark could have allowed both interpretations of the fig tree story to stand in the text is unthinkable to Telford, who finds himself "pressed *ipso facto* towards the view that the sequel to the story of the fig tree has been to some extent subject to a developing hermeneutical process conducted subsequently upon the Markan text."[15] There is, in fact, evidence that at least one such addition has been made to the text: Mark 11:26.

Verse 26 ("But if you do not forgive, neither will your Father who is in heaven forgive your trespasses.") appears in a number of witnesses,[16] but is absent from early representatives of all text-types.[17] Although such an omission could theoretically be explained as homoeoteleuton,[18] the existence of early independent witnesses that lack the verse and its similarity to Matt 6:15 make it very likely that 11:26 is a secondary addition designed to make 11:25-26 conform to Matt 6:14-15.[19]

Telford also wants to eliminate verses 25 and 24 from the text as scribal glosses, although not a single extant manuscript omits either verse. About verse 25, Telford observes (1) that it is similar in content to Matt 6:14,[20] (2) that it contains non-Markan language and grammar,[21] and (3) that it is missing in the Matthean parallel (21:18-22), suggesting that it was missing from the text of

---

[13] Telford, *Barren*, 49; Schweizer, *Mark*, 235-36; Pesch, *Markusevangelium*, 2:193; Bacon, *Beginnings*, 163.

[14] This is the position of Best and Schweizer. See n. 26 below.

[15] Telford, *Barren*, 50.

[16] A (C,D) Θ (f[1.13]) M lat syp.h. bopt and Cyprian.

[17] Bruce Metzger, *A Textual Commentary on the Greek New Testament* (Stuttgart: United Bible Societies, 1971) 110.

[18] Telford, *Barren*, 64 n. 55.

[19] Metzger, *Commentary*, 110. The UBS committee rated the omission of verse 26 "A" or "virtually certain" to be original. Some witnesses add after verse 26 another verse that is identical to Matt 7:7-8 except that the variant in Mark is introduced with the phrase λέγω δὲ ὑμῖν before αἰτεῖτε. See Telford, *Barren*, 50, 64 n. 56.

[20] Telford, *Barren*, 51.

[21] Ibid., 51-54.

Mark used by the author of Matthew.[22] Telford does not make his case, however, as none of his arguments is sufficiently compelling.

In the first place, the clearly secondary verse (11:26) is much closer in wording to Matt 6:15, upon which it is based, than is Mark 11:25 to Matt 6:14.[23] Recognizing that Mark 11:25 contains several elements that are missing in Matt 6:14, such as "when you stand praying," and "if you have anything against anyone." Telford resorts to the suggestion that Mark 11:25 is a "hybrid citation" based on a number of Matthean prayer texts.[24] This is no more likely than the hypothesis of M. D. Goulder that the author of Matthew composed the Lord's Prayer from elements extracted from Mark 11:25, 9:1, and 14:36, 38 and elsewhere.[25] In both cases, the most reasonable hypothesis is that both Mark and Matthew drew upon previously existing prayer teaching in the oral tradition.

In the second place, no one would be surprised to learn that there are "non-Markan" elements in Mark 11:25 since no one supposes that it is a Markan composition. Rather, most scholars hold that the evangelist assembled the collection 11:23–25 from traditional sayings that originally circulated independently.[26] It is completely unremarkable, therefore, that 11:25 should contain non-Markan features such as the indicative after ὅταν and στήκειν rather than ἵστημι, since a brief saying would have been quoted as received rather than re-worked by the

---

[22] Ibid., 54.

[23] Krister Stendahl, "Prayer and Forgiveness," *SEÅ* 22–23 (1957–58) 76 n. 8.

[24] Telford, *Barren*, 53.

[25] M. D. Goulder, "The Composition of the Lord's Prayer," *JTS* 14 (1963) 32–45. See Telford, *Barren*, 55 and 66 n. 84.

[26] Telford (*Barren*, 15) lists Bacon, Bultmann, Montefiore, Klostermann, Hatch, Lohmeyer, Blunt, Rawlinson, Knox, Johnson, Nineham, and Dowda. This is also the position of Haenchen, *Weg*, 391. Some scholars hold that the logia were connected in this cluster in the pre-Markan tradition: Joseph Zmijewski, "Der Glaube und seine Macht," *Begegnung mit dem Wort* (ed. J. Zmijewski and E. Nellessen; FS Heinrich Zimmermann; BBB 53; Bonn: Peter Hanstein, 1980) 90; Joachim Gnilka, *Das Evangelium nach Markus* (2 vols.; EKKNT 2; Zürich: Benziger, 1978–79) 2:133; Cranfield, *Mark*, 360; Münderlein, "Verfluchung," 102. According to Telford (*Barren*, 15) this is also the position of Loisy. Ernest Best ("Mark's Preservation of the Tradition," *The Interpretation of Mark* [ed. W. R. Telford; Philadelphia: Fortress, 1985] 125) thinks that the logia collection was already connected to the fig tree pericope before Mark. So does Schweizer (*Mark*, 235–36). Best, like Telford and most commentators, believes that the prayer teaching and the temple cleansing provide conflicting interpretations of the fig tree pericope. Since I will argue that the whole of Mark 11 makes sense as it stands, how the sayings came to be collected makes no difference for my argument. The discussion of the narrative introduction to the prayer teaching, 11:20–21, will show that the evangelist has shaped the end of the fig tree story so that it prepares for the prayer teaching, which means that the prayer logia were probably not attached to the fig tree pericope prior to Mark. However, even if the sayings had been attached to the fig tree pericope in the tradition as the evangelist received it, he has deliberately left them there while also interpreting the fig tree story as a prophecy of the destruction of the temple.

evangelist. The allegedly Matthean features of 11:25 are not necessarily derived from Matthew at all. The word for sin, παράπτωμα, is *hapax legomenon* not only in Mark,[27] but also in Matthew, where it occurs in the undisputed text only at 6:14-15.[28] Thus, παράπτωμα is hardly Matthean vocabulary.

The reference to God as ὁ πατὴρ ὑμῶν ὁ ἐν τοῖς οὐρανοῖς is not characteristically Markan, whereas Matthew does use "heavenly Father" and "Father who (is) in the heavens" frequently.[29] However, the author of Matthew did not coin this expression; it was in use in his environment and it may have been present in the Lord's Prayer tradition prior to the composition of Matthew.[30] There is no reason to doubt that the expression "Father in heaven" was characteristic of the prayer teachings of the Jesus tradition and therefore could appear in the Markan gospel in one of those traditional sayings without becoming a feature of the evangelist's own style elsewhere. The use of the expression here is not evidence of Matthean influence. Nor does it necessarily reflect the influence of the Lord's prayer.[31] It reflects the influence of Jewish expressions on Christian prayer teaching.

Telford's third argument, that verse 25 is missing from Matthew's version of the teachings on faith and prayer that follow the fig tree pericope, depends for its cogency on the hypothesis of Matthew's literary dependence on Mark. Even if the author of Matthew is assumed to have used Mark, there is no reason to doubt that he could have moved the forgiveness logion from this context to chapter 6, where it follows the Lord's Prayer. Telford thinks that "there is simply no reason' for the evangelist to have omitted the forgiveness logion from the collection of logia that follows the fig tree incident.[32] It is possible, however, that the author of Matthew, like Telford himself, thought that a saying about forgiveness was out of place in the context of Jesus' curse on the fig tree and would only make Jesus' apparent impatience look even worse.[33] He could have omitted the forgiveness logion, as he did the Markan comment that "it was not the season for figs" (Mark 11:13b) in order to reduce the offense of the pericope. He could have rewritten the forgiveness logion (Matt 6:14), added its logical corollary for balance (Matt 6:15) and placed both verses at the end of his version

---

[27] Telford, *Barren,* 52.

[28] Stendahl, "Prayer," 76 n. 8. The variant with παράπτωμα at Matt 18:35 is an expansion derived from 6:14 and is poorly attested, according to Metzger, *Commentary,* 46.

[29] Telford, *Barren,* 52.

[30] Stendahl, "Prayer," 77.

[31] Against G. Biguzzi, "Mc 11, 23-25 e il Pater," *RivB* 27 (1979) 57-68; Wilfrid Harrington, *Mark* (Wilmington, DE: Michael Glazier, 1979) 182; Taylor, *Mark,* 467.

[32] Telford, *Barren,* 54.

[33] Ibid., 49: "At best this story would seem to illustrate the destructive power of a Rabbi's curse. . . . Its tenor is quite alien to the loving and forgiving spirit that is urged on the believer in 11.25, 26."

of the Lord's Prayer in order to emphasize the nature of the messianic community as a community of mutual forgiven-ness.[34]

In order to see verse 25 as a scribal gloss based on Matthew we would have to suppose (1) that a scribe would have had a compelling reason to connect forgiveness with the power of prayer and that he would have added verse 25 to the original text of Mark (2) despite the fact that doing so *decreased* the harmonization with Matthew's version of the fig tree story and (3) despite the fact that adding the logion *increased* the dissonance between Jesus' attitude toward the tree and the attitude urged on disciples. Moreover, this scribal activity, which takes place *after* the writing of Matthew, is supposed to have occurred so early that no correct manuscript of Mark has survived, since all extant texts include verse 25. Telford is asking us to believe too many improbable things before breakfast.

In the case of verse 24, the suggestion that it may be a scribal gloss has nothing at all to recommend it, as Telford himself recognizes.[35] His only arguments for the omission of verse 24 from the Markan text have to do with the non-Markan characteristics of the logion. As we have seen, such arguments mean nothing when Mark is acknowledged to have been using traditional material. In fact, the only reason that Telford insists on eliminating Mark 11:24-25 from the text is that he believes that his view of the Markan anti-temple position is weakened if these verses are allowed to stand as original:

> The crux of the problem . . . lies in the reflection that if Mark himself either found these sayings already attached to the story [of the fig tree] and did not remove them, or conversely, himself connected them to the story, then it is hard to see how he himself could have intended that the story be understood as a specific commentary on the Cleansing account . . . the appended logia do not appear to bring out the significance of this juxtaposition. Taken together, they serve rather to weaken its effect.[36]

If Telford's solution is rejected and 11:24-25 are understood as part of the original text of the gospel, the problem to which Telford draws attention yet remains to be addressed. Can the evangelist have deliberately created a text in which the story about the fig tree has two functions? Does the withering of the tree foreshadow the destruction of the temple *and* illustrate the power available to the praying community which has faith in God? If so, it must be the case that the author of Mark saw a connection between the rejection of the temple cult portrayed in 11:15-19 and the prayer life of the Christian community, for which 11:22-25 provides instruction.

Some commentators suggest that such a connection is to be seen in the hybrid quotation from Isaiah 56:7 and Jeremiah 7:11 that the evangelist puts on the lips of Jesus in 11:17: "And he taught, and said to them, 'Is it not written,

---

[34] Stendahl, "Prayer," 83.
[35] Telford, *Barren*, 54-56.
[36] Ibid., 49.

"My house shall be called a house of prayer for all the nations"? But you have made it a den of robbers.' "[37] Schweizer thinks that for the author of Mark, the prayer logia "illustrate the expression 'house of prayer.' "[38] In its present form chapter 11 emphasizes "the great and crucial transition from a temple which was open only to Israel to one open to all nations."[39]

The theme of a transition also appears in the interpretations of Achtemeier and Harrington, who believe that in Mark the temple cult is replaced by faith and prayer.[40] Giesen and Gnilka emphasize the Christian community as the new "house of prayer" that includes the Gentiles.[41] In his dissertation, which focuses on the testimony of the false witnesses in Mark 14:58, Juel also makes the connection between the failure of the Jerusalem temple to become a "house of prayer for all nations" and its replacement by the Christian community as the temple "not made with hands," which is based on Jesus' death and resurrection.[42]

---

[37] It is unlikely that σπήλαιον λῃστῶν refers to dishonest merchants since λῃστής means "robber," "highwayman," "bandit," or even "revolutionary, insurrectionist" (Juel, *Messiah*, 132). Lloyd Gaston (*No Stone on Another. Studies in the Significance of the Fall of Jerusalem in the Synoptic Gospels* [Leiden: Brill, 1970] 85), following Buchanan, translates σπήλαιον λῃστῶν as "Zealot stronghold," and takes it as a reference to the siege of Jerusalem (Josephus, *Bellum*, 4.151). Whether Mark intended to refer to the Zealots or to the Jewish leaders, it is clear that he intended a negative contrast to "house of prayer," and that he meant to call to mind Jeremiah's prediction of the destruction of the temple. See Juel, *Messiah*, 132–34.

[38] Schweizer, *Mark*, 235.

[39] Ibid., 236.

[40] Achtemeier, *Mark*, 26: "What Mark means to say by this conclusion is simply that the locus of salvation, of God's plan, has shifted from temple to Jesus, and that therefore faith and prayer, not temple cults, are the way to God." Harrington, *Mark*, 181–82: "Faith and prayer, not temple cult, are now the way to God. . . . Jesus has replaced the temple." The confusion in these statements by Achtemeier and Harrington about whether the temple is replaced by "Jesus" or by "faith and prayer" can be traced to a real ambiguity in the gospel itself. The evangelist incorporates earlier Christian conceptions, which results in a mixture of metaphors. According to the false witnesses in 14:58, Jesus claimed to be the builder of the temple "not made with hands," but in the conclusion of the vineyard parable at 12:10–11 the evangelist incorporates the "cornerstone" tradition based on Ps 118, which implies that Jesus is the stone and God is the builder. Gaston (*No Stone*, 176–243) discusses at length the variety of images in New Testament materials and concludes that the older tradition is that of the community as temple, which goes back to Jesus himself, and that the traditions in which Jesus is the temple or the foundation stone are secondary developments. One does not have to be as certain as Gaston is about what Jesus thought and taught to be informed by his collection of the evidence.

[41] H. Giesen, "Der verdorrte Feigenbaum—Eine symbolische Aussage? Zu Mk 11, 12–14. 20f," *BZ* 20 (1976) 110; Gnilka, *Markus*, 2:129–31. See further literature cited in Telford, *Barren*, 35 n. 106.

[42] Juel, *Messiah*, 135–36. Juel attributes the connection to a conversation with Nils Dahl. Adolf Schlatter (*Markus, der Evangelist für die Griechen* [Stuttgart: Calwer

These suggestions have in common the insight that the logia collection in Mark 11:22-25 has an intrinsic link with the judgment on the temple portrayed by the intercalated fig tree and temple "cleansing" narratives. The Jerusalem temple is condemned and replaced by the praying community. The following discussion will lend support to this interpretation by demonstrating that the rejection of the temple by the Christians and its subsequent destruction would have raised precisely the question to which the logia collection provides an answer, namely, the question, "What is it that guarantees the efficacy of prayer?"

THE RELATIONSHIP BETWEEN PRAYER AND TEMPLE: PROBLEMS AND SOLUTIONS IN ANTIQUITY

"Primitive man," according to Friedrich Heiler, "prays at the place where the god dwells. If the god sojourns afar, the worshiper will at least direct hands and eyes towards his dwelling-place."[43] What Heiler calls primitive thinking is, like much of the language and practice of prayer, a derivative of human social relationships. The person who wants to make a request of a ruler or lord must go to the place where that person holds court. That is why the Egyptians, for example, built their temples like palace audience-rooms with orifices in the walls representing the ears of the deity into which prayers and requests were spoken.[44] The religions of the ancient Near East were all characterized by a focus on the importance of identifying the dwelling-place of the deity so that he or she could be visited there.[45]

Prayer and the Temple in the Biblical Tradition

There is ample evidence in the Hebrew scriptures that the sanctuary was regarded as the place where prayer was particularly appropriate and effective.[46] Hannah prays in the sanctuary at Shiloh and her prayer is answered (1 Sam 1:1-29). Hezekiah prays in the temple and the army of Sennacherib is dispersed (2 Kgs 19:14-37). Jonah prays from the belly of the fish and his prayer is said to come "into thy holy temple" (Jonah 2:8). The Psalms stress the importance of the sanctuary as a place for prayer.[47] It was in the sanctuary that the petitioner

Vereinsbuchhandlung, 1935] 215) had suggested as early as 1935 that the significance of the prayer logia in Mark 11 was to assure the disciples that the loss of the temple did not mean for them the loss of the possibility of prayer.

[43] Friedrich Heiler, *Prayer* (trans. and ed. Samuel McComb; London: Oxford, 1932) 112.

[44] Otto Weinrich, *Gebet und Wunder* (Darmstadt: Wissenschaftliche Buchgesellschaft, 1968) 207.

[45] R. E. Clements, *God and Temple* (Philadelphia: Fortress, 1965) 1.

[46] Cf. Solomon Zeitlin, "The Temple and Worship," *JQR* 51 (1961) 235.

[47] T. C. Vriezen, *An Outline of Old Testament Theology* (Newton, MA: Charles T. Branford, 1958) 305.

received from the cult functionary the "salvation oracle," which is thought to be the basis for the change of tone in the individual laments from pleading to the certainty of God's faithfulness to answer the prayer.[48] The priestly practice of giving assurance and instruction to worshipers as they prayed must have contributed greatly toward increased confidence in prayers offered in the temple.[49]

The Deuteronomist links the efficacy of prayer with the temple in the dedication speech attributed to Solomon (1 Kgs 8:14–61).[50] Solomon prays:

> But will God indeed dwell on the earth? Behold, heaven and the highest heaven cannot contain thee; how much less this house which I have built! Yet have regard to the prayer of thy servant and to his supplication, O Lord my God, hearkening to the cry and to the prayer which thy servant prays before thee this day; that thy eyes may be open night and day toward this house, the place of which thou has said, "My name shall be there," that thou mayest hearken to the prayer which thy servant offers toward this place. And hearken thou to the supplication of thy servant and of thy people Israel, when they pray toward this place; yea, hear thou in heaven thy dwelling place; and when thou hearest, forgive. (1 Kgs 8:27–30, RSV)

Here "the accent remains not on how YHWH transcends the temple but on its significance for the worship of YHWH."[51] Solomon's prayer goes on to list seven situations in which prayer is offered: in individual disputes involving a curse (31–32); defeat of the nation by an enemy (33–34); drought (35–36); famine, pestilence and siege (37–40); prayer by a non-Israelite (41–43); defeat in battle (44–45) and exile (46–51). In each case, prayer is to be offered "in" or 'toward" the temple.

S. B. Wheeler believes that the Deuteronomic theology of prayer is based on an old practice that involved prayer in the sanctuary for the removal of a curse inflicted on one individual by another. Appealing to this practice, which had long been believed to be efficacious, the Deuteronomistic theologians extended the idea of the effectiveness of prayer in the temple to the need to remove the effects of the treaty curses so important in their theology.[52]

> . . . the authors wished to convince their audience that the Solomonic temple was especially efficacious as the place where calamity (interpreted as an inflicted curse) could be undone.[53] The attempt to centralize worship in the temple . . . could

---

[48] Hermann Gunkel and Joachim Begrich, *Einleitung in die Psalmen* (2d ed.; Göttingen: Vandenhoeck & Ruprecht, 1966) 245–47. Cf. John H. Hayes, *Understanding the Psalms* (Valley Forge: Judson, 1976) 62–64; Bernard W. Anderson, *Out of the Depths* (rev. ed.; Philadelphia: Westminster, 1983) 77.

[49] Hayes, *Psalms*, 64.

[50] Solomon's prayer "seems to be a free composition of the Deuteronomistic historian," according to Clements, *God and Temple*, 90.

[51] S. B. Wheeler, "Prayer and Temple in the Dedication Speech of Solomon: 1 Kings 8:14–61" (Ph.D. dissertation Columbia University, 1977) 155.

[52] Ibid., 317.

[53] Ibid., 291.

explain the Deuteronomistic authors' concern for the temple and for its significance
for those upon whom the curses of the covenant have fallen.[54]

Wheeler thinks that the main body of the prayer comes from the time of Josiah
or Hezekiah.[55] Later interpolations (verses 44-51, 52-53, and 59-60) show how
the emphasis on the temple had to be modified in light of the exile of Judah and
the still later diaspora situation.[56]

The importance of the temple for the efficacy of prayer did not merely
evaporate when the first temple was destroyed. Ezekiel recognized that distance
from Zion did not necessarily mean absence from Yahweh, but the language he
used to express the presence of Yahweh was temple language. The temple is still
the locus of prayer, even if it is a metaphorical temple.[57]

In the literature from the period of the Second Temple the same emphases
appear.[58] In Judith 4:9-15 the people prostrate themselves in front of the temple
when they pray for protection from Holofernes. In 3 Maccabees the priest and
people rush to the temple to pray in the face of the threat to the Holy of Holies
by Ptolemy Philopator (3 Macc 1:20-24). The high priest prays, "thou didst
promise that if . . . we should come to this place and make our supplication,
thou wouldst hear our prayer." The enemy is struck down (3 Macc 2:1-22). In
2 Maccabees 3:15 the priests pray before the altar as Heliodorus prepares to sack
the temple treasury. In response to the prayer Heliodorus is flattened by a divine
apparition and subsequently converted (2 Macc 3:24-40). After Judas and his
men pray before the altar (2 Macc 10:25-26), the Lord gives them victory over
Timotheus by sending angels into battle with them.

The assumption that effective prayer must be offered toward the temple is
so basic in Josephus' thought that he commits a gross anachronism by introducing the temple into his (somewhat garbled) account of Abraham's prayer for the
recovery of his wife (Gen 12:10-20: ". . . uplifting pure hands towards this spot
which you have now polluted, [Abraham] enlisted the invincible Ally on his side"
(*Bellum* 5.380).

The Problem Posed by the Destruction of the Second Temple

Given this background, it is not hard to see why the destruction of the
Second Temple would cause some rabbis to question whether prayer were any
longer possible:[59]

---

[54] Ibid., 312-13.

[55] Ibid.

[56] Ibid., 315.

[57] Samuel Terrien, *The Elusive Presence* (San Francisco: Harper and Row, 1978) 209.

[58] Norman B. Johnson (*Prayer in the Apocrypha and Pseudepigrapha* [Philadelphia:
Society of Biblical Literature, 1948] 45) lists the references discussed in this paragraph.

[59] On this see Joseph Heinemann, *Prayer in the Talmud* (Berlin: Walter de Gruyter,
1977) 19-21.

R. Eleazar said: From the day on which the Temple was destroyed, the gates of prayer have been closed, as it says, "Yea, when I cry and call for help, He shutteth out my prayer," (Lam 3:8). . . . R. Eleazar also said: Since the day that the Temple was destroyed, a wall of iron divides between Israel and their Father in Heaven; as it says, "And take thou unto thee an iron griddle and set it for a wall of iron between thee and the city." (Ezek 4:3) *b. Ber.* 32b.[60]

The expression "gates of prayer" reflects the idea that the Jerusalem temple was the "gate of heaven":

. . . when a man prays in Jerusalem, it is as though he prays before the throne of glory, for the gate of heaven is in Jerusalem, and a door is always open for the hearing of prayer, as is said, "This is the gate of heaven." (Gen 28:17) *Midr. Ps.* 91:7.[61]

Not only was the temple the "gate of heaven," but it was also the dwelling-place of the Shekhina; for this reason some of the rabbis taught that the destruction of the temple meant that the Shekhina had been withdrawn from Israel:

Rabbi Jonathan said: Three and a half years the Shekhina abode on the Mountain of Olives and proclaimed thrice daily, saying "Return, ye backsliding children, I will heal your backslidings" (Jeremiah 3:22). Since they did not return, the Shekhina began to hover in the air, uttering the verse "I will go and return to My place, till they acknowledge their guilt and seek My face; in their trouble they will seek Me earnestly" (Hosea 5:15).[62]

When the Holy One, blessed be He, wished to destroy the Temple, He said: "So long as I am in it, the Gentile nations will not harm it. I shall, therefore, cease to regard it and I shall swear not to give it heed till the time of the End . . ." At that moment the enemy entered the Temple and burned it. When it was burnt, the Holy One, blessed be He, said, "I no longer have a seat upon earth; I shall remove My Shekhina therefrom and ascend to My first habitation . . ." At that moment the Holy One,

[60] Quotations from the Babylonian Talmud are taken from *The Babylonian Talmud* (ed. I. Epstein; London: Soncino, 1935-1952). In this passage, Baruch M. Bokser ('The Wall Separating God and Israel," *JQR* 73 [1983] 349-74) wants to translate, "The iron wall that was between Israel and its Father in Heaven has come to an end" (352). His argument (357-67) is not likely to convince many, but he is correct in asserting that the passage taken as a whole is an attempt to cope with the loss of the temple while maintaining that Israel still has access to God (371-72). In the same passage we read, "But though the gates of prayer are closed, the gates of weeping are not closed, as it says, 'Hear my prayer, O Lord, and give ear unto my cry; keep not silence at my tears.' "

[61] Here we have the same kind of concretization of the notion of access that is represented by the openings in Egyptian temple walls through which prayers can pass to the ears of the deity. In Lucian's *Icaromenippus* (25-26) the wall openings become holes in the floor of heaven whose covers can be removed to allow the prayers to float up into the audience chamber of Zeus. See H. D. Betz, *Lukian von Samosata und das Neue Testament* (Berlin: Akademie, 1961) 63.

[62] *Pesiqta de-Rav Kahana,* quoted by Ephraim E. Urbach, *The Sages: Their Concepts and Beliefs* (2 vols.; Jerusalem: Magnes Press, 1975) 1:54-55.

blessed be He, wept and said: "Woe unto Me, what have I done! I caused My Shekhina to dwell below for Israel's sake, and now that they have sinned I have returned to my original place."[63]

However, this level of despair was overcome by the necessity of coping with the loss of the temple. R. Samuel b. Nahman is quoted as saying that "The gates of prayer are sometimes open and sometimes closed, but the gates of repentance always remain open." And the following saying is attributed to R. 'Anan:

> The gates of prayer are never closed, for it is written, "As the Lord our God is whenever we call upon Him;" and calling is nothing else but praying, as Scripture in another context has it, "And it shall come to pass that before they call I will answer" (Isa 65:24) *Deut. Rab.* 2.12.[64]

Sometimes it was argued that the Shekhina had not departed from the site of the temple after all:

> R. Samuel b. Nahman said: Before the Temple was destroyed, the Divine Presence dwelt therein, for it says: The Lord is in His holy temple (Ps 11:4); but when the Temple was destroyed, the Divine Presence removed itself to heaven, as it is said: The Lord hath established His throne in the heavens (Ps 103:19). R. Eleazar says: The Shechinah did not depart from the Temple, for it is said: And Mine eyes and My heart shall be there perpetually (2 Chr 7:16) . . . for although it was laid waste, it still retained its holiness. . . . R. Aha said: The Divine Presence will never depart from the Western Wall, as it is said: Behold He standeth behind our wall (Cant 2:9) *Exod. Rab.* 2.2.

Some scholars believe that prayer and sacrifice continued to be offered in the ruins of the Second Temple until Hadrian's response to the Bar Kochba revolt made this impossible.[65] Whether or not that was actually the case, we know that prayers were offered in the direction of the temple (*m. Ber.* 4.5, *y. Ber.* 4.5, *b. Ber.* 30a).[66]

---

[63] *Lamentations Rabba,* proem 24, ed. Buber, p. 13a. Quoted in Urbach, *Sages,* 55.

[64] Heinemann (*Prayer,* 20) cites *b. Pesah.* 85b, where R. Joshua b. Levi is quoted as saying, "Even an iron partition cannot interpose between Israel and their Father in Heaven." However, as Heinemann tacitly acknowledges, this discussion has nothing to do with the possibility of prayer, but is part of an argument over whether a person is to be counted in the minyan if he stands inside or outside the city gate. See Epstein's note 7 on page 450 of the Soncino *Talmud,* Part 2, Vol. 2.

[65] Kenneth W. Clark, "Worship in the Jerusalem Temple After A.D. 70," *NTS* 6 (1960) 269–80; Abraham Kon, *Prayer* (London: Soncino, 1971) 100. The presence of the Shekhina in the Western Wall is the basis for the offering of prayers at that spot up to the present time. Cf. Urbach, *Sages,* 1:57.

[66] Some rabbis opposed a fixed orientation for prayer because it had become the practice of Christians to pray toward Jerusalem or, in some cases, toward the east. Urbach, *Sages,* 1:61–63.

Of course, the presence of the Shekhina in the temple had never meant that it was not also everywhere in the world.[67] Thus the sages were able to assert that even though the temple had been destroyed, the Shekhina was present in the synagogues and houses of study (*y. Ber.* 5.8d).

> It has been taught: Abba Benjamin says: A man's prayer is heard [by God] only in the Synagogue . . . How do you know that the Holy One, blessed be He, is to be found in the Synagogue? For it is said: "God standeth in the congregation of God" (Ps 82:1). And how do you know that if ten people pray together the Divine Presence is with them? For it is said: "God standeth in the congregation of God." *b. Ber.* 6a.[68]
>
> "My Beloved is like a gazelle." Just as a gazelle leaps from mountain to mountain . . . so the Holy One, blessed be He, leaps from one synagogue to another synagogue, from one house of study to another house of study. And why all this? So as to bless Israel. *Cant. Rab.* 2:9.[69]

Sometimes it could be said that the reading of the passages on sacrifice was a substitute for the offering of sacrifice (*b. Ta'an.* 27b), or that deeds of mercy had replaced sacrifice as a means of atonement (*Abot R. Nat.* 4).[70] Finally prayer itself, rather than being made impossible by the loss of the temple, was seen to be all the more necessary.

> Rabbi Isaac says: At this time we have neither prophet nor priest, neither sacrifice, nor Temple, nor altar—what is it that can make atonement for us, even though the Temple is destroyed? The only thing that we have left is prayer![71]

The change of emphasis from sacrifice to prayer and the focus on the synagogues and the houses of study as replacements for the destroyed temple represent the success of rabbinic Judaism in coping with the loss of temple and cult. That it was the Pharisaic party which emerged as the leaders of post-70 Judaism is understandable, since it was the Pharisees who had already envisioned, as Neusner puts it, "a kingdom in which everyone was a priest, a people of whom all were holy—a community which would live as if it were always in the Temple sanctuary of Jerusalem."[72] Thus, the praying and studying community replaced the temple as the center of Jewish life and worship.[73] But this

---

[67] Urbach, *Sages,* 1:53; Walther Eichrodt, *Theology of the Old Testament* (2 vols.; Philadelphia: Westminster, 1961-1967) 2:188-89.

[68] Cf. *Deut. Rab.* 7.2: R. Aibu said: And what is more, when you stand in the synagogue, God stands by your side. Whence this? For it is said, "God standeth in the congregation of God" (Ps 82:1).

[69] Heinemann, *Prayer,* 21.

[70] Gaston, *No Stone,* 3.

[71] Heinemann, *Prayer,* 20.

[72] Jacob Neusner, "Judaism in a Time of Crisis: Four Responses to the Destruction of the Second Temple," *Judaism* 21 (1972) 321-25.

[73] Neusner regards the Mishnah as the "mediating document" in the shift from temple to community. See his "Map Without Territory: Mishnah's System of Sacrifice and Sanctuary," *HR* 19 (1979) 103-27.

transition, forced upon Judaism by the destruction of the Jerusalem temple in 70, had already been made, to some extent, by the Jews of the diaspora, to whom the temple was inaccessible even before it was destroyed.[74] The replacement of the temple by the praying community had also taken place before 70 at Qumran and in some Christian groups. In these cases the shift took place not because the temple had been destroyed, but because it had been rejected.[75]

Communities as Replacements for Temples in Late Antiquity

That the Qumran sectarians thought of their community as a replacement for the Jerusalem temple, which they had rejected as defiled and unworthy, may be regarded as an established result of scholarship and need not be argued here.[76] Specific opposition to the Jerusalem temple seems also to have characterized the Stephen traditions that lie behind Acts 7:44–50.[77] The critique of temples 'made with hands" (χειροποίητος), in Acts 7:48 and found implicitly in Mark 14:58, as well as in other New Testament passages, draws upon a much older Greek tradition that was critical of images and temples as loci for the presence of deity.[78]

[74] Joel Gereboff, *Rabbi Tarfon* (BJS 7; Missoula: Scholars, 1979) 444.

[75] Neusner, "Crisis," 318.

[76] See, for example, Bertil Gärtner, *The Temple and the Community in Qumran and the New Testament* (Cambridge: Cambridge University Press, 1965); Gaston, *No Stone,* 161–76; Juel, *Messiah,* 159–68; R. J. McKelvey, *The New Temple* (London: Oxford, 1969) 46–53.

[77] Gaston, *No Stone,* 154–61; see the literature cited by Juel, *Messiah,* 148 n. 23.

[78] The Greek criticism of worship involving images goes back at least as early as the sixth century B.C.E., and can be seen in surviving fragments of Xenophanes and Heraclitus. Temples were included in this kind of polemic; both images and temples can be characterized as χειροποίητος. In the LXX, the adjective "made with hands" is a technical term in anti-idolatry polemic and can be used of the idols themselves or of a pagan temple.

The Christians took up the contrast "made with hands/not made with hands" and modified it to suit the arguments in which they used it. In some contexts it reflects the traditional Jewish polemic against idolatry (Acts 7:41, 19:26, Rev 9:20). The argument of the Areopagus speech in Acts 17:24–25 is hardly distinguishable from the anti-temple views of the Stoics, but Stephen's speech (Acts 7:48) seems to reflect a specific opposition to the Jerusalem temple. In Hebrews 9:11 χειροποίητος is explicitly defined as having to do with "this creation," and in 9:23–24 the "sanctuary made with hands" is contrasted with the "true" or "heavenly" sanctuary. This distinction between χειροποίητος as earthly or having to do with this creation and ἀχειροποίητος as heavenly, spiritual, miraculous, or of an entirely different order fits the uses in the New Testament epistles (Eph 2:11, Col 2:11, 2 Cor 5:1) and Mark 14:58.

On this, see the following: Harold W. Attridge, *First-Century Cynicism in the Epistles of Heraclitus* (HTS 29; Missoula: Scholars, 1976) 13–23; Bertil Gärtner, *The Areopagus Speech and Natural Revelation* (Uppsala: Gleerup, 1955) 211–12; Ernst Haenchen, *The Acts of the Apostles* (Philadelphia: Westminster, 1971) 522; Juel, *Messiah,* 143–57; Eduard Lohse, "χειροποίητος," TDNT 9 (1974) 436–37; Gottlob Schrenk, "ἱερός," TDNT 3 (1965) 221–83.

The Greek anti-temple polemic was not directed against any particular temple, but against temples in general. Images and temples "made with hands" are contrasted negatively with the beauties of the natural world. Although this tradition has a long history, this kind of critique became especially prominent in the last century B.C.E. and the first two centuries of the Common Era.[79] Seneca, for example, finds natural places or worship, which are not made with hands (*non manu factus*), more inspiring than temples (*Ep.* 41.3). Similarly, for Plutarch and the author of the fourth Epistle of Heraclitus, the whole world is the temple of deity.[80]

The devaluation of temples had implications for attitudes toward the efficacy of prayer, as Lucian's life of Demonax indicates:

> When one of his friends said: "Demonax, let's go to the Asclepium and pray for my son," he replied: "You must think Asclepius very deaf, that he can't hear our prayers from where we are!" (*Demonax* 27).

The Stoic attitude is ably expressed by Seneca:

> We do not need to uplift our hands towards heaven, or to beg the keeper of a temple to let us approach his idol's ear, as if in this way our prayers were more likely to be heard. God is near you, he is with you, he is within you. (*Ep.* 41.1).

The philosophical critique of temples was reinforced by sociological factors in late antiquity. As people in the imperial period became increasingly mobile and cosmopolitan, the various religions were forced, as Jonathan Z. Smith puts it, to develop "modes of access to the deity which transcended any particular place."[81] Sacred places became relatively less important and religious associations became the individual's protection against external hostile powers.[82] The devaluation of temples was accompanied by an emphasis on religious community, not only in diaspora Judaism, in Christianity and at Qumran, but in other Hellenistic religions as well. It is precisely this shift from temple to community, and the implications of the shift for the efficacy of prayer, which explain the apparent ambiguity in the treatment of the fig tree story in Mark 11.

The Markan Community as "House of Prayer"

We have seen how the destruction of the Jerusalem temple raised the question of the continued possibility and efficacy of prayer, and how rabbinic

---

[79] Attridge, *Cynicism*, 16.

[80] Attridge, *Cynicism*, 13–14. Philo sympathizes with the critique, but he still has a place for the temple "made with hands" in Jerusalem. It is a necessary concession to those who wish to offer material sacrifices, but "the highest, and in the truest sense the holy, temple of God is the whole universe" (*Spec.* 1.66–67). See Schrenk, "ἱερός," 241–42.

[81] Jonathan Z. Smith, *Map Is Not Territory. Studies in the History of Religions* (SJLA 36; Leiden: Brill, 1978) xiv. Cf. McKelvey, *New Temple*, 55–56.

[82] Smith, *Map*, 187.

thinkers answered the question by asserting the importance of the synagogues and houses of study as replacements for the temple. Indeed, the importance of community prayer was finally seen to be enhanced by the loss of the temple cult: "The only thing we have left is prayer!" In fact, as J. Z. Smith insists,

> if the Temple had not been destroyed, it would have had to be neglected. For it represented a locative type of religious activity no longer perceived as effective in a new, utopian religious situation with a concomitant shift from a cosmological to an anthropological viewpoint.[83]

From the viewpoint of the author of Mark, the temple had been rejected as a failure long before the Romans destroyed it,[84] but because of its traditional role as the guarantor of the efficacy of prayer, the rejection of the temple required a reassertion of the importance of community prayer and the power available to it. The evangelist has arranged his materials in chapter 11 so as to follow the proleptic destruction of the temple with the necessary assurances about the efficacy of prayer, and he has used the fig tree pericope as a metaphorical clamp to hold the two ideas together.

This strange story about the barren fig tree that Jesus withered with a word serves two purposes in the Markan narrative. As scholars have long recognized, it prefigures the destruction of the temple by framing the "cleansing" account in which Jesus effectively cancels the temple cult. The explicit prediction of the temple's destruction in 13:2 is greatly strengthened by the effect that the fig tree pericope has on the audience. Whatever the Markan Jesus says, happens. If he says there will not be left one stone on another, then the temple is certainly doomed.

But the fig tree story is not merely a threat, but also a promise. As we will see, the evangelist takes pains throughout the gospel to make it clear that the power manifested in Jesus' ministry—the power that withered the tree—was the power of God. That same power, the evangelist insists, is available to the community through believing prayer. He has shaped the sequel to the fig tree pericope, the observation by Peter that the tree has withered (11:20–21), in order to prepare for the prayer teaching.[85] These traditional logia belong here, as far

---

[83] Smith, *Map*, 128.

[84] Kelber (*Kingdom*, 106) thinks that the Roman destruction of the temple forced an anti-Zion theology upon the evangelist. Gaston (*No Stone*, 5, 472–75) thinks that the author of Mark predicts the destruction of the temple before the event. This study neither investigates the dating of the gospel nor does it assume a solution to that issue. It should be noted, however, that the notion of the community as replacement for the temple presupposes the *rejection* of the temple but not necessarily its *destruction*. Cf. Neusner, "Crisis," 319: "Christians experienced the end of the old cult and the old Temple before it actually took place, much like the Qumran sectarians. . . . Whether the essays on that central problem were done before or after 70 C.E. is of no consequence."

[85] See Chapter 3 for the discussion of the Markan features of 11:20–21.

as our evangelist is concerned, because the rejection of the temple *requires* the reaffirmation of prayer. The prayer catechesis is addressed to the Markan community, represented in the narrative by the disciples. They are the "house of prayer for all the nations" that the temple had failed to become.[86]

[86] This is the most that can be said with certainty about the sense in which the Markan community replaces the temple. Donahue and Juel are among those who believe that the author of Mark views the community as a new temple "not made with hands" (Donahue, *Trial*, 103-38; Juel, *Messiah*, 57-58, 145-209, and passim). Certainly some Christian traditions using temple imagery for the community were in circulation before Mark was written; Mark 14:58 preserves one such tradition. Gaston (*No Stone*, 176-243) claims to be able to trace the idea back to the teaching of Jesus, whereas Gärtner (*Temple*, 135-39) argues that the image of the new temple was applied first to Jesus by the Christians, then to the community under the influence of Qumran. However that may have been, the Gospel of Mark does not clearly indicate whether temple imagery is to be affirmed of the Christian community, or whether even the metaphorical sense of "temple" is to be completely rejected.

The problem is that the community-as-temple image appears in the narrative on the lips of the false witnesses at Jesus' trial: "And some stood up and bore false witness against him, saying, 'We heard him say, "I will destroy this temple that is made with hands, and in three days I will build another, not made with hands."' Yet not even so did their testimony agree" (14:57-59). Juel interprets this passage ironically, arguing that the witnesses are false because (according to the evangelist) Jesus never made such a statement, but unknowingly they utter an accurate prediction because Jesus' death will be the end of the temple cult and the risen Lord will "build" a new temple "not made with hands," that is, the Christian community (117-25, 208).

Elizabeth Struthers Malbon objects to this interpretation. Malbon ("TH OIKIA AYTOY: Mark 2.15 in Context," *NTS* 31 [1985] 288) writes: "Even at the metaphorical level of Mark's gospel, temple is rejected, house affirmed. The metaphor of building a temple 'not made with hands' (14.58) is falsely attributed to the Markan Jesus, but the metaphor of the temple as the house of God is on his lips truly, both early and late (2.26; 11.17) . . . may it not be that the house, which replaces the synagogue and stands in opposition to the doomed temple in Mark, does suggest the early Christian community? With the destruction of the temple (13.2) and rejection in the synagogue (13.9), the Christian community must come together in 'house churches.' The sacred structures of temple and synagogue are no longer central; the new community gathers in a house to experience, witness to, and await 'the Lord of the house.' " The details of Malbon's analysis of the significance of οἰκία/οἶκος in Mark may be seen in her *Narrative Space*, 106-140.

Donahue, influenced by Malbon's argument, has begun to place more stress on the communal significance of "house" in Mark. See his The *Theology and Setting of Discipleship in the Gospel of Mark* (Milwaukee: Marquette University, 1983). Ernest Best (*Following Jesus*, 213-29) wants to have it both ways; both the temple "not made with hands" and the "house" are images of the church.

Malbon's analysis of the "house" image in Mark is careful and thorough. The difficulty, as she notes in "Mark 2.15," 291-92 n. 26, lies in moving from literary observations to historical conclusions. In addition, although it is true that the evangelist does not clearly equate the community with the temple "not made with hands," he *is* capable of the kind of irony attributed to him by Juel's interpretation. Also, the "cornerstone" tradition based

CONCLUSION: THE INTEGRITY OF MARK 11

As we have seen, although Mark 11:26 is appropriately omitted from current critical texts as a secondary interpolation, the rest of the prayer logia collection, 11:22–25, is to be regarded as part of the original text. Not only are Telford's arguments against verses 24 and 25 invalid, but the problem that compelled him to attempt to eliminate these verses from the text of Mark has been solved.

The pericope of the withered fig tree functions in Mark 11 *both* to foreshadow the destruction of the temple *and* to illustrate the power of God, which was manifested in Jesus' miracles and promised to the community which replaced the rejected temple as "house of prayer." It is precisely the rejection of the temple that makes the inclusion of the prayer logia at this point in the gospel not only appropriate, but even necessary. Having established the literary and theological integrity of the logia collection in its immediate context, we will focus in chapter 3 on the grammatical and syntactical features of the logia collection as an introduction to an examination of their theological significance.

---

on Ps 118 is treated positively in Mark 12:10–11, and Gaston (*No Stone,* 176–243) thinks that this tradition represents another spiritualization of the temple in early Christianity.

All that is necessary for the argument of this study is the observation that in the Gospel of Mark the community replaces the temple as "house of prayer." That much is not disputed by anyone.

3
The Markan Prayer Logia —
Text and Structure

Before we turn to an examination of the theological aspects of the prayer logia collection in Mark 11, it is necessary to deal with the remaining textual questions and issues of grammar and syntax. We have already observed the way in which the temple "cleansing" story is linked with the prayer logia thematically by the quotation from Isaiah about God's "house of prayer." Between the temple episode and the logia collection stands the conclusion of the story about the fig tree (11:20-21). These two sentences have a dual function in the chapter. They seal the doom of the temple by dramatically establishing the reliability of Jesus' words and actions. The cancellation of the temple cult, signified by his words and actions in 11:15-19, is as certain as the destruction of the fig tree, which stands starkly before the eyes of the audience in 11:20-21. These same two verses also serve as an introduction to the prayer teaching which follows in 11:22-25. The thoroughly Markan vocabulary and syntax of 11:20-21 indicate that the evangelist has carefully shaped the end of the fig tree story to suit his purposes![1]

THE WITHERED FIG TREE: 11:20-21

As they passed by in the morning, they saw the fig tree withered away to its roots. And Peter remembered and said to him, "Master, look! The fig tree which you cursed has withered."

Verse 20 informs the audience that the scene takes place on the day following the temple episode and is set on the road from Bethany to Jerusalem in the vicinity of the Mount of Olives, as in 11:12-14. The Markan narrator employs his favorite copulative, καί, to link this scene with the preceding one and to connect verse 20 to verse 21 and verse 21 to verse 22.[2] The verbs παραπορεύομαι and ξηραίνω are used more frequently by Mark than by any other evangelist.[3] The temporal notice, "in the morning" (πρωΐ), is a part of the redactional three-day

---

[1] Caba, *Oración*, 120; Taylor, *Mark*, 466; Telford, *Barren*, 56-57.

[2] Caba, *Oración*, 120.

[3] παραπορεύομαι: Mark x4, Matt x1, Luke x0, John x0; ξηραίνω: Mark x6, Matt x3, Luke x1, John x1. See Caba, *Oración*, 120.

scheme of chapter 11.[4] That the fig tree is seen to have been completely destroyed (ἐξηραμμένην ἐκ ῥιζῶν)[5] prepares the audience to pay close attention to what follows, since it establishes Jesus as the primary example of one of whom it can be said "that what he says happens" (11:23, cf. 11:14).

This confirmation of the power of Jesus' word is reinforced in verse 21 by the notice that "Peter remembered" (ἀναμνησθεὶς ὁ Πέτρος; cf. 11:14: καὶ ἤκουον οἱ μαθηταὶ αὐτοῦ). Like the similar notice in the denial scene (14:72), it calls attention to the fulfillment of a previous statement by Jesus. As usual in the gospel, Peter speaks for the disciples.[6] The exclamation ἴδε and the use of ῥαββί addressed to Jesus are Markan touches,[7] as is the historical present λέγει in 21 and 22a.[8]

It is worth noting that it is Peter who interprets Jesus' words to the fig tree (11:14) as a "curse" (ἡ συκῆ ἣν κατηράσω). This tells the audience much more about the narrator's characterization of Peter than about the narrator's own view of what happened. Jesus' response, "Have faith in God," and the teaching about prayer that follows show that the evangelist interprets Jesus' words in 11:14 as a prayer.[9]

THE PRAYER TEACHING: 11:22-25

And Jesus answered them, "Have faith in God. Truly, I say to you, whoever says to this mountain, 'Be taken up and be thrown into the sea,' and does not doubt in his heart, but believes that what he says happens, it will be done for him. Therefore I say to you, keep on believing that you received everything that you are praying and asking for, and it will be done for you. And whenever you stand praying, forgive, if you have anything against anyone; so that your Father also who is in heaven may forgive you your trespasses."[10]

Although the observation that the fig tree had withered was made by Peter, the response of the Markan Jesus is directed to the larger group of disciples (αὐτοῖς) and ultimately to the community for which the gospel was written.[11] This shift from an encounter between Jesus and Peter to a saying or teaching section directed to the community is characteristic of the Markan narrative.[12] Verse 22

---

[4] On the three-day scheme see Telford, *Barren*, 39–49.

[5] Taylor, *Mark*, 466: "The use of the perfect illustrates the precision with which he uses this tense, as frequently elsewhere (cf. 3:1, 5:15, 11:17, etc.), to describe abiding results."

[6] Caba, *Oración*, 120–21; Telford, *Barren*, 56.

[7] Telford, *Barren*, 56, Caba, *Oración*, 121.

[8] Caba, *Oración*, 121.

[9] Swete, *Mark*, 259; Ernst Lohmeyer, *Des Evangelium des Markus* (Göttingen: Vandenhoeck & Ruprecht, 1957) 239.

[10] My translation.

[11] Schweizer, *Mark*, 234.

[12] Cf. 8:29–38, 10:28–31, 14:37–38; Caba, *Oración*, 121.

has a transitional character.[13] It concludes the fig tree episode by attributing the power that withered the tree to God, and it introduces the sayings on faith, prayer and forgiveness that follow in 11:23-25.

Problems in 11:22: Text and Translation

A few witnesses[14] insert εἰ before ἔχετε πίστιν θεοῦ in 11:22.[15] The particle εἰ can be either conditional or interrogative.[16] If the variant were read as an interrogative, it would be translated, "Do you have faith in God?"[17] The problem with this reading lies in the introductory ἀποκριθεὶς ὁ Ἰησοῦς λέγει αὐτοῖς. Interrogative εἰ is never introduced by ἀποκρίνομαι in the New Testament. Moreover, the author of Mark uses interrogative εἰ only in indirect questions, never in direct questions.

As a conditional, the variant would be translated, "If you have faith in God, . . ." reading ἔχετε as an indicative. This reading is awkward in combination with the conditional relative clause of 11:23, which is in the third person: "If you have faith in God, truly I say to you that whoever should say to this mountain . . ." The protasis with εἰ is left dangling without an apodosis, since ἔσται αὐτῷ serves as the apodosis for the ὃς ἂν clause in 11:23. Moreover, the asseverative ἀμὴν λέγω ὑμῖν (11:23) is "always introductory and is never preceded by a protasis," as Metzger points out.[18] The most likely explanation for the variant with εἰ is that a scribe has attempted to assimilate Mark 11:22 to Luke 17:6 (εἰ ἔχετε πίστιν ὡς κόκκον σινάπεως) without providing a proper apodosis.[19] The original reading is ἔχετε πίστιν θεοῦ without the particle.[20]

---

[13] It is really not possible to determine whether verse 22 was composed by Mark as Walter Schmithals thinks (*Das Evangelium nach Markus*, 2 vols. [Gütersloh: Mohn, 1979] 2:500), or whether it existed already in the tradition, either as an isolated saying or attached to the (hypothetical) pre-Markan collection of sayings on faith and prayer. See the discussion in Zmijewski, "Glaube," 91-92.

[14] ℵ, D, Θ, f[13], 28, 33[C], 565, 700, pc, it, sy[S].

[15] θεοῦ is missing in a few minuscules. See Caba, *Oración*, 122 n. 78.

[16] Metzger, *Commentary*, 109.

[17] Ibid., 109 n. 1.

[18] Ibid., 109.

[19] Ibid.; Taylor, *Mark*, 466.

[20] Many scholars believe that the earliest form of the saying about the power of faith is the Q version which refers to "faith as a grain of mustard seed." Some, like Telford (*Barren*, 103), regard Matt 17:20 as the more primitive form of the Q saying and some, like Zmijewski ("Glaube," 87), prefer Luke 17:6. See also Caba, *Oración*, 321. The arguments are summarized by Zmijewski, who lists the scholars on each side. Ferdinand Hahn ("Das Verständnis des Glaubens im Markusevangelium," *Glaube im Neuen Testament* [FS H. Binder; BT 57; ed. F. Hahn and H. Klein; Neukirchen-Vluyn: Neukirchener, 1982] 52) thinks that Mark changed the mustard seed clause into the imperative, "Have faith in God." Gerhard Barth ("Glaube und Zweifel in der synoptischen Evangelien," *ZTK* 72 [1975] 276) argues that Mark has replaced the mustard seed with the admonition against

Even after the particle is eliminated as secondary, ambiguity remains as to the mood of ἔχετε, which may be either indicative or imperative. In the synoptic gospels, ἔχω is infrequently found in the imperative; there are only two instances if this verse is excluded. However, one of those imperatives is in Mark 9:50: "Have salt in yourselves . . ." (ἔχετε ἐν ἑαυτοῖς ἅλα). The other is in Luke 14:18-19: ". . . have me excused" (ἔχε με παρῃτημένον). The combination ἔχω πίστιν as a synonym for πιστεύω is found in Mark 4:40, Matt 17:20, Matt 21:21, Luke 17:6, and Acts 14:9, but not in the imperative mood (except here in 11:22). However, it is characteristic of Mark to demand faith: πιστεύω is found in the imperative at 1:15, 5:36, 11:24, and (negated) 13:21. By contrast, πιστεύω is never found in the imperative in Matthew and is used by the author of Luke-Acts only at Acts 16:31. Since Mark 11:22 introduces a series of conditional constructions and imperatives that function as conditions, it makes better sense to read the imperative here than to read the indicative.

The translation, "Have faith in God," which is the choice of the RSV and the majority of Markan scholars, depends not only on the interpretation of ἔχετε as an imperative, but also on the interpretation of θεοῦ as an objective genitive. As such, it is unique in the New Testament. The Western text has πίστις τοῦ θεοῦ at Acts 19:20, which is an example of the objective genitive with the intervening article. At Rom 3:3, πίστιν τοῦ θεοῦ is subjective: "the faithfulness of God."[21] Most of the debate on whether or not the objective genitive can be read after πίστις when there is no intervening preposition (such as εἰς) has been focused on Paul's use of πίστις with Χριστοῦ and equivalents.[22] There have been a few attempts to read the genitive in Mark 11:22 in another way, but none has gained much support.

D. W. B. Robinson attempts to argue against the existence of the objective genitive after πίστις in Mark 11:22, Acts 3:16, Col 2:12, and 2 Thess 2:13.[23] His translation of Mark 11:22 is "be firm as God is firm." However, the context does not call for fidelity or faithfulness in the sense of the Hebrew אמן, but for confidence in the power of God.

W. L. Lane suggests the translation, "you have the faithfulness of God," reading the indicative instead of the imperative and the subjective genitive. His argument is not grammatical, but theological:

doubt. The theories of Hahn and Barth require the assumption that Mark knew the Q version of the saying. The resolution of these issues regarding sources is outside the scope of the present study.

[21] Rudolf Bultmann, "πιστεύω," TDNT 6 (1968) 206 n. 243.

[22] For the literature on this debate see R. B. Hayes, The Faith of Jesus Christ (SBLDS 56; Chico: Scholars, 1983).

[23] D. W. B. Robinson, " 'Faith of Jesus Christ'—a New Testament Debate," RTR 29 (1970) 78-79.

On this understanding the solemnly introduced assurances of verses 23-24 are grounded explicitly on God's faithfulness and not on the ability of a man to banish from his heart the presumption of doubt.[24]

As we will see in Chapter 5, the author of Mark is concerned about the theological problems connected with faith as a condition for the activity of God, but the evangelist deals with the problems in a way that is different from Lane's proposal. His translation is not convincing for at least two reasons.

In the first place, "have faith" in 11:22 should be equivalent to "believe" in 11:23 and 11:24, where, as Lane himself recognizes,[25] the community is being summoned to confidence in the power of God. In the second place, in all the instances in which ἔχω occurs with πίστις the noun means either (1) confidence in the power of God to perform miracles (Matt 17:20, Matt 21:21, Mark 4:40, Luke 17:6, Acts 14:9, 1 Cor 13:2), (2) confidence in one's standing before God (Rom 14:22), or (3) a Christian doctrinal position (1 Tim 1:19, Jas 2:1, Jas 2:18, cf. Jas 2:19). In no case does ἔχειν πίστιν mean "to be the beneficiary of (the) faithfulness (of someone else)." Such a construction would ordinarily include the article before θεοῦ, as in Rom 3:3 (τὴν πίστιν τοῦ θεοῦ).

Philip Carrington apparently regards the construction as ambiguous. In *According to Mark*[26] he writes:

> The answer of Jesus might be understood as a check to the eagerness in Peter's impulsive remark. It is not very easy to translate it: "Hold firm or hold fast, a faith (which comes) from God" (or even "You have [indeed] a faith from God"): literally "of God." It might be a word of admonition designed to have a sobering effect on Peter's excitement.

However, on the next page Carrington translates the sentence, "Have faith in God,"[27] and still later, "Hold firm your faith in God."[28] Commenting on 11:24, he writes:

> The primary thing is the unwavering faith in God which originates from God; the man who has this pure faith "from God" in his heart, without any doubt or uncertainty, has on his side the greatest power in the world. He *then* finds himself asking God for something, and because the faith has preceded the asking, and comes from God, the asking is a form of faith and will be effective.[29]

Carrington's comments point toward a translation of θεοῦ not so much as a subjective genitive (God's faith) as a genitive of origin[30] or what the

---

[24] W. L. Lane, *The Gospel According to Mark* (Grand Rapids: Eerdmans, 1974) 409-10.
[25] Ibid., 410.
[26] Carrington, *Mark*, 240.
[27] Ibid., 241.
[28] Ibid., 242.
[29] Ibid., 244.
[30] F. Blass and A. Debrunner, *A Greek Grammar of the New Testament and Other Early*

older grammarians used to call an ablative of source.[31]

Apparently, Carrington regards the construction as deliberately ambiguous: "faith in God which originates from God." Reading the genitive of origin brings the Gospel of Mark within the sphere of Paul's view of miracle-working faith as a charism, and prevents faith from being viewed as a human achievement. As attractive as Carrington's proposal is, however, it remains the case that his original assessment stands: "It is not very easy" to translate ἔχετε πίστιν θεοῦ as "Hold firm a faith which comes from God." The context weighs heavily in favor of the imperative, and once the imperative is conceded, the genitive of origin can be read only with great difficulty. None of the alternative proposals is as strong as the traditional translation: "Have faith in God!"[32]

Standing as it does at the head of the collection of logia, 11:22 exercises the important function of controlling the interpretation of the individual sayings. Thus, "to believe" in verses 23 and 24 means specifically to believe in God—to have confidence in God's power.[33] As we will see in Chapter 4, only God has power to do the impossible, symbolized in 11:23 as "taking up" a mountain and "throwing" it "into the sea." The passives ἄρθητι and βλήθητι imply a divine agent; that implication is reinforced by 11:22, which specifies God as the one who moves the mountain.[34]

The parallel expressions ἔσται αὐτῷ in 11:23 and ἔσται ὑμῖν in 11:24 must be understood, because of 11:22, to mean "it will be done for him (you) by God." The use of λαμβάνω in 11:24 also points to God as the giver, as in Matt 7:8, Matt 21:22, Luke 11:10, and John 16:24.[35] Thus, the references of the commentators to the "omnipotence of faith,"[36] and their anxieties about "autosuggestion"[37] are

---

Christian Literature (rev. A. Debrunner; trans. and ed. R. W. Funk; Chicago: University of Chicago Press, 1961) 89–90. This grammar is hereinafter cited as BDF.

[31] A. T. Robertson, *A Grammar of the Greek New Testament* (Nashville: Broadman, 1934) 514–15.

[32] Malachy Marrion ('Petitionary Prayer," 91) reads the subjective genitive without arguing for it. His interpretation depends upon the concept of divinization, which Marrion attributes to Aquinas: ". . . the basis of Markan prayer is 'the faith of God,' Mk 11:22, which gradually divinizes the believer: as the believer grows in this faith, God's own power more and more becomes his own" (91–92; references to Aquinas are in note 27, page 92). Of course, this line of argument is anachronistic.

[33] Rudolf Bultmann, *The History of the Synoptic Tradition* (trans. J. Marsh; New York: Harper and Row, 1963) 91; Gnilka, *Markus*, 2:134. That "faith" here means confidence in the power of God will be argued in chapter 5.

[34] Cook, "Text Linguistic Approach," 257. See the section on the mountain-moving logion as an ἀδύνατον in chapter 4.

[35] G. Delling, "λαμβάνω," *TDNT* 4 (1967) 7.

[36] For example, Kelber, *Oral and Written*, 176.

[37] Haenchen, *Weg*, 391; Gnilka, *Markus*, 2:134.

without warrant in the Markan text. The author makes it clear in the way he introduces the prayer teaching that the agent of miracle is God, not faith, or the person who has faith.[38]

Prayer and Faith: 11:23-24

Verse 23 makes a general statement about the relationship between faith and the power of God; verse 24 applies the principle to the prayers of the community. The connective διὰ τοῦτο, "on this account," indicates that the prayer instruction in verse 24 is based on the preceding verse. To reinforce the connection, the two sayings are made parallel in structure. Both are introduced with λέγω ὑμῖν, shortened in verse 24 by the omission of the asseverative ἀμήν. Both employ the verb πιστεύω followed by a ὅτι clause indicating the activity of God, and both end with a short apodosis promising a response to believing prayer: ἔσται αὐτῷ (11:23), ἔσται ὑμῖν (11:24). The pair may be diagrammed as follows:

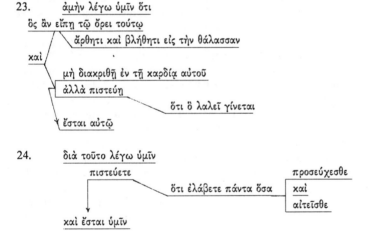

The ὃς ἄν construction in verse 23 introduces a general third-class condition that expects the situation in the apodosis to occur if the condition of the protasis is fulfilled.[39] The condition is expressed by the three subjunctive verbs: εἴπῃ, (μή) διακριθῇ, πιστεύῃ.

[38] Ethelbert Stauffer, *New Testament Theology* (trans. J. Marsh; New York: Macmillan, 1955) 169: "What is it that distinguishes this faith from the self-intoxication that, in the words of Björnson, 'is beyond one's powers' and makes a man and his work end up in a fiasco? The 'faith' of Mark 11:23f. is a faith that prays . . . Prayer is the source of its power, and the means of its strength—God's omnipotence is its sole assurance, and God's sovereignty its only restriction."

[39] H. E. Dana and J. R. Mantey, *A Manual Grammar of the Greek New Testament* (New York: Macmillan, 1927) 290.

The command to the mountain, as we shall see in chapter 4, is a figure of speech that is common in Mark's environment, and represents something thought to be impossible. Whether or not the deity had the power to do the impossible was a widely debated issue in the Hellenistic-Roman world. Magicians often claimed that *they* could do the impossible. The placement of the saying about the mountain between the exhortation, "Have faith in God!" and the saying about communal prayer in 11:24 thus clarifies the evangelist's position on two issues. Against those who say that some things are impossible even for God, the author of Mark asserts that God *can* do the impossible (move a mountain). Against those who might accuse Christian miracle-workers of magic, the evangelist places the emphasis on *God* as the doer of the impossible. The parallel structures of verses 23 and 24 specify the command to the mountain in verse 23 as a prayer,[40] and prevent its being interpreted as a magic spell.[41]

The coordination of μὴ διακριθῇ with πιστεύῃ by the adversative ἀλλὰ makes the two expressions equivalent. To believe is to refuse to doubt in one's heart. Thus "not doubting" does not represent an especially strong faith,[42] but is rather a definition of faith,[43] the force of which carries over into the parallel πιστεύετε in verse 24. The use of the present imperative in verses 24 and 25 creates an implied condition. In verse 24, "believe that you received" replaces the protasis and "it will be done for you" describes the result.[44]

Each instance of πιστεύω is followed by a ὅτι clause. In verse 23, the one who speaks to the mountain believes "that what he says happens," that is, that God performs the "impossible" act of removing a mountain from its place (αἴρω) and throwing it (βάλλω) into the sea. The parallel ὅτι clause in verse 24, "that you received everything whatsoever you are praying and asking for" is based on the premise of verse 24, as the connecting διὰ τοῦτο indicates. Since everything is possible for God, everything whatsoever (πάντα ὅσα) the community prays for can be regarded as already given by God and, in that sense, already received by the community.

The aorist ἐλάβετε in 11:24 is a more difficult reading than the present λαμβάνετε (A, f¹³, and the majority text) or the future λήμψεσθε (D, Θ, f¹, 565, 700,

---

[40] Lohmeyer (*Markus,* 239) thinks that the command to the mountain is a prayer. See also Pesch, *Markusevangelium,* 2:208 and Cook, "Text Linguistic Approach," 256.

[41] It is, of course, not possible to know for certain the extent to which the evangelist may have been attempting to protect Christian miracle-workers against charges of magic. That such a defense might have been necessary is suggested by the similarity of the attitudes advocated by 11:23 and by a magic spell preserved in Albrecht Dieterich, *Abraxas* (Leipzig: Teubner, 1891) 196, lines 17– 18: "What I say must happen" (ὃ ἔνειπω, δεῖ γενέσθαι). Magicians claimed to be able to force the gods to do their bidding. In chapter 7 we will see how the category "will of God" could be used as a defense against this aspect of magical practice.

[42] Against Barth, "Glaube," 276.

[43] Schweizer, *Mark,* 234; Schlatter, *Markus,* 215; Gnilka, *Markus,* 2:134.

[44] Robertson, *Grammar,* 948–949, 1022–1023; Swete, *Mark,* 261; Taylor, *Mark,* 467.

the Latin versions and Cyprian). It is to be preferred both because it is extremely unlikely that the present or future would have been changed to an aorist and because the aorist is attested by Sinaiticus, Vaticanus, and other important witnesses.[45] The value of the variants is that they indicate that this aorist was understood by early readers of the gospel as a past tense and regarded as erroneous or offensive.[46] The contrast in the original tenses is emphasized in the proposed translation at the beginning of this section by translating the present tenses progressively: "Keep on believing that you received everything that you are praying and asking for, and it will be done for you."

Prayer and Forgiveness: 11:25

Verse 25 adds the further condition of forgiveness.[47] The connection with what precedes is not merely the catchword "prayer." On the contrary, there is understood to be an intrinsic connection between forgiveness and effective petitionary prayer, as we will see in chapter 6. The adverbial phrase, "whenever you stand praying," indicates that the condition to follow must be fulfilled if the dramatic results promised in 23 and 24 are to be realized.[48] The condition is again implied by the imperative, as in verse 24,[49] and a ἵνα clause substitutes for the apodosis.[50] The forgiveness of the sins of the praying community is made dependent upon their forgiveness of each other. Both are necessary in order for the community to receive everything they pray and ask for.

It is worth noting that it is assumed that prayer is offered by a community. The singular ὃς ἄν of the mountain-moving saying in 11:23 is overshadowed by the plurals in the other sayings: ἔχετε (11:22), προσεύχεσθε, καὶ αἰτεῖσθε, πιστεύετε, ἐλάβετε, ἔσται ὑμῖν, (11:24), στήκετε προσευχόμενοι, ἀφίετε, ἔχετε, ὑμῖν, ὑμῶν (11:25). No doubt a carryover from Jewish practice, in which even the individual praying alone uses the first person plural,[51] this emphasis on the communal character of

---

[45] C, L, W, Δ, 892, pc, sa^mss, bo^mss.

[46] Metzger (Commentary, 110) thinks that the copyists found the aorist too bold. The future may have been influenced by Matt 21:22. Taylor (Mark, 467) writes, "ἐλάβετε points back to something that has already happened."

[47] Zmijewski, "Glaube," 90; Stendahl, "Prayer," 85–86; Swete, Mark, 261; Lane, Mark, 411.

[48] ὅταν is found with the present indicative only infrequently according to Robertson, Grammar, 972–973. Mark uses it with the imperfect in 3:11 and with the aorist indicative in 11:19. Since the usual sense of ὅταν with the indicative in past tenses is indefinite repetition (Robertson, Grammar, 973), Swete (Mark, 261) translates it "whenever" in 11:25. Although the tense of στήκετε is present, the context implies repeated action. Taylor (Mark, 228) however, insists on the simple "when." On standing as a prayer posture, see Swete, Mark, 261; Marrion, "Petitionary Prayer," 42 n. 88; Heinrich Greeven, "εὔχομαι," TDNT 2 (1964) 779.

[49] See the references in note 44.

[50] Matt 7:1: μὴ κρίνετε, ἵνα μὴ κριθῆτε.

[51] Heinemann, Prayer, 15, 250.

prayer may be another attempt to distinguish Christian prayer from magic, which tended to be private and individualistic.[52] Although the Markan Jesus sometimes prays alone (1:35, 6:46, 14:35), he does not instruct his disciples to pray "in secret," as does the Matthean Jesus (Matt 6:5-6). It is not the private room (Matt 5:6) which replaces the temple as the "house of prayer" in Mark, but the praying community.

SUMMARY: TWO CONDITIONS FOR EFFECTIVE PRAYER

The prayer teaching in Mark 11 is prepared for by the Markan editing of the end of the fig tree pericope. The introductory exhortation, "Have faith in God" (11:22) controls the interpretation of the logia in 11:23-25. The coordinated pair of sayings, 11:23-24, emphasize faith as a condition for effective prayer. In chapters 4 and 5 we will discover the significance of the claim made in 11:23 that God will move mountains in response to prayer, and the relationship between such a claim and the πίστις/πιστεύω word group, as it would have been understood by the audience of Mark.

Mark 11:25 emphasizes forgiveness as a condition for effective prayer. In chapter 6 we will explore the relationship between forgiveness and petitionary prayer.

---

[52] David E. Aune, "Magic in Early Christianity," *ANRW* 2.23.2 (1980) 1512 (citing the work of W. J. Goode). On the scholarly debate over whether or not ancient magic can be distinguished from ancient religion, see pages 1508-16 of Aune's article and the discussion in chapter 7 of this study. Also of interest is Adalbert Hamman, "La prière chrétienne et la prière païenne, formes et différences," *ANRW* 2.23.2 (1980) 1230-31.

PART II

THE THEOLOGY OF THE
MARKAN PRAYER LOGIA

4
Prayer to the God
Who Moves Mountains

One of the most striking aspects of the Markan prayer teaching is the extravagance of the promises that are made to the praying community in 11:23-24. In response to prayer God will cause a mountain to "be taken up and thrown into the sea." In fact, the community may expect everything (πάντα) they ask in prayer to be done for them by God. These claims are mutually reinforcing: to say that God is able to move a mountain is to claim that God is able to do something that is impossible in the normal course of things. God can do the impossible because, as the author of Mark insists throughout the gospel, "everything is possible for God." In this chapter we will investigate the cultural context within which the evangelist makes such claims in an attempt to understand how this aspect of the prayer teaching would have been understood by the audience of the gospel.

THE MOUNTAIN-MOVING LOGION AS AN ἀδύνατον

Although modern theologians may sometimes be tempted to regard the ancients as naive and superstitious, it is nevertheless clear that the evangelists and their contemporaries had their own notions of what kinds of events were to be expected in the regular course of things and what would be regarded as extraordinary or impossible[1] One of the indicators of ancient notions of the impossible is the literary device known as the ἀδύνατον or "impossibility," which was used by both Greek and Latin writers in a variety of ways.[2] The discussion

---

[1] The standard work on this topic is Robert M. Grant, *Miracle and Natural Law in Graeco-Roman and Early Christian Thought* (Amsterdam: North-Holland, 1952). More recently, Harold Remus (*Pagan-Christian Conflict over Miracle in the Second Century* [Cambridge, MA: Philadelphia Patristic Foundation, 1983]) has contributed a helpful analysis of the categories and bases for ancient views of the ordinary and the extraordinary as they relate to the concept of miracle.

[2] The following discussion is dependent on H. V. Canter, "The Figure ΑΔΥΝΑΤΟΝ in Greek and Latin Poetry" *American Journal of Philology* 51 (1930) 32–41 and Ernest Dutoit, *Le Thème de L'Adynaton dans la Poésie Antique* (Paris: Société d'Edition "Les Belles Lettres," 1936).

which follows will demonstrate that Mark 11:23 is an example of one of the typical uses of the ἀδύνατον device in antiquity.

The ἀδύνατον as a Literary Device

The most common use of the ἀδύνατον involves the juxtaposition of two events or conditions, one of which is regarded by common consent as utterly impossible. The effect is to render the other member of the pair impossible or unthinkable as well. So Herodotus (5.92) has Socles tell the citizens of Sparta that "the heaven shall be beneath the earth and the earth aloft above the heaven, and men shall dwell in the sea and fishes where men did dwell before, now that you . . . are destroying the rule of equals and making ready to bring back despotism into the cities . . ." Pindar asserts that it is no more possible for the Locrians to fail to be wise and brave than for the fox or the lion to change its nature.[3] An epigram attributed to Lucian says, "You will sooner find white crows and winged tortoises than a Cappadocian who is an accomplished orator."[4]

This kind of appeal to what is typical or expected in the natural world is quite common. Since the regularity of nature is something that can be depended upon, it is appealed to in the composition of oaths. In Ovid's *Metamorphoses* 14.37–39, Glaucus insists that before he changes his mind about his love for Scylla, trees will grow on the sea and seaweed on the mountains. Horace's sailors swear not to give up on their mission until rocks float, until the Po river flows backward, and until the Apennine mountains rush down to the sea (*in mare seu celsus procurrerit Appenninus*).[5] Luke's sycamine tree, which is "uprooted and planted in the sea" (17:6) and Mark's mountain that can be ordered to "be taken up and cast into the sea" (11:23) represent "impossibilities" which depend for their force on common-sense notions about the regularity of nature.[6] The reversal of rivers is often found in ἀδύνατα, as is the notion of the "impossible count," which is illustrated by the number of stars, grains of sand, or pebbles on the shore.[7] Homer says that there were as many Achaean soldiers arrayed against Troy as there are flies around a dairy in the spring.[8]

Of course, similar views of the impossible are found in Hebrew literature. Jeremiah 13:23 says, "Can the Ethiopian change his skin or the leopard his spots? Then also you can do good who are accustomed to do evil." Isaiah 49:15 says that even if a mother should reject her own child (which is unthinkable), Yahweh will not forget Zion. Proverbs 6:27-29: "Can a man carry fire in his bosom and his clothes not be burned? Or can one walk upon hot coals and his feet not be scorched? So is he who goes in to his neighbor's wife; none who

---

[3] *Olympian Ode* 11. 20–21.

[4] *The Greek Anthology*, LCL, 11. 436.

[5] *Epode* 16. 25–35; Dutoit, *L'Adynaton*, 85.

[6] Remus, *Conflict*, 24.

[7] Canter, "ΑΔΥΝΑΤΟΝ," 39.

[8] *Iliad* 2. 467–71.

touches her will go unpunished." The "impossible count" appears in Genesis 15:5, where Yahweh says to Abram, "Look toward heaven, and number the stars, if you are able to number them . . . so shall your descendants be."

The normal literary use of the ἀδύνατον is the one illustrated above. The "semi-scientific common sense"[9] of the audience is appealed to in order to make the point that the action in question is just as impossible or unthinkable as the ἀδύνατον. But the saying in Mark 11:23 belongs to a second classification of ἀδύνατον usage in antiquity. In this class of references to events popularly regarded as impossible, the sense of the ἀδύνατον is reversed![10] Instead of using the ἀδύνατον to emphasize how impossible it is that something should happen, the figure is used to assert that an impossible action *can* be performed or has been performed by a deity or by a human assisted by divine powers.

Dio Chrysostom gives examples of impossible things that only a god can do: "to have men walk dryshod over the sea, to sail over the mountains, to drain rivers by drinking . . ."[11] Lists of ἀδύνατα are found in texts that describe magicians, witches, or priests who have access to divine power and can therefore do the impossible. Claudian's magician claims to know how the Chaldeans "impose their will upon the subject gods" (*qua gens Chaldaea vocatis imperet arte deis*) and claims, by virtue of this access to divine power, to be able to cause trees to walk and rivers to flow backward![12] Ovid's Medea claims to reverse the course of streams, uproot rocks and trees, move forests, shake mountains, calm angry seas, disturb calm waters and cause ghosts to come forth from their tombs![13] Similar lists are found in Apuleius, *Met.* 1.3, Tibullus 1.2.41-52, Virgil, *Aeneid* 4.483-93, Propertius, *Elegies* 4.5.5-18![14] The control of the weather and of the movements of the heavenly bodies are elements often found in such lists.

Again, similar acts are attributed to God and to the "men of God" in Hebrew literature. A few that resemble the ἀδύνατα found in pagan sources are stopping the flow of seas or rivers (Exod 14:21-22, Josh 3:15-17), control of heavenly bodies (Josh 10:12-14), control of weather (Exod 9:23-24; 1 Kgs 17:1), causing iron to float (2 Kgs 6:7). In Job 9:5-7, God is described as "he who removes mountains, who shakes the earth . . . who commands the sun, and it does not rise; who seals up the stars." Rabbinic literature knows the reversal of rivers and the uprooting of trees (*b. B. Mes.* 58b-59b), the control of weather (*b. Ta'an.* 23a-25b, *b. Yoma* 53b), and the uprooting of mountains (*b. Sota* 9b).

When the saying about the mountain in Mark 11:23 is understood as an ἀδύνατον, it must be read as a claim that the power of God to do the impossible

---

[9] Grant, *Miracle,* 58.
[10] Canter, "ΑΔΥΝΑΤΟΝ," 32 n. 1.
[11] *Oration,* 3. 30.
[12] *In Ruf.* 1. 145-63.
[13] *Met.* 7. 199-206.
[14] See also A. S. Pease, *Publi Vergili Maronis Aeneidos IV* (Darmstadt: Wissenschaftliche Buchgesellschaft, 1967) 401-6, for additional examples.

is available to the believing community through prayer (11:24).[15] However, the objection has been raised that the mountain-moving saying is *not* about the power available to prayer, but is rather an eschatological prediction which has been attached to the prayer logia in violation of its intent. Therefore, it is necessary briefly to consider this line of argument.

The Eschatological Interpretation of 11:23

W. R. Telford thinks that the evangelist treats the mountain-moving saying as an announcement that the events of the last days are taking place in his present. Mountains were expected to be moved in the last days, Telford argues, and the evangelist predicts that the temple mount ("this mountain") is about to be cast down![16] He agrees with R. E. Dowda:

> The temple is the mountainous obstacle which is to vanish before the faith of the gospel movement. The temple system, with its corrupt clericalism and vested interests, is to be removed in the eschatological era, which is now being experienced![17]

In order to interpret the saying in this way, Telford first has to excise verses 24 and 25 from the Markan text![18] Then he has to make "this mountain" equivalent to the temple![19] He can show that in two places in the Talmud "this mountain" is a reference to the temple: *b. Pesah.* 87b; *b. Git.* 56b.[20] He has not demonstrated that "this mountain" would have been understood as a reference to the temple as early as the time of Mark.

In Isa 2:2 and Mic 4:1, "the mountain of the house of the Lord" will be *established* in the Messianic age, not *removed* as in Mark 11:23. The mountains which are to be leveled to make way for the Lord (Isa 40:4–5) or for Cyrus (Isa 45:2) are not removed or cast into the sea. According to Zech 4:6–10 a mountain will be leveled so that the temple can be *restored.*

In fact, the only instance Telford can cite in which the moving of mountains is associated with the *destruction* of the temple is *b. B. Bat.* 3b where there is a discussion about whether Herod acted illegally by tearing down the old temple before the new one was built. The response is:

---

[15] So, for example, Cranfield, *Mark,* 361; Zmijewski, "Glaube," 100.

[16] Telford, *Barren,* 119.

[17] R. E. Dowda, "The Cleansing of the Temple in the Synoptic Gospels" (Ph.D. dissertation, Duke University, 1972) 250. This allegorical interpretation is borrowed from Carrington, *Mark,* 243.

[18] See the section, "W. R. Telford: Mark 11:24–25 as Interpolation," in chapter 2.

[19] Telford, *Barren,* 59, with C. H. Dodd, *The Parables of the Kingdom* (London: Nisbet, 1935) 63. See also Edwin K. Broadhead, "Which Mountain Is 'This Mountain'? A Critical Note on Mark 11:22–25," *Paradigms* 2 (1986) 33–38.

[20] Telford, *Barren,* 170 n. 65.

... if you like I can say that the rule does not apply to Royalty, since a king does not go back on his word. For so said Samuel: If Royalty says, I will uproot mountains, it will uproot them and not go back on its word.

Telford argues that since the idea of uprooting mountains appears in a discussion about the temple, then the temple mount is understood to be the mountain that a king can uproot with impunity.[21]

The problem with this argument is that "one who uproots mountains" is a technical term in rabbinic literature for a person so skilled in argumentation that he can solve legal problems that appear to be insoluble. Telford discusses this usage,[22] but refuses to admit that the passage about Herod's illegal action is an example of "uprooting mountains" in the sense of solving impossible legal problems — in this case by royal fiat. Of course, the use of this image to express the idea of the impossible is further proof that the moving of a mountain would have been understood as an ἀδύνατον by the audience of Mark.

A final observation about Telford's argument is that since in the Markan narrative the setting for 11:23 is somewhere outside Bethany (11:12-13) "at the Mount of Olives" (11:1), τῷ ὄρει τούτῳ should refer to the nearer mountain, i.e., the Mount of Olives.[23] A reference to the more distant mountain, on which the temple stood, would have read τῷ ὄρει ἐκείνῳ.

R. M. Grant takes "this mountain" as a reference to the Mount of Olives, but he too gives the verse an eschatological interpretation. According to Grant, the mountain-moving saying is a mistranslation into Greek of a word of Jesus based on the prophecy of Zechariah 14:4:[24]

On that day his feet shall stand on the Mount of Olives which lies before Jerusalem on the east; and the Mount of Olives shall be split in two from east to west by a very wide valley; so that one half of the Mount shall withdraw northward, and the other half southward.

Since the Hebrew "the west" (יָמָּה) literally means "the sea," Grant argues that Mark 11:23 is Jesus' own version of the messianic woes predicted in Zechariah 14:4 and Psalm 46:3: "we will not fear, though the earth change and the mountains be moved[25] into the heart of the seas . . ." The verse therefore is to be understood eschatologically. Several observations may be made about this suggestion.

First, Grant's interpretation is really an interpretation of the intent of the historical Jesus, not an interpretation of Mark. Second, the messianic woes

---

[21] Ibid., 112.

[22] Ibid., 110-12.

[23] M.-J. Lagrange, *Évangile selon Saint Marc* (Paris: Gabalda, 1966) 923.

[24] Grant, *Miracle,* 167, based on R. M. Grant, "The Coming of the Kingdom," *JBL* 67 (1948) 300. Gaston (*No Stone,* 475 n. 3) attributes a similar view to C. F. Evans and William Manson.

[25] RSV: "though the mountains shake in the heart of the sea."

cannot by any stretch of the imagination be understood as something initiated by a human command, and yet the Markan Jesus says, "Whoever says to this mountain . . . it will be done for him." Third, the faith required in the time of the messianic woes is the faith to endure them, not faith to cause them: Ps. 46:1 "God is our refuge and strength, a very present help in trouble." Fourth, the Zechariah prophecy speaks of the Mount of Olives being split from east to west, but *moving* north and south, so the "mistranslation" of "to the west" as the direction of movement is irrelevant.[26] Finally, Grant ignores the fact that the moving of mountains is an ἀδύνατον: Horace speaks of mountains rushing down to the sea. Grant recognizes the ἀδύνατον in Luke 17:6[27] but misses the fact that the Markan version has exactly the same function, which is to assert that faith gives access to God's ability to do the impossible.

This is the way the saying was understood in the early church. Before Mark, Paul understood the saying as an example of the impossible things that a Christian might do by faith (1 Cor 13:2). That is also the way the saying was interpreted in Matt 17:19-20, 21:21 and Luke 17:5-6. It still meant that through faith Christians could do the impossible in the *Acts of Paul*.[28] Cyril of Alexandria and Chrysostom found it necessary to respond to charges by Porphyry that the apostles were lacking in faith, since they moved no mountains.[29] The *Gospel of Thomas* (48, 106) understands the saying as an ἀδύνατον but does not connect it with faith.[30] Rufinus reports that when Gregory the Thaumaturge wanted to have a church built in a location that was too narrow, he quoted the Matthean version of the saying to the Lord in prayer one night and went out the next morning to discover that the mountain had moved aside to make room for the church.[31] Neither Grant nor Telford is able to find an ancient interpretation of

---

[26] Gaston, *No Stone*, 475 n. 3. Gaston, following C. H. Dodd, suggests that "the sea" means "the Gentiles." Thus, the church prays that the temple (Mount Zion = this mountain) may go to the Gentiles ('the sea') since the Gentiles cannot make their prophesied pilgrimage to Mount Zion (474-76, cf. 83-84). When we start down the primrose path of allegory, anything can mean anything.

[27] Grant, *Miracle*, 167.

[28] E. Hennecke and W. Schneemelcher, eds., *New Testament Apocrypha* (2 vols.; trans. R. McL. Wilson; Philadelphia: Westminster, 1963-65) 2:382.

[29] Grant, "Kingdom," 302.

[30] Texts in Telford, *Barren*, 118.

[31] To his translation of Eusebius' *Church History*, Rufinus added four anecdotes about St. Gregory Thaumaturgus at Book 7, chapter 28. The story about St. Gregory and the mountain is the second story in that series. The text may be seen in *Eusebius*, Bd. 2, T. 2 (GCS; ed. Eduard Schwartz; Leipzig: Hinrichs, 1908) 954. The following translation is by Robert Ulery, Department of Classics, Wake Forest University, Winston-Salem, NC, 1985:

"There is recorded yet another more outstanding and divine act of his. In a certain locality of narrow countryside, when the situation demanded the construction of a church, a certain cliff of a nearby mountain jutting forth on the east, and on the other side a river flowing by, denied them the space sufficient for a church. And since there was no other

Mark 11:23 that corresponds with his own reading; thus, if the original intent was to predict the eschaton rather than to teach about the power available to believing prayer, the message was not received by any ancient interpreter.

The best solution is to read the mountain-moving saying as an ἀδύνατον in the "reverse" sense of an impossible occurrence that is possible only for a deity or for a human who has access to divine power. That the author of Mark could use ἀδύνατα in this way is confirmed by two other instances in which he does so: 2:1-12 and 10:23-27.

Markan ἀδύνατα in 2:1-12 and 10:23-27

The healing of the paralytic in 2:1-12 is combined with a controversy over the forgiveness of sins. The scribes' objection is appropriate: only God can forgive sins (2:7).[32] Jesus' response is in the form of an ἀδύνατον similar to the "sooner . . . than . . ." type:[33] "Which is easier to say to the paralytic, 'Your sins are forgiven,' or to say, 'Rise, take up your pallet and walk'?" The obvious answer is that the former is easier, since the latter is impossible. The Markan Jesus proves his (divine) authority to forgive sins by performing an impossible task; if he has God's power to do the latter, then he has God's right to do the former. That Jesus' power and authority are from God and not produced by magic is confirmed by the response of the bystanders (2:12): "They were all amazed and glorified God."

This reverse sense of the ἀδύνατον is present again in Mark 10:23-27. In 10:25 the Markan Jesus says, "It is easier for a camel to go through the eye of a needle than for a rich person to enter the Kingdom of God." This saying taken alone is an ἀδύνατον in the original sense.[34] Something universally recognized to be impossible (that a camel should go through the eye of a needle) is juxtaposed with an event the possibility of which is not known (that a rich person should

---

place whatever and everyone was very gloomy, because they did not have the ground for construction of a church, he, full of faith, is said to have spent the night in prayer and to have faithfully reminded the Lord Jesus of His promise, in which He said, 'If you have faith like a grain of mustard seed you will say to this mountain, "Begone and cast yourself into the sea," and it will surely be done.' And since he demanded these things in full faith and devotion, when the people came together at daybreak the troublesome cliff was found to have receded just (far enough to provide the) space required for laying the foundations of the church."

Some of the Fathers interpreted the mountain-moving saying metaphorically or made a moral application. In the *Clementine Recognitions* it refers to the conquest of human passions. Origen takes the mountain as a symbol of Satan in the *Commentary on Matthew* 16.26 (Grant, "Kingdom," 301-2). As usual, this kind of patristic interpretation is intended to reveal a level of meaning other than the level of the text itself.

[32] Robbins, *Jesus*, 118.

[33] Grant, *Miracle*, 133; Canter, "ΑΔΥΝΑΤΟΝ," 33-35.

[34] Grant, *Miracle*, 133.

enter the kingdom of God). The effect is to assert: It is impossible for a rich person to enter the kingdom of God.[35]

In the dialogue with the disciples the Markan Jesus reverses the sense of the ἀδύνατον by asserting that God can accomplish the impossible, i.e., cause a rich person to enter the Kingdom of God (10:27). In its present form 10:23–27 is arranged in such a way that this reversal provides the dramatic climax to the dialogue.[36] In 10:17–22, the failure of the inquirer to follow Jesus is explained with a typical Markan γάρ clause: "for he had a great many possessions." Jesus generalizes the man's situation in 10:23: "How hard it will be for those who have riches to enter the kingdom of God!" The disciples react to this saying with amazement (ἐθαμβοῦντο, 10:24a).

The audience overhearing this dialogue would have understood the amazement of the disciples. In the Greco-Roman world, riches were a religious asset, not a liability. The wealthy could be initiated into more mysteries and offer more and better sacrifices in support of their prayers to various deities. In the Jewish tradition, the Deuteronomic equation of prosperity with the blessing of God had been reinforced by the wisdom school. There were protests, of course, the book of Job and Cynic asceticism, for example, but here the disciples represent the popular opinion: A rich person should not have difficulty entering the Kingdom of God.

In 24b–25 Jesus repeats and intensifies his assertion. Entry into the Kingdom is difficult. In fact, for a rich person it is impossible. At this the disciples are even more astonished (περισσῶς ἐξεπλήσσοντο, 10:26a). The intensification from difficult to impossible is matched by an intensification in the

[35] For subsequent attempts to reinterpret the saying so that the salvation of the rich is difficult, but not impossible, see Grant, *Miracle*, 132–33 and Taylor, *Mark*, 431.

[36] It is not necessary to rearrange the order of the verses, as the Western text does, on the grounds that the ἀδύνατον in 25 must follow 23 (Bultmann, *History*, 22). It is also incorrect to interpret 24b as a broadening of 23, as Taylor does: "It is particularly hard for a rich man, but hard indeed for anyone to enter into the Kingdom of God" (*Mark*, 431). Instead, 24b is a condensed repetition of 23; the secondary τοὺς πεποιθότας ἐπὶ [τοῖς] χρήμασιν of A C D Θ, etc., though it does not belong in the Markan text, nevertheless correctly understands 24b as repetitious. The ἀδύνατον of 25 then intensifies the situation from difficult to impossible.

The Western rearrangement is not more logical than the present text, as Lagrange (*Marc*, 269) thinks, because the Western text leaves the intensification of the disciples' reaction ("they were exceedingly astonished," 26a) after the second statement of Jesus, which in the Western text is actually an amelioration of 23. The "logic" of the Western text is: (1) Jesus says that it is difficult, even impossible, for rich people to enter the Kingdom. (2) The disciples are amazed. (3) Jesus says that, after all, it is only those who trust in their riches who will have difficulty. (4) The disciples are even more amazed. According to the Western text, the disciples are more shocked after the less shocking statement. See also Metzger, *Commentary*, 105–6.

reaction.[37] Their question, "Then who can be saved?" means, "If the rich, who have the most potential, cannot be saved (enter the kingdom) then who can?"[38] It is at this point that the Markan Jesus reverses the ἀδύνατον of 10:25; the impossibility applies only to humans, not to God. Everything is possible for God: παρὰ ἀνθρώποις ἀδύνατον, ἀλλ' οὐ παρὰ θεῷ· πάντα γὰρ δυνατὰ παρὰ τῷ θεῷ.[39]

Both in 2:9 and in 10:27 the ἀδύνατα function to affirm the ability of God to effect a change in the spiritual (and therefore unseen) status of persons. In 2:1-12, Jesus' authority to forgive sins is established by his ability to perform an impossible act, i.e., an act of God. In 10:23-27, God's ability to do the impossible is invoked to make it possible for rich people to be saved (enter the Kingdom).[40] By implication, if God can cause even the rich to enter the kingdom, then anyone can be saved. Salvation (entrance into the Kingdom) is impossible for all humans but is made possible by God. This appeal to God's ability to effect spiritual or moral change that no human effort can effect is also found in Philo. No amount of asceticism can convert an idolatrous soul, "but only God, with whom that is possible which is impossible with us" (θεὸς δὲ μόνος ᾧ δυνατὰ τὰ παρ' ἡμῖν ἀδύνατα).[41]

In 10:23-27 the connection between the reversed ἀδύνατον and the formula "everything is possible for God" is explicit. God can do the impossible because God can do anything. In 11:22-25 we find the claim that God will do the impossible for the person who has faith in God. This claim is also grounded in the omnipotence of God, implicitly behind the πάντα of 11:24. Because (διὰ τοῦτο) God can do the impossible (move a mountain) for one who has faith, the praying community is instructed to believe that they have received everything (πάντα) they ask in prayer. In 14:36, the Markan Jesus begins his prayer with an appeal to the omnipotence of God: "everything is possible for you!" It is clear that the evangelist regards the affirmation of divine omnipotence as essential to his view of prayer. To affirm God's power to act in the world in response to the prayers of the community, the author of Mark employs a formula with a rich heritage in the Greek religious and philosophical traditions: πάντα δυνατὰ παρὰ τῷ θεῷ.

---

[37] Rolf Busemann, *Die Jungergemeinde nach Markus 10* (Bonn: Peter Hanstein, 1983) 46.

[38] Not, as Haenchen thinks, (*Weg,* 354) "Which rich person can be saved?"

[39] The soteriological position that emerges here contradicts not only the equation of prosperity with blessing, but also the position of ascetic moralism that requires the renunciation of riches for salvation. The Markan text asserts that God is able to save even the rich.

[40] In the Acts of Peter and Andrew, Peter pacifies a rich man who is offended by this saying by miraculously causing a camel to pass through the eye of a needle (P. J. Achtemeier, "Jesus and the Disciples as Miracle Workers in the Apocryphal New Testament," *Aspects of Religious Propaganda in Judaism and Early Christianity* [ed. E. Schüssler Fiorenza; Notre Dame: University of Notre Dame Press, 1976] 186 n. 127).

[41] *Spec.* 1. 282.

The following discussion of the ways in which this formula was used by Greek and Latin authors and the critique of the formula by certain of the philosophical schools will contribute to our understanding of the importance of the notion of omnipotence for the Markan theology of prayer.

DIVINE OMNIPOTENCE AND INTERVENTION:
A HELLENISTIC DEBATE

The assumption in Greek literature that omnipotence is inherent in the definition of deity is at least as early as Homer: [Zeus] can do anything (δύναται γὰρ ἅπαντα — Od. 4.237, Od. 14.445); the gods have power to do all things (θεοὶ δέ τε πάντα δύναται — Od. 10.306). Inscriptional evidence confirms the importance of this idea for popular piety. An inscription in Phrygia reads, "I give thanks to Mother Leto because out of impossibilities she makes possibilities" (εὐχαριστῶ Μητρὶ Λητῷ ὅτι ἐξ ἀδυνάτων δυνατὰ πυεῖ).[42] The magical papyri also stress power as a divine attribute: δύναται γὰρ πάντα ὁ θεὸς οὗτος.[43] Similar formulas are sometimes found in Greek and Roman prayers. In an appeal to the oracle of Phoebus Apollo, Virgil's Aeneas says, ". . . you are able to do everything" (potes namque omnia)[44] and a prayer to Serapis asserts, ". . . nothing is impossible for you" (οὐδέν γε σοὶ ἀδύνατον).[45] A prayer to Apollo in the Iliad informs the god, ". . . but you have power everywhere to hearken" (δύνασαι δὲ σὺ πάντοσ' ἀκούειν)[46] and Ovid has Pygmalion pray to Venus, ". . . if you are able to give all things . . ." (si di dare cuncta potestis).[47] According to Pseudo-Callisthenes 3.26, Alexander addresses the deity with the formula, "nothing is impossible for you" (ἀδυνατεῖ δὲ οὐδέν σοι).[48] Often the vocabulary of power (posse, δύναμαι) is found in prayer and hymn texts which, although they fall short of claims to absolute omnipotence, nevertheless remind a particular deity that the request being made falls within his or her sphere of influence and ability.[49]

The idea that the gods could and would intervene in the world for the benefit of their devotees was the basis for the traditional sacrifices of the state religion, for divination and the consultation of oracles, and for the practical piety of the common people. The average person in the imperial period knew what was ordinary and what was impossible; the effectiveness of the ἀδύνατον as

---

[42] W. M. Ramsay, The Cities and Bishoprics of Phrygia (2 vols.; Oxford: Clarendon, 1895) 1:153.

[43] Leiden Pap. J 395 in PGM 2:119, line 713. See additional references in Grant, Miracle, 128 n. 1.

[44] Aeneid 6. 116f.

[45] Aelius Aristides, In Serap. 1 (87D). Cited by van Unnik, "Mk 14,36," 28.

[46] Iliad 16. 515.

[47] Met. 10. 274.

[48] van Unnik, "Mk 14,36," 32.

[49] See further examples and discussion in van Unnik, "Mk 14,36," 28–29.

a literary device depends upon this common-sense view of reality.[50] At the same time, the expectation that the gods or their intermediaries could and did act on the world in extraordinary ways was widespread,[51] not merely among the masses, but even in certain of the philosophical schools.[52]

However, the omnipotence and intervention of the gods was denied by representatives of other philosophical traditions. This debate was a significant factor in the cultural context in which the author of Mark wrote and cannot be ignored if his own use of the claim, πάντα δυνατὰ παρὰ τῷ θεῷ, is to be understood. Although our knowledge of the issues is derived from literary sources, we know that the nature of the gods and their relationship to events in the world were debated in the public forums of cities throughout the empire.[53] Thus it is likely that both the author of the gospel and his audience would have been aware that to claim omnipotence for one's god—as the evangelist does explicitly in 10:27 and 14:36 and implicitly in 9:23 and 11:22-25—was to locate oneself with respect to alternative views of reality.[54] Although an exhaustive discussion of the issues is impossible in this study, a sketch of the debate will illustrate the diversity of the world-views that were competing for adherents during the period in which our evangelist was trying to teach his community how to pray.

The Epicurean Position

The philosophical community founded by Epicurus (341-271 B.C.E.) seems to have peaked in influence shortly before the end of the republican period, but it remained strong at least until 200 C.E.[55] Epicurus believed that human unhappiness was caused by mistaken beliefs, those about the gods being among the most harmful.[56] Epicureanism combated the superstition and fear engendered by these mistaken beliefs by denying that the gods have any influence over natural events or human affairs.[57] That the gods exist, and that they are immortal, sublimely happy and of human shape is proven by the fact that these things are universally believed,[58] but to be sublimely happy means

[50] Remus, *Conflict*, 7; Grant, *Miracle*, 58.

[51] Remus, *Conflict*, 74.

[52] See Grant, *Miracle*, chapters 4 and 5 on the increasing credulity among philosophers. According to Grant, "the tide had already turned" by the end of the first century B.C.E. (41). This is, of course, the "failure of nerve" described by Gilbert Murray in *Five Stages of Greek Religion* (3d ed.; Garden City, NY: Doubleday, Anchor, 1951) 119-65. For the attitude of philosophers toward miracle in the second century C.E., see Remus, *Conflict*.

[53] See Lucian's parody of such a debate, *Zeus Rants*.

[54] This is not to claim that the evangelist is a systematic philosopher. It is merely to assume that he is not a hermit.

[55] A. A. Long, *Hellenistic Philosophy* (London: Duckworth, 1974) 17.

[56] Ibid., 14.

[57] Ibid., 41-42.

[58] Ibid., 44-45.

to be free from all pain and to live in uninterrupted tranquility.[59]

The Epicurean in Cicero's dialog *De Natura Deorum* asserts, "God is entirely inactive and free from all ties of occupation; he toils not, neither does he labour, but he takes delight in his own wisdom and virtue . . ."[60] In effect, then, as Cicero's Academic critic charges, the Epicureans boast of freeing humans from superstition, but they achieve this by depriving the gods of all power (*omnem vim*).[61] The Epicurean Lucretius ridicules religious persons who revert to "the old superstitions, taking to themselves cruel taskmasters, whom the poor wretches believe to be almighty (*omnia posse*); not knowing what can be (*quid queat esse*) and what cannot (*quid nequeat*) . . ."[62] Epicureanism thus denies both providence and miracle. Petitionary prayer is ruled out on principle, but one may derive benefit from contemplating the divine tranquillity and beatitude.[63]

The Academic Objection to Omnipotence

The New Academy (c. 265 B.C.E.–c. 77 B.C.E.) was influenced by Scepticism.[64] On the issue of the relationship of the gods to the world, as on other issues, the Academic philosophers of this period concentrated their efforts on the criticism of the various positions without articulating a dogmatic position of their own.[65] Even Antiochus of Ascalon (first century B.C.E.), who rejected scepticism in favor of an eclectic combination of Stoicism with Platonic and Aristotelian views, parted company with the Stoics on the issue of omnipotence: "For who will have granted you either that the deity is omnipotent (*omnia deum posse*) or that even if he can do as described, he will?"[66]

There was an Academic objection to omnipotence that was not merely sceptical, however. Plato had made it clear in the *Timaeus* that the demiurge, like a human craftsman, is not omnipotent, but achieves only those results that are possible, given the limitations of the material with which he works.[67] So for Plato, "the generation of this universe was a mixed result of the combination of Necessity (ἀνάγκη) and Reason (νοῦς). Reason overruled Necessity by persuading

[59] Ibid., 44.

[60] *N.D.* 1. 19. 51.

[61] *N.D.* 1. 42. 117.

[62] *De Rerum Natura* 5. 86–90.

[63] Long, *Hellenistic Philosophy*, 48–49.

[64] Ibid., 92.

[65] H. Rackham, *Cicero De Natura Deorum* (LCL; London: Heinemann, 1933) x.

[66] Cicero *Ac.* 2 (Luc.) 16. 50. See Grant, *Miracle*, 129.

[67] F. M. Cornford, *Plato's Cosmology* (Indianapolis, IN: Bobbs-Merrill, 1975) 165. On the Platonists' debate with Stoicism see R. Walzer, *Galen on Jews and Christians* (London: Oxford University Press, 1949) 28–37.

her to guide the greatest part of the things that become towards what is best . . ."[68]

Plato gives a concrete illustration of this principle in *Timaeus* 73E–74B, where he discusses the properties of bone. Bone must be hard in order to protect the marrow and the brain. Because it is hard, however, bone is also inflexible and brittle. Unfortunately, it breaks easily and is subject to decay. Thus, the properties of bone are not ideal, but they are "what is best" under the circumstances. Aristotle repeats this argument: ". . . nature never does anything without a purpose . . . but creates all things with a view to the best that circumstances allow."[69] This argument became important in the period of Middle Platonism.

In about 170 C.E. the physician Galen appeals to the position of Plato and Aristotle against the view of "Moses" that "everything is possible for God" (πάντα . . . τῷ θεῷ δυνατά).[70] On the contrary, Galen says, "We say that some things are impossible by nature (ἀδύνατα φύσει), and that God does not undertake these things, but rather chooses the best out of the possibilities of becoming (τῶν δυνατῶν γενέσθαι)."[71] Galen is not criticizing the doctrine of creation out of nothing, although he could have, since that doctrine is incompatible with Platonic cosmology. Rather, as a scientist, Galen objects to the belief that God can do anything that is contrary to the ordinary course of nature.[72]

The assertions that "what is impossible with humans is possible with God" and "everything is possible for God" figured prominently in early Christian apologetic for the resurrection.[73] Such arguments infuriated the Middle Platonist Celsus, who countered with the argument that God "is not able to do anything contrary to reason or to his own character" and the resurrection of anything as contemptible as a corpse is both unreasonable and shameful.[74] Origen agrees that God cannot do that which is incompatible with the divine nature (*c. Cels.* 5.23), and in another context he complains that simple Christians

---

[68] *Timaeus* 47E–48A.

[69] *I.A.* 12. 711a18–19: ἡ φύσις οὐδὲν δημιουργεῖ μάτην, . . . ἀλλὰ πάντα πρὸς τὸ βέλτιστον ἐκ τῶν ἐνδεχομένων.

[70] For this formula in Hellenistic Judaism, see the discussion below.

[71] Text and translation in Walzer, *Galen*, 11–13.

[72] Grant, *Miracle*, 130. In taking the position that Galen is here talking not about creation, but about miracle, Grant believes that he opposes Walzer's position. However, Walzer recognizes the point that Grant wants to make when he writes: "According to Moses there are no limitations to God's power; everything is possible for Him, and He can undoubtedly work miracles which transcend the laws of nature. But in the established order of Galen's universe there is no miraculous intervention of God. Our world is the best possible world; God observes the unchanging laws of nature and will never even attempt what is by nature impossible" (28).

[73] Henry Chadwick, "Origen, Celsus, and the Resurrection of the Body," *HTR* 41 (1948) 84.

[74] *Cels.* 5. 14.

often take refuge in the assertion of divine omnipotence because they have no better arguments.[75] The argument that God does nothing contrary to reason is related to a Peripatetic argument which is frequently found in debates over divine omnipotence.

The Peripatetic Objections to Omnipotence

Aristotle's careful observations of the natural world contributed to the common-sense notions in antiquity that nature was orderly and rational. This sense of order was enhanced by his discussion of causality,[76] and his logical treatises clarified the circumstances under which affirmations and denials were valid. From the work of Aristotle, the Peripatetic school developed arguments that were used to "demythologize" the ancient narratives about the gods and to refute excessive claims about divine omnipotence. Among these arguments are: mathematical truths are unchangeable, the past cannot be altered, and things do not happen contrary to the usual course of nature.[77]

In a discussion of choice in ethical decisions, Aristotle explains that there can be no choice about past events:[78]

> What has happened cannot be made not to have happened. Hence Agathon is right in saying, "This only is denied to God, the power to make what has been done undone."

Aristotle is citing the poet in support of what is actually a principle of logic: "In the case of that which is or which has taken place, propositions, whether positive or negative, must be true or false."[79] Similarly:

> In the case of positives and privatives . . . change in both directions is impossible. There may be a change from possession to privation, but not from privation to possession. The man who has become blind does not regain his sight; the man who has become bald does not regain his hair; the man who lost his teeth does not grow a new set.[80]

Aristotle also held that the final cause controls the changes that take place in a natural being. A human being produces a human being. Its "nature," then

[75] Chadwick, "Resurrection," 84–85. The assertion that God does not act contrary to God's nature is found in the New Testament at Heb 6:18, with which compare 2 Tim 2:13.

[76] *Ph.* 2. 3. 194b17–195b30.

[77] Grant (*Miracle,* 47–48, 130–31) consistently refers to these arguments as Peripatetic without showing how they derive from Aristotle. It seems to be the case that since these arguments are found in Alexander of Aphrodisias, the second-century (C.E.) lecturer and commentator on Aristotle, they are therefore Peripatetic arguments.

[78] *E.N.* 6. 2. 6.

[79] *Int.* 18a, 27–28.

[80] *Cat.* 10. 13a. 31–37.

is to be human.[81] Implicitly, it cannot become something other than a human being. In the same vein, the Peripatetic Alexander of Aphrodisias argues that "according to nature," humans generate humans and horses generate horses. Anything else would be "contrary to nature."[82] This kind of reasoning may have been the basis for Palaephastus' earlier rejection of the existence of centaurs: the "natures" of horse and man cannot be mixed.[83] Similarly, Actaeon cannot have been turned into a stag, as the myth claims, although Palaephastus makes a tongue-in-cheek concession to the mythological tradition by remarking that of course the goddess Artemis is able to do whatever she wishes![84]

The elder Pliny makes use of a list of things impossible for God (*ne deum quidem posse omnia*): God cannot commit suicide, make mortals immortal, recall the deceased, change the past, or cause twice ten not to be twenty. According to Pliny, such facts "demonstrate the power of nature and prove that it is this that we mean by the word 'god.' "[85] The argument from the truth of mathematics is also found in Alexander of Aphrodisias: the gods cannot make the diagonal of a parallelogram equal in length to its side or make twice two equal to five.[86]

Against these challenges to the omnipotence and intervention of the gods, there were those who continued to argue that "nothing is impossible for God." Perhaps the most influential of these groups were the Stoics.

The Stoic Position on Omnipotence

According to Cicero, the motto of Stoicism was, "There is nothing which God is unable to do" (*Nihil est . . . quod deus efficere non possit*).[87] In the dialogue on divination, Cicero has the Academic critic of the Stoic position remark that if God were indeed omnipotent, he should have made the Stoics wise, so that they would not be so superstitious! The charge of superstition was brought against the Stoics because of their belief in divination, oracles, and portents, which was a corollary of their more basic belief in divine providence.[88]

---

[81] *Ph.* 2. 1. 193b8–194a30.

[82] Grant, *Miracle,* 130.

[83] Ibid., 47.

[84] Ibid., 48.

[85] *H.N.* 2. 5. 27. Cf. Plutarch (?) *Cons. ad Apollon.* 26 (115A) "for not even God can undo what has been done": τὸ μὲν γὰρ γεγενημένον οὐδὲ θεῷ δυνατόν ἐστιν ποιῆσαι ἀγένητον.

[86] Grant, *Miracle,* 130. See additional examples in A. S. Pease, *M. Tulli Ciceronis De Natura Deorum* (2 vols.; Darmstadt: Wissenschaftliche Buchgesellschaft, 1968) 2:687–88, 761–62.

[87] *N.D.* 3. 39. 92; *Div.* 2. 41. 86. This was apparently the teaching of Chrysippus: *SVF* 2. 1107.

[88] In the following discussion I am indebted to Long, *Hellenistic Philosophy,* 107–209; E. V. Arnold, *Roman Stoicism* (New York: Humanities Press, 1958); J. N. Sevenster, *Paul and Seneca* (Leiden: Brill, 1961); W. W. Tarn, *Hellenistic Civilization* (3d ed.; Cleveland: World, 1952) and Pease's commentary on Cicero's *De Natura Deorum.*

The Stoics argued in this fashion: If the gods exist at all, they must be superior in power, wisdom, and activity to everything else, and subject to no other power. To be a god is to be superior to everything and to rule and direct all nature and history.[89] In fact, for the Stoics, God is equivalent to nature as the λόγος or creative reason which pervades everything;[90] God acts on the world as easily as the mind acts on the body.[91] Cicero recognizes that the Stoic position is not, in fact, mere superstition, but metaphysical theory:

> Nor do you say this as some superstitious fable or old wives' tale, but you give a scientific and systematic account of it (*physica constantique ratione*): you allege that matter, which constitutes and contains all things, is in its entirety flexible and subject to change, so that there is nothing that cannot be molded and transmuted out of it however suddenly, but the molder and manipulator of this universal substance is divine providence, and therefore providence, whithersoever it moves, is able to perform whatever it will (*efficere posse quiquid velit*).[92]

The Stoics believed that all parts of the universe were related to one another by the all-pervasive λόγος. This universal interdependence was called cosmic "sympathy."[93] Because of cosmic sympathy, all events are causally related.[94] If this is so, then divination is legitimate because events in the present are causally related to future events. All that is required to predict the future is a right understanding of things that can be observed in the present: the flight of birds, the entrails of animals, phenomena in the heavens, or extraordinary happenings (portents) by which God seeks to warn human beings and enable them to make the appropriate response.[95]

It must be kept in mind, however, that Stoicism is both monistic and deterministic.[96] If deity is said to be the cause of signs and portents that is because deity is the cause of everything that happens. Seneca writes, "We Stoics look for a primary and universal cause. This must be single because matter is single. We ask what that cause is? The answer is 'creative reason,' that is God."[97] So, when Seneca remarks that the gods are an active influence in human life,[98] or that they give assistance to humans[99] he means that the λόγος is at work in the human self![100]

[89] *N.D.* 2. 30. 76–77.
[90] Long, *Hellenistic Philosophy*, 163–65.
[91] *N.D.* 3. 39. 92.
[92] Ibid.
[93] Long, *Hellenistic Philosophy*, 163.
[94] Ibid., 212.
[95] Arnold, *Stoicism*, 227.
[96] Sevenster, *Seneca*, 41.
[97] *Ep.* 65. 12; Long, *Hellenistic Philosophy*, 165.
[98] *Ep.* 95. 50; *Ben.* 4. 32. 1; *Prov.* 4. 7.
[99] *Ep.* 41. 2, 5.
[100] Sevenster, *Seneca*, 43.

The contrast with Mark becomes clear when we see that the true Stoic never prays for a miracle. In fact, the truly wise man does not even wish for anything other than what providence has decreed for him. Seneca writes to Marcia, "Prayers and struggles are all in vain; each one will get just the amount [= length of life] that was placed to his credit on the first day of his existence."[101] This is, of course, consistent with Stoic determinism![102] Seneca preserves a place for prayers and vows only when he is polemicizing against the Epicurean position,[103] and it appears that in the cases in which one might speak of "answered prayer," Seneca thinks that it was fated that the person should pray and thus fated that the result should correspond with the prayer![104]

It is no doubt the case that many Stoics participated in traditional prayers and sacrifices. They were conservative and opposed the impiety of the Epicureans, but their monism resulted in the transformation of the traditional Olympians into symbols for the physical principles![105] Whatever claims for divine omnipotence they made were tempered by the Academic and Peripatetic limitations: the intransigence of matter and necessity![106]

Besides the Stoics there was another philosophical group in the first century that stressed belief in providence and divination. They were the followers of Pythagoras.

Neopythagorean Views on Omnipotence

The Pythagorean tradition breaks off in the fourth century B.C.E., and little is heard from it until its revival by Nigidius Figulas in the first century prior to the Common Era.[107] Nigidius was a senator and a man of considerable learning and influence, whose knowledge of grammar, theology, and natural science earned him the respect of the cultured elite![108] Other Neopythagoreans included

---

[101] *Marc.* 21. 6.

[102] Cf. *Nat.* 2. 35. 1, 2; *Ep.* 41. 1; *Ep.* 60. 1.

[103] *Ben.* 4. 4. 2.

[104] *Nat.* 2.35–2.38; Cf. Sevenster, *Seneca*, 48–49.

[105] Arnold, *Stoicism*, 230–31.

[106] Cf. *Nat.* 1 Pr. 16: quantam deus possit; materiam ipse sibi formet an data utatur; utrum utro sit prius, materiae supervenerit ratio an materia rationi; deus quicquid vult efficiat an in multis rebus illum tractanda destituant et a magno artifice prave multa formentur, non quia cessat ars, sed quia id in quo exercetur saepe inobsequens arti est? (How powerful is God? Does he form matter for himself or does he merely make use of what is already there? Which comes first: does function determine matter, or does matter determine function? Does God do whatever he wishes? Or in many cases do the things he treats fail him, just as many things are poorly shaped by a great artist not because his art fails him but because the material in which he works often resists his art?) See Arnold, *Stoicism*, 208.

[107] C. J. De Vogel, *Pythagoras and Early Pythagoreanism* (Assen: Van Gorcum, 1966) 28.

[108] De Vogel, *Pythagoras*, 51; A. S. Pease, *M. Tulli Ciceronis De Divinatione*

the Sextii, Apollonios of Tyana, Moderatus of Gades, Nikomachos, Numenius and Iamblichus.[109] Between its revival by Nigidius and its virtual merger into Neoplatonism after the third century C.E.,[110] the movement exercised considerable influence, affecting the thought of Cicero,[111] Plutarch,[112] and Philo of Alexandria.[113]

Basic to the Pythagorean tradition were the concepts of divine omnipotence and providence.[114] Clement of Alexandria quotes the Pythagorean Epicharmus with approval: "Nothing escapes the divine; this is necessary for you to know. He is our observer. There is nothing that God is unable to do" (ἀδυνατεῖ δὲ οὐδὲν θεός).[115] Although they were pantheistic like the Stoics,[116] the Neopythagoreans believed not only in divination but also in miracles.[117] Apollonios of Tyana was known as a miracle worker, and miracle stories were commonly told about the disciples of Pythagoras.[118]

According to Iamblichus, the Pythagorean belief in miracles was a corollary of the belief in divine omnipotence. He follows up two accounts of singing and conversation by dead persons with an explanation that the Pythagoreans did not regard such stories as stupid, but rather thought anyone stupid who disbelieved them (ἀπιστοῦντας):

> For they did not conceive that some things are possible to God but others impossible (τὰ μὲν δυνατά τῷ θεῷ, τὰ δὲ ἀδύνατα), as those believe who reason sophistically; but they believed that all things are possible (ἀλλὰ πάντα δυνατά)![119]

Similarly:

> Pythagoras always proclaimed that nothing admirable pertaining to the gods or divine dogmas should be disbelieved, because the gods are able to accomplish all things (πάντα τῶν θεῶν δυναμένων)![120]

(Darmstadt: Wissenschaftliche Buchgesellschaft, 1973) 12.

[109] Holger Thesleff, *An Introduction to the Pythagorean Writings of the Hellenistic Period* (Åbo: Åbo Akademie, 1961) 54.

[110] De Vogel, *Pythagoras,* 29.

[111] Ibid., 49–50.

[112] Frederick E. Brenk, *In Mist Apparelled: Religious Themes in Plutarch's Moralia and Lives* (Leiden: Brill, 1977) 82; S. K. Heninger, *Touches of Sweet Harmony* (San Marino, CA: Huntington Library, 1974) 206.

[113] R. M. Berchman, *From Philo to Origen* (Chico: Scholars, 1984) 82.

[114] De Vogel, *Pythagoras,* 183.

[115] Strom. 6. 100. 6–10.

[116] Cicero, *N.D.* 1. 11: Pythagoras conceived of God as one soul, mixing with and pervading all nature.

[117] De Vogel, *Pythagoras,* 184.

[118] Grant, *Miracle,* 62.

[119] *V.P.* 28. 139.

[120] *V.P.* 28. 148.

The Neopythagoreans were more eclectic than systematic, taking support
for their ideas wherever they could find it![121] Among the sources that influenced
the Neopythagorean Numenius and possibly some of his predecessors were the
scriptures of Hellenistic Judaism, which claimed explicitly that "everything is
possible for God."[122]

Omnipotence in Hellenistic Judaism

Of the competing world-views that were current when the Gospel of Mark
was written, the world-view of Hellenistic Judaism was perhaps the one based
most solidly on the omnipotence and intervention of God. The following discussion of the three principal bodies of Hellenistic Jewish literature, the Septuagint,
Josephus, and Philo, provides evidence that the philosophical debate over
omnipotence influenced the way in which Jewish affirmations of divine power
were expressed.

The Septuagint (LXX)

In at least three instances the LXX significantly strengthens the claims of
the Hebrew text in the direction of divine omnipotence, and in one instance it
completely alters the sense of the Hebrew![123] Genesis 18:14 is the *locus classicus*
for the biblical insistence on God's power; its influence may be seen on Philo,
Josephus, and on the Lukan birth narrative![124] Here Yahweh rebukes Sarah's
laughter at the promise of a child with the question, "Is anything too hard for
the LORD?" (הֲיִפָּלֵא מֵיְהוָה דָּבָר).[125] The LXX translates, "Is anything impossible
for God?" (μὴ ἀδυνατεῖ παρὰ τῷ θεῷ ῥῆμα).

In the book of Job, Job's reply to Yahweh begins at 42:2, where the Hebrew
reads, "I know that thou canst do all things, and that no purpose of thine
can be thwarted" (יָדַעְתָּ כִּי־כֹל תּוּכָל וְלֹא־יִבָּצֵר מִמְּךָ מְזִמָּה). The LXX strengthens
the second member of the parallelism by making the negative restatement
repeat the vocabulary of the first line: "I know that you can do everything;
nothing is impossible for you." (οἶδα ὅτι πάντα δύνασαι, ἀδυνατεῖ δὲ σοι οὐθέν).
In Zechariah 8:6 the Hebrew reads, "Thus says the Lord of hosts: *If it is
marvelous in the sight of the remnant of this people* in these days, *should
it also be marvelous in my sight,* says the Lord of hosts?"[126] (. . . נַּם בְּעֵינַי יִפָּלֵא
. . . כִּי יִפָּלֵא בְּעֵינַי שְׁאֵרִית הָעָם הַזֶּה). The LXX translates, "Thus says the Lord,
the Ruler of all, 'If it is impossible in the sight of the remnant of this people

---

[121] *Oxford Classical Dictionary,* 2d ed., s.v. "Neopythagoreanism," by E. R. Dodds.

[122] Walzer, *Galen,* 22.

[123] van Unnik, "Mk 14,36," 31.

[124] Luke 1:37: οὐκ ἀδυνατήσει παρὰ τοῦ θεοῦ πᾶν ῥῆμα. On the interpretation of Gen. 18:14
in Philo and Josephus, see the discussion below.

[125] In this section, English translations of the Hebrew follow the RSV.

[126] That is, that Jerusalem shall again be filled with old people and children (8:4–5).

. . . should it also be impossible in my sight?' . . ." (τάδε λέγει κύριος παντο-κράτωρ· Διότι εἰ ἀδυνατήσει ἐνώπιον τῶν καταλοίπων τοῦ λαοῦ τούτου . . . , μὴ καὶ ἐνώπιον ἐμοῦ ἀδυνατήσει; . . .). Here the epithet κύριος παντοκράτωρ and the use of ἀδυνατήσει emphasize divine omnipotence. The contrast between human and divine ability is also found in Homer, *Od.* 10. 305–6: (about a medicinal root) "It is hard for mortal men to dig it up, but the gods have power to do all things" (χαλεπὸν δὲ τ᾽ ὀρύσσειν ἀνδράσι γε θνητοῖσι· θεοὶ δὲ τε πάντα δύναται).

A striking development takes place in the translation of Job 10:13. Job's first reply to Bildad closes with a section of direct address to God (10:2–22). In the Hebrew, 10:13 reads, "Yet these things thou didst hide in thy heart; I know that this was thy purpose" (וְאֵלֶּה צָפַנְתָּ בִלְבָבֶךָ יָדַעְתִּי כִּי־זֹאת עִמָּךְ). The LXX translates, "You hold these things in yourself; I know that you are able to do everything; nothing is impossible for you." (ταῦτα ἔχων ἐν σεαυτῷ, οἶδα ὅτι πάντα δύνασαι, ἀδυνατεῖ δὲ σοι οὐθέν). Here the idea of omnipotence is introduced into a text without any warrant in the original. Gillis Gerleman thinks that here, as elsewhere in Job, the Greek translator finds Job's accusations against God offensive and modifies them:[127] "The accusation against God, that he should have hid in his heart his evil designs against Job, in the LXX has been turned into an acknowledgement of God's omnipotence."[128] But against this explanation it must be noted that the LXX *retains* the idea that God has held enmity toward Job (ταῦτα=the contents of the verses immediately preceding) within himself: ταῦτα ἔχων ἐν σεαυτῷ. Another explanation presents itself when the whole passage is examined more closely.[129]

In 10:8–12, Job is arguing that it is senseless for the Creator to destroy his work: "Your hands fashioned and made me, and now you turn and destroy me. Remember that you fashioned me of clay; you are returning me to earth again" (10:8–9, LXX). It is possible that the translator of Job, who was apparently quite familiar with Greek pagan literature,[130] would have recognized that to have Job say that God had made him from clay would have evoked a storm of protest from philosophically minded readers.

We know that by the second century C.E., a Greek philosopher-scientist knew about and objected to Jewish ideas about the ability of God to make men and animals out of inanimate materials. In the passage cited earlier, *De usu partium* 11.14, Galen is discussing the wisdom of the creator in the design of eyebrows:

[127] Gillis Gerleman, *Studies in the Septuagint Book of Job* (Lund: C. W. K. Gleerup, 1946) 53.

[128] Ibid., 54.

[129] van Unnik does not discuss possible reasons for the alteration by the Greek translator.

[130] H. B. Swete, *An Introduction to the Old Testament in Greek* (2d ed.; Cambridge: Cambridge University Press, 1914) 316.

For it was certainly not sufficient merely to will their becoming such: it would not have been possible for him to make a man out of stone in an instant, by simply wishing so . . . For [Moses] it seems enough to say that God simply willed the arrangement of matter and it was presently arranged in due order; for he believes everything to be possible with God, even should he wish to make a bull or a horse out of ashes. But . . . we say that certain things are impossible by nature . . [131]

That God makes people from stones or horses and bulls from ashes is not claimed in any extant Jewish tradition. Walzer suggests that an otherwise unknown Jewish tradition may lie behind the saying attributed to John the Baptist in Q: "God is able from these stones to raise up children for Abraham."[132] Of course, it is not really necessary that there be a Jewish tradition with this content. If Galen knew some form of the Q saying he could have failed to make the distinction between a Jewish source and a Christian source. Elsewhere he lumps together "the school of Moses and Christ" as though Jewish and Christian ideas were identical.[133] In Genesis 2:7, God makes humanity from the dust of the earth, (χοῦν ἀπὸ τῆς γῆς) and in 2:19 he makes animals from earth (ἐκ τῆς γῆς). Galen may have these passages in mind when he objects to "Moses' " views on divine omnipotence.[134]

As we saw earlier, Galen's position is as old as Plato's view that the creator has to do his best within the limits imposed by his material. And Aristotle had said that humans come from other humans (that is, the form is the deciding factor in becoming). The arguments Galen brings against "Moses" were the ones that had been used for a long time against the Stoics by Academics and Peripatetics.[135] There is no reason to suppose that the translator of Job would have been ignorant of such arguments. The change in 10:13, then, could have been motivated by the need to justify such a claim for God. God can make a human being out of clay if God wants to and then destroy that same human if God decides to, because nothing is impossible for God. Of course, such speculation about the motives of the translator of LXX Job can be no more than that. What is established, however, is that the Scriptures of Hellenistic Judaism deliberately emphasized the claim that "everything is possible for God."

Josephus

Miraculous events are an important feature of the *Antiquities* of Josephus[136] and portents and prophecy are found in the *Jewish Wars*.[137] In the

[131] Walzer, *Galen,* 12.
[132] Ibid., 27 n. 4.
[133] Ibid., 14–15.
[134] Ibid., 27 n. 4.
[135] Ibid., 28.
[136] H. W. Attridge, *The Interpretation of Biblical History in the Antiquitates Judaicae of Flavius Josephus* (HDR 7; Missoula: Scholars, 1976) 19. See also George MacRae, "Miracle in the *Antiquities* of Josephus," *Miracles* (ed. C. F. D. Moule; London: Mowbray, 1965) 129–47; G. Delling, "Josephus und das Wunderbare," *NovT* 2 (1958) 291–309.
[137] E.g., 3. 399–404; 6. 288–309.

Antiquities, Josephus makes it clear that God is able to do things that are impossible from a human point of view.

According to Josephus' account of the prediction of the birth of Isaac, Sarah smiled upon hearing the prophecy and said that child-bearing was impossible, given her advanced age and that of Abraham (ἀδύνατον εἶναι τὴν τεκνοποιίαν).[138] Nevertheless, the birth takes place at the time predicted by the messengers of God.[139] When Saul sets David the task of procuring the heads[140] of two hundred Philistines as the marriage present for his daughter Michal,[141] Josephus tells us that David did not stop to consider whether or not the task were possible, but performed it easily, "for God was the one who made everything possible and easy for David" (θεὸς γὰρ ἦν ὁ πάντα ποιῶν εὐμαρῆ καὶ δυνατὰ τῷ Δαυίδῃ).[142]

When Samaria is besieged by the Syrians, the prophet Elisha predicts a sudden turn of events. A captain who hears the prophecy mocks: "Incredible (ἄπιστα) are the things you are saying, O prophet. And, as impossible (ἀδύνατον) as it is for God to rain down from heaven torrents of barley or fine flour, just so impossible is it for the things of which you have now spoken to happen."[143] Nevertheless, God causes the Syrian army to flee in confusion and the city is saved.

In Josephus' version of Daniel 2, when Nebuchadnezzar demands that his court magicians tell him his forgotten dream, they inform him that such a thing is impossible for humans: ἀδύνατον εἶναι . . . ἀνθρώποις τοῦθ' εὑρεῖν.[144] When God reveals the dream to him, Daniel addresses the king as follows:

> . . . no less than my sorrow for ourselves who had been condemned to death by you was my concern for your good name, seeing that you had unjustly ordered these men to be put to death . . . on whom you had imposed a task which is by no means within the limits of human wisdom, and demanded of them something which only God can do (οἷς οὐδὲν μὲν ἀνθρωπίνης σοφίας ἐχόμενον προσέταξας, ὃ δ'ἦν ἔργον θεοῦ τοῦτο ἀπήτεις παρ' αὐτῶν).[145]

That which is impossible for human beings is possible for God. In the work of Philo of Alexandria, this confession achieves the status of a δόγμα.

---

[138] *A.J.* 1. 198.
[139] *A.J.* 1. 213–14.
[140] Josephus' more delicate version of the assignment. Cf. 1 Sam. 18:25.
[141] Josephus: Μελχάν LXX: Μελχόλ.
[142] *A.J.* 6. 203.
[143] *A.J.* 9. 73.
[144] *A.J.* 10. 196.
[145] *A.J.* 10. 204.

Philo

Galen was apparently correct in his belief that the omnipotence of God, and the formula that expressed it, were of central importance in the theology of Hellenistic Judaism, because we learn from Philo that πάντα δυνατὰ θεῷ was a doctrine taught to Jewish children. This information is found in Philo's version of Sarah's response to the prediction of Isaac's birth (*Abr.* 112-13).

Sarah laughs, according to Philo, because at first the promise appears incredible (ἀπίστου).[146] When the strangers rebuke her with the question, "Is anything impossible with God?" (μὴ ἀδυνατεῖ παρὰ θεῷ πᾶν ῥῆμα) she becomes ashamed and denies her laughter, "for she knew that all things were possible with God (πάντα γὰρ ᾔδει θεῷ δυνατά), a doctrine (δόγμα) which she had learned almost from the time she was in swaddling cloths."[147] Van Unnik observes correctly that this editorial comment on Sarah's childhood training must reflect the practice of the Judaism of Philo's day, which "formulated one of its basic tenets in this way."[148]

For Philo, God's omnipotence is manifested both in creation and in the history of God's saving acts. In *Op.* 45-46 he comments on the order of creation in the Genesis account. Observing that plants were created on the third day and the sun and moon not until the fourth day, Philo seizes the opportunity to berate the "sophistry" of those who worship the heavenly bodies, thinking that they cause the cycle of vegetation to repeat itself year after year. Obviously, Philo argues, God is superior to the sun and moon since God was able to produce vegetation before they were ever created. ". . . he guides all things in what direction he pleases as law and right demand, standing in need of no one besides: for all things are possible to God" (πάντα γὰρ θεῷ δυνατά).[149]

The same formula appears repeatedly as Philo retells the story of God's saving acts on behalf of God's people. "Everything is possible" for the God who gives Abraham and Sarah a child in their old age![150] As he walks with his son to the place of sacrifice, Philo's Abraham responds to Isaac's question about their lack of a victim to sacrifice with the biblical answer, "God will provide," followed by our formula: "but know that to God all things are possible, including those that are impossible or insuperable to men" (πάντα δ' ἴσθι θεῷ δυνατὰ καὶ ὅσα ἐν ἀμηχάνῳ καὶ ἀπόρῳ κεῖται παρ' ἀνθρώποις).[151] Philo's Joseph informs his repentant brothers, "he who turned my condition of extreme calamity into . . . good fortune was God to whom all things are possible" (θεὸς . . . ᾧ πάντα δυνατά).[152]

---

[146] *Abr.* 111.

[147] *Abr.* 112-13. My translation.

[148] van Unnik, "Mk 14,36," 34.

[149] *Op.* 46.

[150] *Abr.* 112-13.

[151] *Abr.* 175.

[152] *Jos.* 245. In a discourse on Joseph's dream, Philo says that such reversals happen only "by the power of God who alone can do everything" (κράτει θεοῦ τοῦ μόνου πάντα δυνατοῦ) *Som.* 2. 136.

When the Israelites are trapped at the Red Sea by the advancing Egyptians, Philo has Moses say to them, "Do not lose heart, . . . God's way of defense is not as that of men . . . It is his special property to find a way where no way is. What is impossible to all created being is possible to him only, ready to his hand" (ἐν ἀπόροις πόρον εὑρεῖν ἴδιον θεοῦ· τὰ ἀδύνατα παντὶ γενητῷ μόνῳ δυνατὰ καὶ κατὰ χειρός)![153] In another place Philo informs us that there were two reasons why the Israelites were given so much quail to eat that they became ill: "First to show that all things are possible to God who finds a way out of impossible difficulties (ὅτι πάντα θεῷ δυνατὰ πόρον ἐξ ἀμηχάνων καὶ ἀπόρων ἀνευρίσκοντι), and secondly to punish those who let their belly go uncontrolled and rebelled against holiness."[154]

Philo uses the same formula of omnipotence in discussions of moral and spiritual improvements that present special difficulties. God discloses sins that have been concealed, "For to God all things are known even as all things are possible (πάντα γὰρ ὡς δυνατά, οὕτως καὶ γνώριμα θεῷ)![155] Cowardice is a disease of the soul that cannot be eliminated unless it is healed by God: "For all things are possible to God" (πάντα γὰρ θεῷ δυνατά).[156] Prostitutes at least give up their vice when they are forced to do so by old age, "but as for the soul, when by constant familiarity with incontinence it has been schooled into harlotry, what agelong stretch of years can convert it to decent living? Not even the longest, but only God, with whom that is possible which is impossible with us" (θεὸς δὲ μόνος, ᾧ δυνατὰ τὰ παρ' ἡμῖν ἀδύνατα).[157]

Summary

In the introduction to a recent collection of essays entitled *God's Activity in the World: The Contemporary Problem,* Owen C. Thomas makes an assertion that is not uncommon in modern scholarship: "These questions [about the relationship between God's activity and the natural and historical causal nexus] were not especially pressing in the early period of Christian thought."[158] In the brief survey above we have observed just how pressing such questions in fact were among pagan and Jewish thinkers in the period in which the Gospel of Mark was written. Harold Remus' excellent analysis details the variety of ways in which divine agency was conceptualized, affirmed, or denied in the phenomena deemed

[153] *Mos.* 1. 174.

[154] *Spec.* 4. 127.

[155] *Som.* 1. 87.

[156] *Virt.* 26.

[157] *Spec.* 1. 282. The extent to which Philo's assertions about divine omnipotence were in tension with his Platonism needs to be addressed. Such an undertaking is, however, beyond the scope of this brief survey.

[158] O. C. Thomas, ed., *God's Activity in the World: The Contemporary Problem* (Chico: Scholars, 1983) 1.

extraordinary by the ancients. These were pressing questions for the author of Mark as well as for his contemporaries.

We have seen that the assertion of God's activity in the world in ways impossible for humans, that is, the assertion that "everything is possible for God," was the subject of widespread debate in the Greco-Roman world at the time of the writing of the Gospel of Mark. This assertion of divine omnipotence was usually associated with an affirmation of divine agency in events that violated the widely-held canons of the ordinary; in other words, the affirmation of omnipotence usually accompanied a belief in miracles, or at least a belief in the validity of divination.[159] Moreover, these affirmations were not made naively; rather, they represented positions adopted self-consciously, in the full recognition that there were other possible positions with respect to the relationship between the agency of God(s) and events in the world.

According to Philo, Alexandrian Judaism emphasized divine omnipotence as a part of the formative training of its children. In the categories of the discipline known as the sociology of knowledge, the Alexandrian Jews provided for their adherents a "plausibility structure"—a world—in which the members of the religious community lived and by means of which they interpreted their experiences.[160] The importance of the twin tasks of world-construction and world-maintenance is heightened in periods of pluralism when religions and philosophies are in competition.[161] Members of diverse religious communities encounter each other in the traffic of daily life and worlds collide. Each religious community must not only win new adherents, but must also hold the loyalty of old members. Evangelism and the "care of souls" present the same set of problems.[162]

When we return to the Gospel of Mark, we can see that what literary critics have come to call "Mark's narrative world" is not merely that; rather, the gospel functions as the narrative version of the plausibility structure within which the Markan community must live and interpret its experience. The telling of the gospel story creates the world of the praying community. In this world, the God who is addressed in prayer is able to respond by acting in ways that are "impossible"—thus the mountain-moving saying. The God whom the Markan Jesus addresses as "abba" is the God for whom everything is possible (14:36). Affirmation of the omnipotence of God and of God's agency in the world is essential

[159] The phrase "canons of the ordinary" is Harold Remus' (*Conflict,* 7 and see chapter 2, "The Ordinary and the Extraordinary"). It is a better designation than any use of the word "nature," because such constructs as "laws of nature" or "natural law" were quite fluid in antiquity and often referred to moral canons, rather than to physical theories. See Grant, *Miracles,* chapters 1 and 2.

[160] Berger, *Canopy,* 3–51.

[161] Berger, *Canopy,* 49.

[162] Berger, *Canopy,* 51; E. Schüssler Fiorenza, "Miracles, Mission and Apologetics: An Introduction," *Aspects of Religious Propaganda in Judaism and Early Christianity* (ed. E. S. Fiorenza; Notre Dame: University of Notre Dame Press, 1976) 2–3.

to Mark's theology of prayer; that is why the prayer logia collection begins with the saying about the mountain. As we shall see in the next chapter, affirming the community's world-view is what Mark means by "faith."

5
Prayer, Faith, and Power

In the "house of prayer" that replaces the temple, there are two basic conditions which govern the efficacy of the community's prayers. They are, as we saw in chapter 3, faith and forgiveness. In this chapter we will examine the gospel to discover in what sense faith is a condition for prayer and a condition for the miracles with which the omnipotent God responds to prayer.

Studies of the instances of πίστις/πιστεύω in Mark have demonstrated that the evangelist has not attempted to force the variety of uses in his tradition into a single mold.[1] As a result, "faith" has more than one meaning in the gospel. In 1:15 and 9:42, to believe means to accept the kerygma, to be a Christian.[2] In 11:31, 13:21 and 15:32, to believe means to make a positive assessment of someone's claim to speak and act for God.[3] We will argue that in the Markan miracle stories and prayer teaching, faith means confidence in the power of God to do the impossible on behalf of the community. In the following discussion it will become clear that it is illegitimate to read into every instance of the word "faith" in Mark the total sum of religious meaning that the word has acquired over centuries of Christian thought. This is especially evident when the observation is made that "faith" is not synonymous with membership in the Markan community.

In Mark, the category which designates a total response to Jesus is not "faith" but "following."[4] Disciples follow Jesus (1:16–20, 2:14, 6:1, 10:28), but they do not always have faith (4:40). In 5:36, where Jairus is urged, "Do not fear, only believe," the call is not to become a disciple but to trust in Jesus' power to help. After a miracle Bartimaeus becomes a follower (10:52)[5] but others who are

---

[1] E.g. Hahn, "Verständnis"; Barth, "Glaube"; Dieter Zeller, "Jesus als Mittler des Glaubens nach dem Markusevangelium," *BibLeb* 9 (1968) 278–86.

[2] Bultmann, "πιστεύω," 210, 214 n. 296; Hahn, "Verständnis," 62, 67; Barth, "Glaube," 291; Pesch, *Markusevangelium,* 1:103, 2:114; Gnilka, *Markus,* 2:64.

[3] Hahn, "Verständnis," 61–62; Pesch, *Markusevangelium,* 2:488, 2:211; Gnilka, *Markus,* 2:139–40. The same idea is present in the Pharisees' demand for a sign in 8:11 where πιστεύω does not appear (Hahn, "Verständnis," 61).

[4] Hahn, "Verständnis," 63.

[5] P. J. Achtemeier (" 'And He Followed Him': Miracles and Discipleship in Mark 10:46–52," *Semeia* 11 [1978] 116–25) argues that the Bartimaeus story is not a miracle story but a call story. However, the text makes it clear that it is because Bartimaeus receives his sight that he follows Jesus "on the way" to the cross. Noting this, V. K. Robbins ("The

healed do not follow, and some people follow Jesus who are not linked with miracles or with "faith" by the narrator: the tax collectors and sinners of 2:15 and the Galilean women of 15:40–41.[6]

Ernest Best and Elizabeth Struthers Malbon have demonstrated that a major function of the Markan narrative is to hold up before the community the promise and the pitfalls of Christian discipleship. Malbon writes, "Only by such a composite and complex image of followers is the author of the Markan gospel able to communicate clearly and powerfully to the reader the twofold message: anyone can be a follower, no one finds it easy."[7] Followers may find it difficult to keep believing in the power of God when faced with danger (4:40), illness (5:36), or especially difficult cases of exorcism (9:14–29). Their failure to believe does not exclude them from the community of followers. It may not even exclude them from God's miraculous help (4:40, 6:5, 6:35–44, 8:1–10), because, as we shall see later in this discussion, the author of Mark links faith with miracles in a positive way without introducing the correlative negative idea that lack of faith limits the freedom of God to act. The relationships established in the text between the power of God to do the impossible, faith as confidence in God's power, and prayer as the practice which provides access to God's power need to be understood if the theology of the evangelist is to be appreciated fully.

THE RELATIONSHIP BETWEEN FAITH AND POWER

The author of Mark establishes a positive relationship between the power of God and confidence in that power in the bold claim of 9:23: πάντα δυνατὰ τῷ πιστεύοντι, which is a condensed version of the claims made in the prayer logia collection. Everything is possible for God, and God will do the impossible for those who ask with confidence in God's power. The credibility of this claim would have depended upon the assent of the audience to the major premise: Everything is possible for God. As we have seen, not everyone in the first century would have agreed with the premise. However, even the skeptical linked the word group πίστις/πιστεύω with the idea that the impossible is possible for a deity. In this section we will document the relationship between divine power and "faith" in the thought-world of the Markan audience.

Faith as Confidence that God Can Do the Impossible

In Hellenistic-Roman views of miraculous healing, the confidence that the

---

Healing of Blind Bartimaeus [10:46–52] in the Marcan Theology," *JBL* 92 [1973] 224–43) writes, "In the Bartimaeus story faith which leads to healing and faith which issues in discipleship converge."

[6] Malbon, "Disciples," 108–9.

[7] Malbon, "Fallible," 46. See Best, *Following Jesus*.

deity was able to heal was labeled πίστις.[8] The literature and inscriptions connected with the Asclepius cult provide us with examples.

Faith and Power in the Cult of Asclepius

Strabo reports that in Epidaurus, Asclepius is believed (πιστευμένου) to cure diseases of every kind (8.6.15), and that similar practices are connected with the Serapis cult at Canobus. Even the most reputable men believe (πιστεύειν) and go to the temple to sleep and be healed (17.1.17).[9] The third inscription from Epidaurus tells about a man with a paralyzed hand who did not believe (ἀπίστει) in the cures and made fun of the inscriptions. But while sleeping in the sanctuary, the man dreamed that the god healed his hand and then lectured him on his scepticism:

> Since, then, formerly you were incredulous (ἀπίστεις) of the cures, though they were not incredible (ἀπίστοις), for the future, he said, your name shall be "Incredulous" ἄπιστος).

This attitude of incredulity on the part of suppliants is attested in some of the other inscriptions. Ambrosia of Athens is said to have "laughed at some of the cures as incredible and impossible" (ἀπίθανα καὶ ἀδύνατα).[10] Another suppliant, named Cephisias, is said to have laughed at the cures and to have denied the power of Asclepius:

> If the god says he has healed lame people he is lying; for, if he had the power (εἰ δύναμιν ε[ἶχε]) to do so, why has he not healed Hephaestus?

In the inscription, this attitude is labeled "insolence" (ὕβριος).[11] Clearly, the inscriptions are intended to combat the attitude that miraculous cures are impossible or that Asclepius does not have the power to heal. In the third inscription the one who lacks confidence in the power of the god is called ἄπιστος.

This unbelief is overturned in the inscriptions by the miraculous cures. Even the physician Galen, who insisted that "some things are impossible by nature" became a believer in Asclepius after he was healed of an abscess by the god, and

---

[8] Theissen, *Miracle Stories*, 130–33; V. K. Robbins, "The Woman who Touched Jesus' Garment: Social-Rhetorical Analysis of the Synoptic Accounts," paper presented at the southeastern regional meeting of the Society of Biblical Literature, Chattanooga, TN, 21 March, 1986, 4.

[9] Theissen (*Miracle Stories,* 131) wants to make a distinction between the meaning of πιστεύω here in 17.1.17 and the meaning in 8.6.15. It seems to me, however, that in both cases the belief is in the healing power of the deity at the sanctuary.

[10] Inscription 4. Here, πείθω appears rather than πιστεύω. This and other inscriptions from Epidaurus are collected by Emma and Ludwig Edelstein, *Asclepius: A Collection and Interpretation of the Testimonies* (2 vols.; Baltimore: Johns Hopkins, 1945).

[11] Inscription 36.

he reported on the healings of other people![2] The evidence we have indicates that the beneficiaries of Asclepius' healing power were by no means limited to the gullible lower classes. The wealthy and the educated also sought his help![3] The widespread confidence in Asclepius' power was due to the high success rate at his temples![4] Seeing was believing. This quasi-empirical appeal to experience as justification for belief in divine power was common in the Hellenistic-Roman period, as we will see clearly in Lucian of Samosata.

From the Asclepius cult we learn two things that are relevant for our study. In the first place, we find the root πιστ- connected directly with confidence and lack of confidence in a deity's power to perform miracles. In the second place, we find the practice of relating miracle stories as an encouragement to suppliants. The steles at Epidaurus preserved the testimonies of the healed in order to evoke faith and courage in the sick![5] The suppliants believed that the god had power to heal them because the god had healed others like them.

Faith and divine power in Plutarch's Coriolanus

As in every age, there were those in the first century whose sense of the ambiguities of life led them to leave open many issues which touched upon the extraordinary. Plutarch was one such person.

Plutarch, who was in his twenties when Mark was written, was influenced by Platonism and by Peripatetic thought![6] He could easily have written the phrase in the disputed letter of consolation: "not even God can undo what has been done" (τὸ μὲν γὰρ γεγενημένον οὐδὲ θεῷ δυνατόν ἐστι ποιῆσαι ἀγένητον)![7] He did write a treatise against superstition in which he complains that superstitious people live in a dream-like world where fear dominates and reason is asleep![8] But

---

[12] Remus, *Conflict*, 39; Edelstein and Edelstein, *Asclepius*, 1:263–64.

[13] Theissen, *Miracle Stories*, 235–36.

[14] Dieter Georgi, "Socioeconomic Reasons for the 'Divine Man' as a Propagandistic Pattern," *Aspects of Religious Propaganda in Judaism and Early Christianity* (ed. E. Schüssler Fiorenza; Notre Dame: University of Notre Dame Press, 1976) 31; See also Edelstein and Edelstein, *Asclepius* 2:157, 160–61.

[15] Theissen, *Miracle Stories*, 283: "they are intended to give suppliants comfort and confidence, to increase expectations and cushion disappointments." R. Herzog, *Die Wunderheilungen von Epidauros* (Leipzig: Dieterich, 1931) 60: "Sie sollten die Geschichten lesen . . . um Hoffnung und Mut zu bekommen. Mit dem Glauben sollte auch der Wille zur Heilung gestärkt werden. . . . Denn die Kranken kamen ja, weil die Hilfe der menschlichen Ärzte versagt hatte, zu dem Gott, dem das Unmögliche möglich ist" (Cf. Ibid., 71). See also H. C. Kee, "Self-Definition in the Asclepius Cult," *Self-Definition in the Greco-Roman World* (ed. B. F. Meyer and E. P. Sanders; Philadelphia: Fortress, 1982) 122.

[16] Frederick Copleston, *A History of Philosophy*, vol. 1: *Greece and Rome*, Part 2 (New rev. ed.; Garden City, NY: Doubleday, Image Books, 1962) 197.

[17] *Cons. ad Apollon.*, 26 (115A).

[18] *De Superstitione* 166 C.

Plutarch was also influenced by Stoicism and, more importantly, by Neopythagoreanism.[19] So, in an essay against the Epicureans, Plutarch can quote with approval from one Hermogenes: "These gods, he says, who know everything and can do everything . . ." (οὗτοι γάρ, φησίν, οἱ πάντα μὲν εἰδότες πάντα δὲ δυνάμενοι θεοί . . .).[20] He believes that dreams can be prophetic, he defends the validity of divination, and he gives credence to miracles and apparitions.[21] His real objection to superstition seems to be that the people he calls superstitious attribute evil motives and actions to the gods. The gods, Plutarch insists, act only for the good of humanity.[22]

Given this level of ambiguity in Plutarch's thought, it is not surprising to find him attempting to reconcile opposing explanations of extraordinary phenomena. In his life of Pericles (6.2–4) Plutarch tells about a one-horned ram which was brought to Pericles. The seer (μάντις) Lampon told Pericles that the ram was a sign (σημεῖον) from the deity that Pericles was to become the one master of Athens. But Anaxagoras, a natural philosopher (φυσικός) cut open the ram's skull and argued that the one horn was caused by the peculiar shape and location of the ram's brain. Plutarch informs the reader that both explanations were correct. Anaxagoras explained the cause (τὴν αἰτίαν) of the single horn, but Lampon understood the purpose (τέλος).[23]

Two observations may be made about this passage. One is that the Aristotelian classification of causes has been absorbed into Middle Platonism[24] and can here be used to defend divination. The other is that Plutarch accepts the Stoic notion of cosmic "sympathy," according to which events as disparate as a one-horned ram and the career of Pericles can be causally related.[25] Of course, history vindicated the seer, as Pericles did become master of Athens.[26]

A striking example of Plutarch's ambiguity occurs in his discussion of talking statues in *Coriolanus* 37–38. After telling a story about a statue which was supposed to have spoken on two occasions, Plutarch says that this "probably never happened and is difficult to believe" (ἀγενήτοις ὅμοια καὶ χαλεπὰ πεισθῆναι). Then he goes on to explain that statues which seem to sweat, bleed, and shed tears are really affected by mold and atmospheric conditions. Perhaps an internal rupture could cause a sound like a moan or a groan, but articulate speech cannot

[19] Copleston, *Greece and Rome,* 197; Brenk, *Mist,* 80–82.

[20] *Non posse suav.* 22.

[21] Brenk, *Mist,* 80.

[22] B. S. Mackay, "Plutarch and the Miraculous," *Miracles* (ed. C. F. D. Moule; London: Mowbray, 1965) 97.

[23] Remus, *Conflict,* 42; Grant, *Miracle,* 66, 67.

[24] Grant, *Miracle,* 67.

[25] Ibid.; Brenk, *Mist,* 209.

[26] The elder Pliny gives a "both-and" explanation of earthquakes. Earthquakes are caused by winds, but they are also omens (Remus, *Conflict,* 43–44).

be produced by an inanimate object (ἐν ἀψύχῳ) and no spiritual entity can speak without a body and vocal cords. Maybe the impression that a statue spoke was merely subjective "as, for instance, in sleep, when we think we see and hear, although we neither see nor hear." So far, so good.

But now Plutarch leaves the realm of common-sense explanation and begins to talk like a Neopythagorean:

> However, those who cherish strong feelings of goodwill and affection for the deity and are therefore unable to reject or deny anything of this kind, have a strong argument for their faith (πίστιν) in the wonderful and transcendent character of the divine power (δυνάμεως). For the deity has no resemblance whatever to man, either in nature, activity, skill or strength (ἰσχύν); nor, if he does something that we cannot do, or contrives something that we cannot contrive, is this contrary to reason (παράλογον ἐστιν); but rather, since he differs from us in all points, in his works most of all is he unlike us and far removed from us. But most things pertaining to deity, as Heraclitus says, "escape our knowledge through unbelief" (ἀπιστίη).[27]

Harold Remus calls Plutarch's position a "both-and explanation" of the extraordinary.[28] Whatever the modern reader may think of Plutarch's solution, the discussion in *Coriolanus* serves to remind her that not all ancient believers in miracles were naive about causation in the natural world.

So, in a contemporary of the author of Mark, we find the attitude which regards it as possible for a deity to act upon a concrete object in the world labeled "faith." By contrast, the opposite point of view is called "unbelief." Later the same usage may be observed in a man who shared none of Plutarch's credulity: Lucian of Samosata.

Possibility and Faith in Lucian of Samosata

Lucian was one of those persons in the second century whose experience included nothing which contradicted their common-sense view of the possible. At the beginning of his *True Story*, a parody of the kind of fantastic accounts popular in his day, Lucian writes,

> Be it understood, then, that I am writing about things which I have neither seen nor had to do with nor learned from others—which in fact do not exist at all and, in the nature of things, cannot exist (ἔτι δὲ μήτε ὅλως ὄντων μήτε τὴν ἀρχὴν γενέσθαι δυναμένων). Therefore my readers should on no account believe in them (μηδαμῶς πιστεύειν αὐτοῖς).[29]

In *Alexander the False Prophet* (17) Lucian is discussing one of Alexander's fake miracles. He comments that any sane philosopher, even without knowing how the trick was done, would have been convinced beforehand (προπεισμένου)

---

[27] *Coriolanus* 38. 3–4.
[28] Remus, *Conflict*, 42–46.
[29] *V.H.* 4.

that the whole business was a fraud (ψεῦδος) and could not happen (γενέσθαι ἀδύνατον). However, Lucian claims that only the Epicureans detected Alexander's trickery. The Platonists, Stoics and Pythagoreans believed in him (25).

In the *Lover of Lies*, Lucian portrays a Platonist, a Stoic, a Peripatetic and a physician (ἰατρός) exchanging miracle stories beside the bed of a sick friend (6). Their credulity is challenged by one Tychiades, clearly a mouthpiece for Lucian himself. In response to the scepticism of Tychiades, the Peripatetic makes the following speech:

> I myself was formerly more incredulous (ἀπιστότερος) than you in regard to such things, for I thought it in no way possible that they could happen (οὐδενὶ λόγῳ δυνατὸν γίγνεσθαι); but when first I saw the foreign stranger fly—he came from the land of the Hyperboreans, he said,—I believed (ἐπίστευσα) and was conquered after long resistance. What was I to do when I saw him soar through the air in broad daylight and walk on the water and go through fire slowly on foot?[30]

After another series of such stories and accounts of magic spells, the Peripatetic again says, "If you had seen that, Tychiades, you would no longer have doubted" (εἰ ταῦτα εἶδες . . . οὐκ ἂν ἔτι ἠπίστησας, *Philops.* 15). Lucian's response to these testimonies is predictable: "I am the only one of all who does not see them; if I saw them, I should believe in them, of course, just as you do!" (30).

So, although Lucian has no use for "faith," he uses the terminology in much the same way that it is used by Plutarch and by the previously cited references to the Asclepius cult. To hold to the possibility of miracles is to "believe." To deny that possibility is to be "unbelieving." And again, as in the Asclepius cult, the difference between believers and unbelievers is personal experience.

Neopythagorean Faith according to Iamblichus

The Neopythagoreans were far from sceptical, but Iamblichus reports that even they did not believe miracle stories merely because they were told by others, but they "tested many [similar] things for themselves" (πολλὰ δὲ καὶ αὐτοὶ πειρῶνται).[31] According to his account, followers of Pythagoras believe (πιστεύουσι) every kind of miracle story, "disbelieving (ἀπιστοῦντες) nothing which may be referred to divinity."[32] Those who disbelieve (ἀπιστοῦντας) miracle stories, the Pythagoreans regard as stupid (εὐήθεις).[33] Pythagoras taught that because everything is possible for the gods, nothing marvelous concerning them should be disbelieved (περὶ θεῶν μηδὲν θαυμαστὸν ἀπιστεῖν).[34]

Here the explicit connection is made between the world-view which holds that "everything is possible for God" and the concept of "faith." Faith is

30 *Philops.* 13.
31 *V.P.* 138.
32 Ibid.
33 *V.P.* 139.
34 *V.P.* 148.

confidence in the unlimited power of deity to intervene in the world; thus, faith in divine omnipotence entails believing miracle stories. To believe is to hold a view of the God-world relationship in which anything is possible because of divine omnipotence. The Neopythagoreans share this understanding of faith with Lucian, but they regard faith as admirable, whereas Lucian regards it as reprehensible and ridiculous.

Faith and Omnipotence in Hellenistic Judaism and Christianity

Just a few examples will be enough to show that the literature of Hellenistic Judaism and early Christianity shares with other Hellenistic-Roman literature the use of the πίστις/πιστεύω word group to mean confidence in the power of deity to perform the impossible. In chapter 4 we saw that Philo and Josephus can use the term ἄπιστος in passages that portray incredulity at the idea that God can perform a miracle which seems impossible.[35] This understanding of faith is also found in the LXX.

In Psalm 78:19 (LXX 77:19) the Israelites are portrayed as asking, "Can God spread a table in the wilderness?" (Μὴ δυνήσεται ὁ θεὸς ἑτοιμάσαι τράπεζαν ἐν ἐρήμῳ). The use of μὴ in the interrogative construction implies a negative answer: God is not able to supply food. This attitude betrays absence of faith (v 22): "they did not believe in God (οὐκ ἐπίστευσαν ἐν τῷ θεῷ) or hope in his saving power (σωτήριον)." To deny the power of God to do the impossible (provide food in the wilderness) is to disbelieve. The same connection between faith and miracle is made in the summary statement at Exodus 14:31: "And Israel saw the great work which the LORD did against the Egyptians, and the people feared the LORD; and they believed in the LORD (ἐπίστευσαν τῷ θεῷ) and in his servant Moses."

In the New Testament and early Christian literature, faith as confidence that God can do the otherwise impossible is often expressed by πιστεύω followed by a ὅτι clause.[36] This sense is explicit in Hermas, Vision 4.2.6: "Believe on the Lord, you who are double-minded, that he can do all things: πιστεύσατε τῷ κυρίῳ, οἱ δίψυχοι, ὅτι πάντα δύναται. The construction "believe that . . ." appears in the same sense in Luke 1:45 and Acts 27:25. In both these cases, the ὅτι clause designates something which is apparently impossible. In Luke 1:45 Mary is blessed because she believed the angel's promise that she would become pregnant without sexual intercourse. In Acts 27:25 Paul believes an angel's promise that he and the entire ship's crew will be saved although everything else indicates that all will be lost (27:20).

In Romans 4:20-21 Paul says of Abraham that he was strong in faith (ἐνεδυναμώθη τῇ πίστει), which is equivalent to being "fully convinced that the one who promised (that his barren wife would bear a son) is powerful and will do

---

[35] Philo, Abr. 111; Josephus, A.J. 9. 73. See "Omnipotence in Hellenistic Judaism," chapter 4.

[36] Bultmann, "πιστεύω," 203.

it" (πληροφορηθεὶς ὅτι ὃ ἐπήγγελται δυνατός ἐστιν καὶ ποιῆσαι). Similarly, in Matt 9:28, Jesus asks the two blind men, "Do you believe that I am able to do this?" This sense of πιστεύω as confidence that the impossible is possible through the power of God is the sense we find in the Markan prayer logia collection.

Each instance of πιστεύω in the logia collection is followed by a ὅτι clause:

11:23: πιστεύῃ οτι ὃ λαλεῖ γίνεται
(believes that what he says happens)
11:24: πιστεύετε ὅτι ἐλάβετε
(believe that you received)

The content of "what he says" is the command to the mountain, so here again, to believe is to have confidence in God's power to do the impossible, since, as we have seen, 11:22 ("Have faith in God") specifies the mover of the mountain as God and the command as a prayer. Verse 24 generalizes the principle: if God can do the impossible task of moving a mountain, then God can give everything (πάντα) the community asks in prayer.

Summary

In a study of the relationship between faith and miracles in Mark, Walter Schmithals asserts that the concept of "faith" in the gospel does not involve "holding something to be true."[37] By making this assertion, Schmithals emphasizes the existential and relational aspects of faith. However, our comparison of the use of πίστις/πιστεύω in the Markan prayer teaching with the use of this word-group in pagan, Jewish and early Christian literature, and in the Epidaurus inscriptions, forces us to disagree with Schmithals' assertion. In Mark 11:22-24, "to believe" or "to have faith" *does* mean to "hold to be true" the world-view that asserts God's power to affect events in the world in ways that are impossible for humans and for other natural agents.[38] The specific cognitive content of this "faith" is the δόγμα (to use Philo's term) that "everything is possible for God." By contrast, then, to doubt is to lack confidence in God's power to intervene in the world.

"Doubt" and "Unbelief" in Mark and Other Early Christian Texts

In Mark 11:23 "to believe" is clarified by contrast with "to doubt in one's heart" (διακριθῇ ἐν τῇ καρδίᾳ αὐτοῦ).[39] Faith and doubt are often found in dialectical relationship in contexts in which faith means confidence in the miraculous

[37] Schmithals, *Wunder und Glaube,* 90.
[38] D. Lührmann, *Glaube im frühen Christentum* (Gütersloh: Mohn, 1976) 23, 28.
[39] This does not mean, as Barth thinks, that mountain-moving faith is an especially strong faith ("Glaube," 276). "Not doubting" here does not modify or qualify faith but defines it by contrast.

power of God.[40] This is a Christian appropriation of the middle voice of διαχρίνω, found only in the New Testament and other early Christian literature.[41] This usage, usually translated "to doubt" or "to waver," carries the sense of being inwardly divided or uncertain.[42] Thus, James can interpret διαχρινόμενος as δίψυχος (double-minded).[43] This inward division is graphically illustrated in James 1:6 as a condition which makes a person "like a wave of the sea that is driven and tossed by the wind."

It is interesting to note, however, that the negative sanction behind the command to believe and not doubt, although found in James, is missing from Mark. James 1:7 reads: "Let that person [the doubter] not suppose that he will receive anything from the Lord." This is a much stronger threat than Mark's "whoever . . . does not doubt, but believes in his heart . . . it will be done for him."

Paul also employs the contrast between doubt and faith. In Romans 4:20-21, Abraham's being strong in faith (ἐνεδυναμώθη τῇ πίστει) is contrasted with doubting in unbelief (οὐ διαχρίθη τῇ ἀπιστίᾳ). As we saw earlier, to believe and not to doubt here means to be "fully convinced that the one who promised is powerful and will do it."[44] In Paul's discussion about Abraham, the temptation to doubt or waver inwardly is related to the impossibility of having a child in old age (4:19).[45] Here, as in Mark 11:23, doubt is a lack of confidence in God's ability to do the apparently impossible.

Doubt or double-mindedness as an obstacle to receiving from God that for which one prays is the subject of *Mandate* 9 of the *Shepherd of Hermas*. Here the cause of doubt may be the petitioner's sense of unworthiness (9:1) or a delay in God's response (9:8). When an answer is delayed, Hermas is advised in 9:7-8:

. . . do not be doubleminded (διψυχήσῃς) because you have not received (ἔλαβες) the request of your soul speedily . . . do not therefore cease from making the request of your soul, and you shall receive it. But if you grow weary and are doubleminded in your request, blame yourself and not him who gives to you.

[40] Barth, "Glaube," 269.

[41] Friedrich Büchsel, "διαχρίνω," *TDNT* 3 (1965) 947.

[42] Ibid. Similarly, Adolf Schlatter (*Der Glaube im neuen Testament* [5th ed.; Stuttgart: Calwer, 1963] 124) writes: "Das ist die innere Teilung, nicht Glaubensverweigerung, aber auch nicht Glaube, der die Haltung der Person bestimmt, sondern ein Zusammenbestehen entgegengesetzter Eindrüke und Erwartungen." Schlatter thinks that the disciples' surprise that the fig tree had withered is an expression of their doubt.

[43] For a discussion of the concepts of doubt and faith in James see Martin Dibelius, *James* (rev. H. Greeven; trans. M. A. Williams; Philadelphia: Fortress, 1976) 70-83, 219, 254-55.

[44] Büchsel, "διαχρίνω," 947.

[45] On this passage, see Hendrikus Boers, "Polarities at the Roots of New Testament Thought: Methodological Considerations," *PRS* 11 (1984) 65-69.

An interpretation like this may be the basis for the use of the aorist ἐλάβετε in Mark 11:24, where the future or even the present would have been less surprising, as the variants indicate. If the aorist is being used to interpret the lack of response as a delay, then 11:24 would be translated, "Keep on believing that you received everything that you are praying and asking for and it will be done for you." The present tenses are interpreted progressively. The effective aorist (ἐλάβετε) and the future (ἔσται) both refer to the granting of the petition and both are deliberately contrasted with the present tenses. While the praying and asking continue, the community is to believe that the response which still lies ahead was given with the first request.[46]

The one who believes and does not doubt, then, is one who is not inwardly divided, but whole. This is explicit in *Mandate* 9:6:

> Those who are whole (οἱ ὁλοτελεῖς ὄντες) ask in faith for all things, trusting in the Lord, and they receive because they ask without doubting, and are double-minded in nothing.

The emphasis in Mark 11:23 on overcoming the obstacle of inward division again points us in the direction of understanding faith in terms of world-view. For the Markan community to pray in faith for the impossible means that they understand reality from the point of view of the omnipotence of God and resist the temptation to waver on this point. The doubter thinks that God may not have power to do what she asks. The community is encouraged to trust the world-view by which it interprets its existence in terms of the active power of God.

The other terms that the author of Mark uses to indicate a lack of confidence in God's power are ἄπιστος and ἀπιστία. Both appear in the pericope about the demon-possessed boy, Mark 9:14–29. In this story ἄπιστος and ἀπιστία are equivalent in meaning to διακρίνομαι in 11:23. The "faithless generation" of 9:19, which includes the father of the boy, lacks confidence that the boy can be healed. Again the idea of delay is present. The father has made one request which was not successful. His unbelief is expressed in the second, now conditional, request, "If you can do anything, have pity on us and help us" (9:22). The noun ἀπιστία in 9:24, then, merely labels the attitude that has already been clearly delineated by the narrative and the dialogue.

The use of ἀπιστία in 6:6a, however, is not so clear. The narrator's comment, "And he marveled because of their unbelief," follows the information in 6:5 that Jesus "could do no mighty work there, except that he laid his hands upon a few sick people and healed them." Commentators usually follow Matthew in assuming that the people's unbelief is given as the reason for the paucity of healings.[47] It is important to note, however, that in this instance ἀπιστία does not involve a lack of confidence in the possibility of mighty works. On the contrary, the people

---

[46] Swete, *Mark,* 261.

[47] Gnilka, *Markus,* 1:233; Schmithals, *Wunder und Glaube,* 95; Swete, *Mark,* 114; Lane, *Mark,* 204.

of Nazareth remark with astonishment upon Jesus' power (6:2). Their unbelief consists of their refusal to acknowledge that it is God who is at work in Jesus' ministry.[48] Their speculative question, "Where did this man get all this?" (6:2) is intended to evoke from the audience of the gospel the correct response: "From God!"[49] But the comments of the people of Nazareth upon Jesus' humble origins (6:3) let the audience know that their attitude is the same as that of the family and the scribes in 3:20-22.[50] They acknowledge that Jesus has power, but they do not recognize that God is the source of Jesus' power.[51]

In the narrative structure of this pericope, "they took offense at him" (ἐσκανδαλίζοντο ἐν αὐτῷ) is made equivalent to "their unbelief" (τὴν ἀπιστίαν αὐτῶν).[52] They take offense, or make the wrong response to God's activity in Jesus, because they cannot reconcile Jesus' ordinariness ("Is not this the carpenter, the son of Mary . . .?") with the power and wisdom he exercises.[53] Like Peter, who could not reconcile God's power with suffering and rejection (8:32), the people of Nazareth think the things of humans, not the things of God (8:33).

This is an important passage for our understanding of the evangelist's view of the relationship between faith and power. Recognizing miracle-working power but refusing to acknowledge the power as God's is not πίστις in Mark but ἀπιστία. Thus, the faith of the miracle stories and the prayer teaching is always faith in God (11:22) who works through Jesus and through Mark's church. The comment of 6:5b, which qualifies Jesus' inability to do any miracles in the presence of ἀπιστία, shows a reluctance to make faith a condition for miracle in any sense which limits the freedom of God, a reluctance that is manifested in other places in the Markan narrative, as we will see. Later in this discussion we will see how Jesus' freedom to perform miracles even in the presence of unbelief renders faith itself a gift rather than a human achievement.

The discussion of doubt and unbelief has carried us out of the logia collection and into the Markan miracle stories. Since it is generally agreed that the

---

[48] Pesch, *Markusevangelium,* 1:318; Haenchen, *Weg,* 214. But Fridrichsen (*Problem,* 80) and Aune ("Magic," 1536) think that the unbelief of the people consists of their refusal to request help from Jesus.

[49] Haenchen, *Weg,* 214.

[50] Pesch, *Markusevangelium,* 1:318.

[51] See the discussion of 3:20-35 in chapter 7.

[52] Gnilka, *Markus,* 1:232.

[53] In Mark, σκανδαλίζω and its derivatives have the sense of failure to persevere in discipleship. In 9:42 we have a warning against causing a believer, i.e., a Christian, to stumble. As in 6:1-6a, stumbling is contrasted with faith. The contrast continues in 9:43, 45 and 47. In 4:17 and 14:27-29 the failure to continue in discipleship is caused by suffering and persecution, either that of Jesus, or that of the community. In 6:1-6a, it is not suffering but the ordinariness of Jesus' identity as "Mary's boy, the carpenter" which causes the people to reject the idea that God could be at work in Jesus.

sense of πίστις and πιστεύω is the same in the miracle stories as in the prayer teaching,[54] we will now turn our attention to the relationship between faith and power in the Markan miracles.

Faith and Power in the Markan Miracle Stories

It has become almost axiomatic in New Testament studies that in the synoptic miracle traditions, and in Mark in particular, faith leads to miracles, but miracles do not lead to faith.[55] Frequently New Testament miracle stories are contrasted with pagan stories with respect to faith; while faith may be a *consequence* of a miracle in pagan stories, in the New Testament stories faith is the *condition* for miracles.[56] R. M. Grant disputes this distinction, asserting that, ". . . (a) sometimes faith is necessary in the miracle stories, sometimes it is not; and (b) sometimes outside Christianity faith is necessary too."[57] The scope of the present study does not permit examination of more than the Markan miracles, but in order to understand the evangelist's view of the relationship between faith and power in the prayer teaching, we will have to consider the evidence of the miracle stories as well.

Faith is attributed to the recipient of Jesus' aid in only two of the Markan miracles: the story of the hemorrhaging woman (5:24b–34) and the story of blind Bartimaeus (10:46–52). In both of these stories the Markan Jesus says to the healed person, "Your faith has made you well" (ἡ πίστις σου σέσωκέν σε). In the story of the paralytic (2:1–12) the narrator calls attention to the faith of those who devised a way of getting the paralytic to Jesus in spite of the crowd: ἰδὼν ὁ Ἰησοῦς τὴν πίστιν αὐτῶν (2:5).[58]

In the story of Jairus' daughter (5:21–24a, 35–43) the Markan Jesus exhorts Jairus, "Do not fear, only believe" (5:36). To be afraid is to lack confidence in Jesus' power. Similarly, in 4:40 Jesus rebukes the disciples for their cowardice in the face of the storm at sea and asks, "Do you not yet have faith?"[59] The

---

[54] Tagawa, *Miracles*, 116; Dibelius, *James*, 81; Gerhard Ebeling, "Jesus and Faith," *Word and Faith* (trans. J. Leitch; Philadelphia: Fortress, 1963) 230–32.

[55] H. J. Held ('Matthew as Interpreter of the Miracle Stories," *Tradition and Interpretation in Matthew*, by G. Bornkamm, G. Barth and H. J. Held [trans. P. Scott; Philadelphia: Westminster, 1963] 276) thinks this is true of the relationship between faith and miracles in the synoptic tradition generally. Schmithals (*Markus*, 1:303) thinks it is true of Mark in particular. In a discussion of Mark 10:46–52, Achtemeier (" 'And He Followed,' " 134) contrasts Mark with Luke in respect to the relationship between miracles and faith.

[56] W. Grundmann, "δύναμαι," *TDNT* 2 (1964) 302–3; Theissen, *Miracle Stories*, 132; Pesch, *Markusevangelium*, 1:305.

[57] Grant, *Miracle*, 173; See also his "Miracle and Mythology," *ZRGG* 4 (1952) 123–33.

[58] Gnilka (*Markus*, 1:99) wants to include the paralytic among those whose faith Jesus "sees" in 2:5.

[59] Reading οὔπω ἔχετε πίστιν; with Nestle-Aland[26]. The RSV translates, "Have you no faith?" perhaps reading πῶς οὐκ with A, C, K, II, 33, etc. See Metzger, *Commentary*, 84.

implication is that if they had had confidence in God's power to protect them, they would not have been afraid of the storm.

The story of the demon-possessed boy (9:14–29) contains the instances of ἄπιστος and ἀπιστία discussed above, as well as two instances of πιστεύω. In 9:23 the Markan Jesus links faith with the formula of omnipotence: "All things are possible to him who believes" (πάντα δυνατὰ τῷ πιστεύοντι). The father responds with the well-known cry, "I believe; help my unbelief!" (πιστεύω· βοήθει μου τῇ ἀπιστίᾳ). This is an important pericope for the Markan view of faith and will be discussed at some length below.

Let us examine the consensus positions stated at the beginning of this section by testing them against the Markan miracle stories. First, is it the case that faith leads to miracles, but miracles do not lead to faith? Second, is it the case that in Mark faith is a requisite condition for miracles? The second question is obviously important for the interpretation of the prayer logia collection, since the grammatical structure of the logia in 11:23–24 does make faith a condition for God's response to the prayers of the community.

It is certainly the case that the evangelist advocates faith on the part of those who seek healing or exorcism. This is clear in the story of the hemorrhaging woman, the story of blind Bartamaeus, and the story of the paralytic. When the Markan Jesus urges Jairus to believe, the implication is that if he believes, as the woman did, then his daughter will be healed, even as the woman was healed. The father of the demon-possessed boy interprets Jesus' "If you can! All things are possible to him who believes" to mean that if he had faith, his faith would lead to the healing of his son. That is why he responds as he does in 9:23. Clearly, faith leads to miracles in Mark.

The assertion that miracles do not lead to faith is based on formal considerations. In the stories in which faith is attributed to persons who seek miraculous help, their faith is clearly prior to the miracle. The Markan miracles do not have any formal characteristics which correspond to the Johannine epilogue: "This . . . sign Jesus did . . . and . . . they believed in him" (2:11, Cf. 7:31, 9:38, 11:45). After receiving his sight, Bartimaeus follows Jesus, but, as we have seen, "following" and "believing" are not synonymous in Mark. Some follow who have trouble believing and some who believe do not follow. There is a real sense, however, in which miracles do lead to faith in the sense of confidence in the possibility of miracles, or confidence in Jesus' power to help.

In the Markan narrative it is clear that the people who come to Jesus seeking miraculous help do so because of his reputation as a miracle-worker. In 2:1–12, the four men who bring the paralytic are part of the crowd which is gathered in Capernaum (2:1–3) as a result of Jesus' reputation as a healer and exorcist, both in Capernaum and in "all Galilee" (1:21–45). About the hemorrhaging woman, the narrator tells us that "she had heard the reports about Jesus" (5:27), and that the explanation (γάρ) for her touching his garment was that she said, "If I touch even his garments I shall be made well" (5:28). The woman is portrayed as knowing Jesus' reputation, which now included the fact that people were healed by touching him (3:10).[60] Similarly, Mark tells us that Bartimaeus begins to cry out "when he heard that it was Jesus of Nazareth."[61] There is a direct connection between the reputation of the healer and the faith of those seeking healing. They believe that Jesus can heal them because they have heard about his healing others. Here we have a parallel with the Epidaurus inscriptions and a clue as to how the Markan miracles are expected to function in the community: they inspire faith in the power of the cultic Lord. In Mark, then, faith leads to miracles and miracles lead to faith.

In what sense is it correct to say that in Mark faith is a condition for miracles? Certainly, from the point of view of the narrator, those who sought help from Jesus would not have done so, had they not put some credence in the miracle stories they had heard. Moreover, the repetition in the text of the omnipotence formula reminds the audience that believing the miracle stories is predicated on the world-view that the deity from whom help is expected actually has the power to do anything, even the apparently impossible. That is why the father of the demon-possessed boy can say, "I believe" (9:24). Had he not put some credence in the view that an omnipotent deity can intervene through a miracle-worker, he would have stayed home. Faith is a condition for miracle in Mark in the sense that maintenance of the world-view is essential for the ongoing experience of the community. Christians, Jews, Neopythagoreans and followers of Asclepius tell miracle stories. Epicureans do not tell miracle stories. The difference lies in the respective world-views.

We have already observed that although James and the Shepherd of Hermas state explicitly that those who doubt will not receive what they ask in prayer, Mark demands faith and forbids doubt without going on explicitly to exclude doubters from God's miraculous help. In 6:5b, Jesus' inability to do any miracles in Nazareth is qualified with the words, "except that he laid his hands upon a few sick people and healed them." When we examine the Markan miracle stories carefully we discover that faith cannot be said to be a condition for miracles in any absolute sense.

In the story of the stilling of the storm (4:35–41), the text states explicitly that the beneficiaries of the miracle did not have faith either prior to or as a result of the miracle. In the second sea miracle, 6:45–52, the disciples are again in trouble in a boat, they are again afraid, and Jesus rescues them again (6:51). Faith is not mentioned in this story and it certainly is not demonstrated by the behavior of the disciples. In some of the miracle stories where faith is not mentioned, people nevertheless behave in ways that indicate that they have confidence in Jesus' power to heal or exorcise. In that sense, people like the

---

[60] Swete, *Mark,* 103.

[61] The RSV interprets ἀκούσας temporally ("when he heard"), but the participle also has a causal sense. Bartimaeus does not cry out, "Son of David, have mercy on me!" to every passerby; he begins this cry because "he heard that it was Jesus of Nazareth."

Syrophoenician woman are legitimately cited by scholars as examples of faith.[62] However, in other miracle stories no one evidences any confidence in Jesus' power or any expectation of his help prior to a miracle. This is the case in both the feeding accounts (6:35–44, 8:1–10). Thus, it is not the case that faith is an absolute prerequisite for miracles in Mark. The story of the demon-possessed boy provides a dramatic example of a miracle that is given in response to a request made in unbelief.

In this pericope, the father, along with the scribes and the crowd is characterized as ἄπιστος. This evaluation is confirmed by the form in which the father makes his request to Jesus: "if you can do anything, (εἴ τι δύνῃ) have pity on us and help us" (9:22). His request stands in sharp contrast to that of the leper in 1:40: "If you will, you can make me clean."[63] Jesus' response to the father makes it clear that to regard as conditional the possibility of the requested miracle is to be unbelieving. In the context of this narrative the father's scepticism is grounded in the disciples' unsuccessful attempt to exorcise his son (9:18).[64] Thus the Markan Jesus' emphasis on faith seems to be a call for persistence in maintaining the community's world-view even in the face of unanswered prayer. When the requested miracle does not happen, the power of God is still not to be questioned. Lagrange correctly paraphrases, " 'If you can'! That is not the question!"[65] Jesus repeats the father's words in order to challenge them.[66]

The sense of the second part of Jesus' response is much debated, because of the ambiguity of the phrase πάντα δυνατὰ τῷ πιστεύοντι. Is Jesus demanding faith from the father, or is he saying that his own ability to exorcise the boy comes from his faith?[67] Of course, in the narrative the father interprets Jesus'

---

[62] E. Schweizer, "The Portrayal of the Life of Faith in the Gospel of Mark," *Interpreting the Gospels* (ed. J. L. Mays; Philadelphia: Fortress, 1981) 177; Malbon, "Fallible," 36–37; Tagawa, *Miracles*, 117–18.

[63] Pesch, *Markusevangelium*, 2:92.

[64] Theissen, *Miracle Stories*, 136.

[65] Lagrange, *Marc*, 241. Taylor (*Mark*, 399) writes, "The article has the force of inverted commas or an exclamation mark." The ambiguity of the phrase generated the addition of πιστεῦσαι in order to make the father the subject of δύνῃ. This led to the omission of the article, according to Metzger (*Commentary*, 100).

[66] Metzger, *Commentary*, 100.

[67] Schmithals (*Markus*, 2:418) lists Lohmeyer and Schniewind among the commentators who read Jesus' response as a reference to his own faith. See also Gnilka, *Markus*, 2:48 and Ebeling, "Jesus and Faith," 234. Achtemeier ("Miracles and the Historical Jesus: A Study of Mark 9:14–29," *CBQ* 37 [1975] 480–81) argues that one of the two original stories that have been combined in 9:14–29 contrasted Jesus' faith with the father's unbelief. Later, the idea that Jesus' power came from his faith was unacceptable to the church, with the result that the lament of verse 19 was added to identify Jesus more closely with God, according to Achtemeier.

response as a call for him to have faith.[68] But this still leaves open the question of whether faith is required of the father in order for him to become a miracle-worker and thus heal his son[69] or whether the father in this story corresponds to the friends of the paralytic and to Jairus as the patient's representative who is expected to have faith. Elsewhere Mark attributes the necessary faith to the recipient of healing (5:34, 10:52).

The question of whether miracle-workers or patients or both must have faith is resolved when we remember that from the evangelist's point of view the healer and the patient have the same status with respect to miraculous power.[70] It is not the case that one human is the worker of the miracle and another the recipient. Rather, both are recipients. The miracle is always, so the author of Mark thinks, done by God. That is why he can allow 11:23, which seems to refer to one who performs a miracle, to stand next to 11:24, which refers to those who receive (ἐλάβετε). In both sayings, the effective result of the prayer is expressed in identical dative constructions which point to God as the agent: ἔσται αὐτῷ (11:23), ἔσται ὑμῖν (11:24).[71] The phrase πάντα δυνατά, as we have seen, is always an attribute of God.[72] The transformation of τῷ θεῷ into τῷ πιστεύοντι in 9:23 is equivalent to the use of the ἀδύνατον in 11:23 in connection with πίστις. The "one who believes" is the one who lives within the world-view in which everything is possible for God, thus, the one who believes in God (11:22).

Rudolf Pesch holds that the reference of τῷ πιστεύοντι in 9:23 is deliberately ambiguous, referring to the father, as the father realizes in the narrative, but also to Jesus.[73] Ebeling points out that the connection of the fig tree pericope with 11:22-25 implies that Jesus is an example of one who has faith in the God who is able to move mountains.[74] Certainly in the Gethsemane prayer scene the Markan Jesus is portrayed as one who has faith, since he begins his prayer with the omnipotence formula (πάντα δυνατά σοι). Schweizer thinks that the Markan stress on following Jesus means that Jesus' life and death are to be understood as enabling the community to live and die faithfully. Jesus is not merely an example to be imitated, but a leader to be followed.[75] It is likely, then, that "the one who believes" in 9:23 is deliberately ambiguous. Jesus has faith and he calls the father to have faith.

---

[68] Hahn, "Verständnis," 58; Theissen, *Miracle Stories*, 137.

[69] Barth, "Glaube," 279 (following Lohmeyer).

[70] D. Lührmann, "Glaube," *RAC* 11 (1981) 66-67.

[71] E. D. O'Connor, *Faith in the Synoptic Gospels* (Notre Dame: University of Notre Dame Press, 1961) 13: "It is always God who works the miracle, even when a creature serves in some sense as His instrument. Faith confers on its possessor no power but that of praying in such a way as to be heard; the believer who 'works' a miracle is really only obtaining it from God."

[72] Theissen (*Miracle Stories*, 137) calls attention to this fact in his discussion of 9:23.

[73] Pesch, *Markusevangelium*, 2:92.

[74] Ebeling, "Jesus and Faith," 234.

[75] Schweizer, "Faith," 175-77.

We have seen that the father's initial request, which expressed doubt about Jesus' ability to help, received from Jesus a rebuke and a demand for faith. At this point in the narrative (9:24), the father makes a new request. He cries out,[76] "I believe (πιστεύω); help my unbelief (βοήθει μου τῷ ἀπιστίᾳ)." Jesus' response to this cry for help is to exorcise the boy (9:25-27).

F. G. Lang believes that the father's cry, which he correctly interprets as a prayer,[77] indicates that the father moves from unbelief to faith prior to the healing of his son.[78] Achtemeier, however, disagrees:

> The response of the father—that his faith is insufficient—is never corrected. Nowhere is there any indication that the father's faith rose above its ambiguity. In their present form, vss. 23-24 present the contrast between the powerful wonder worker and the impotent seeker. Jesus is powerful because of his faith, as vs. 23 clearly implies, and the faith of the father, far from ultimately proving sufficient (a point nowhere made in the narrative), is a clear counter-point to the effective faith of Jesus which alone, through the expulsion, is proved sufficient.[79]

Achtemeier is correct in his recognition that Jesus functions in this story as an example of one who has faith in God and for whom therefore everything is possible. He is also correct in pointing out that the narrator does not comment on the father's faith again after 9:24. However, the father's cry is more ambiguous than Achtemeier allows.

In the first place, Achtemeier ignores the fact that the father's cry is not merely a confession that his faith is insufficient, but at the same time a request: "Help my unbelief." That is why most commentators interpret the cry as a recognition by the father that the faith which is demanded of him is not a human possibility and that he must receive faith as a gift.[80] In that case, this pericope would indicate that the author of Mark agrees with Paul in the view that the faith connected with miracle is a charism (1 Cor 12:9, 13:2).[81] Gerhard Barth argues

---

[76] κράξας; Cf. Bartimaeus, 10:47, 48.

[77] F. G. Lang, "Sola Gratia im Markusevangelium: Die Soteriologie des Markus nach 9, 14-29 und 10, 17-31," *Rechtfertigung* (FS E. Käsemann; ed. J. Friedrich, W. Pöhlmann and P. Stuhlmacher; Tübingen: Mohr, 1976) 325. Lang, however, also thinks that this is the prayer to which Jesus refers in 9:29 and that the disciples are not seen by Mark as in any way at fault in this story. He writes, ". . . das Unvermögen der Jünger im Unglauben des Vaters der ja v 24 eingestanden ist begründet zu sehen. Und dafür kann man die Jünger ebensowenig verantwortlich machen wie Jesus für den Unglauben in seiner Vaterstadt (6,6)." However, 9:18 and 9:28 require that the pericope be read as requiring prayer for a miracle as well as prayer for faith, which is the way Lang interprets the father's request.

[78] Lang, "Soteriologie," 326.

[79] "Miracles," 480.

[80] Schmithals, *Markus,* 2:419; Pesch, *Markusevangelium,* 2:93; Swete, *Mark,* 200; Taylor, *Mark,* 399-400; Lang, "Soteriologie," 326; Schweizer, *Mark,* 188-89.

[81] Zmijewski ("Glaube," 97) points out that this is also the view of the "apostles" in Luke 17:6 who ask Jesus to increase their faith. Jesus, however, responds that a tiny faith is enough without having to be increased.

that the dialogue between Jesus and the father, which ends with the father's dramatic request, is included in this pericope prior to 11:22-25 in order to forestall a misunderstanding of faith which would regard it as a human achievement. Instead, faith is represented in 9:24 as recognizing its inadequacy and asking for help.[82]

According to Barth, the earliest form of the logion preserved in 11:23 was Matthew 17:20, where faith the size of a grain of mustard seed is enough to move a mountain.[83] The comparison with a mustard seed, Barth thinks, was intended to discourage speculation about how much faith was needed for a miracle.[84] However, experiences of unanswered prayers and unsuccessful exorcisms led to a re-examination of the promise, with the result that the prohibition of doubt was inserted into the logion—thus Mark 11:23, which means that only a very strong faith receives the promise.[85] In Barth's view, then, Mark 9:24 is a correction of 11:23. Faith is not to examine itself but to recognize that it always exists only in the context of the temptation to doubt.[86]

We can agree with Barth that 9:24 is intended to protect against the notion of faith as human achievement. This is the majority opinion because it reflects the plain sense of the text. Thus the father's cry is not a mere confession of unbelief as Achtemeier reads it. However, we have seen earlier that the construction of 11:23 sets μὴ διακριθῇ ἐν τῇ καρδίᾳ parallel to πιστεύῃ so that "not doubting" *defines* "believing" rather than functioning as a qualifier which designates an especially strong faith.[87] Nowhere in the Markan narrative is a saying attributed to Jesus which the evangelist regards as needing correction. We cannot agree with Barth that 11:23 regards miracle-working faith as a human achievement, but we can agree with him that 9:24 explicitly denies that faith is a work.

It should be noted at this point that we are still talking about praying faith, or the faith which expects the impossible from God. We are not dealing with a concept of faith as constitutive of Christian existence. This tends to be forgotten when 9:14-29 is appealed to in support of a soteriology of grace.[88] There is grace in this passage, but it is the grace that gives a miraculous healing to one who confesses that he is not able to believe and has the humility to ask for the miracle anyway.

---

[82] Barth, "Glaube," 281.

[83] Barth, "Glaube," 275. This is also the position of Telford (*Barren,* 98-104) and Ebeling ("Jesus and Faith," 228).

[84] Barth, "Glaube," 275.

[85] Ibid., 272, 276, 290.

[86] Ibid., 282, 290.

[87] See the discussion in chapter 3, especially note 43.

[88] As Lang ('Soteriologie," 328, 335-37) does. Soteriology is explicitly the subject of 10:17-27 where the call is to "follow," not to "believe." In 9:14-29 prayer and faith are in the foreground and soteriology is, at most, implicit.

This brings us to Achtemeier's correct observation that the narrative neither gives any indication of an increase in the father's faith, nor is there any response from Jesus which pronounces his faith adequate. The help which Jesus gives to his unbelief is the miracle itself; Jesus makes no other response to his request. That what the father requests in 9:24 is not more faith, but the miracle which will strengthen his faith, is evident in the vocabulary. In 9:22, his first request is, "Have pity on us and help us" (βοήθησον ἡμῖν). This obviously means, "Heal my son." In 9:24, his request is similar: βοήθει μου τῇ ἀπιστίᾳ. Like the previous verse, 9:23, this request in 9:24, "Help my unbelief," is ambiguous. It can be interpreted to mean, "Heal my son, even though I cannot believe,"[89] but it can also be understood to mean, "Help me to believe by healing my son." On the latter reading, the requested miracle would be understood as help, not only for the boy's condition (possession by a demon) but also for the father's condition (unbelief).

If the miracle is understood as help for the father's unbelief, then the relationship between faith and miracle in this story is very much like the relationship between faith and miracle in the Epidaurus story about the man with the crippled hand. In both stories, the protagonist approaches the healer, but does not really regard it as possible that the desired healing can take place. The healer reproaches the protagonist's unbelief, but performs the healing. Not only does the sceptic receive the requested miracle, but he also (it is implied) believes in the power of the healer as a result of the miracle.

Both aspects of the current consensus on the relationship between faith and miracles in the Gospel of Mark need to be qualified. In the first place, although it is the case that faith leads to miracles in Mark, it is not the case that miracles do not lead to faith. In the Markan narrative, some people have faith in Jesus' power because they have heard miracle stories. The reporting of miracles is expected to lead to faith in the possibility of miracles (not necessarily to discipleship, however). In the story about the demon-possessed boy, it is possible that the experience of a miracle is understood as an encouragement to faith. In the second place, it is not the case that faith is always a condition for miracles in Mark. The narrative preserves the freedom of God to intervene when faith is not present, and even when unbelief is present. The miracle stories and the prayer teaching illustrate faith and call for faith without limiting the freedom of God.

Miracle Faith as "Faith in God" (11:22)

According to 11:22, the faith which prays for and receives miracles is faith in God, but the faith of persons seeking help in the miracle stories is clearly confidence in the power of Jesus.[90] It is clear throughout the Markan narrative, however, that Jesus is not an autonomous miracle-worker; rather his power and

---

[89] Schlatter, *Markus*, 170.

[90] Bultmann, "πιστεύω," 206 n. 240; Hahn, "Verständnis," 55; Ebeling, "Jesus and Faith," 235; Aune, "Magic," 1535.

authority come from God. Because the Markan portrait of Jesus is partly
derived from the disciple-gathering teacher familiar to Hellenistic-Roman audiences,[91] the Markan Jesus does not, like the biblical prophet, preface his teaching
with "thus says the Lord."[92] Nevertheless, the influence of the Hebrew scriptures
on the portrait of Jesus is pervasive. In fact, the Markan Jesus takes over many
of the role functions that would normally be assigned to Yahweh in biblical
literature.[93] In the miracle stories especially, Jesus is portrayed in the same way
that Yahweh is portrayed in the Psalms that celebrate the mighty deeds of
Yahweh.[94] The narrator also stresses in a number of other ways that it is God's
power that is at work in Jesus.

Jesus' very first act of power, the exorcism in the Capernaum synagogue, is
recognized as a reflection of the power of God by the public cry of the demon,
"I know who you are, the Holy One of God" (1:24). At the end of this first cycle
of miracles, Jesus heals a leper (1:40–45), an act which, according to Jewish tradition, only God could do.[95] The leper's request is framed in such a way that the
audience is made to understand that Jesus' ability to help is unlimited: ἐὰν θέλῃς
δύνασαί με καθαρίσαι. This is the sort of accolade which in Hellenistic Judaism is
addressed to God: "You have only to will, and your power is there" (LXX
Wisdom 12:18: πάρεστιν γάρ σοι, ὅταν θέλῃς, τὸ δύνασθαι).

Only God can forgive sins, but Jesus both forgives and heals the paralytic
(2:1–12). The "choral response" attributes the miracle to God: "they were all
amazed and glorified God" (2:12). The source of Jesus' power is again the issue
when the scribes accuse him of magic in 3:22; they say he is conjuring the
demons by Beelzebul.[96] But the author of Mark makes it clear that although
Jesus has indeed bound the strong one, i.e., Satan,[97] he has done so by the power
of the Holy Spirit (3:39). Not to recognize the Holy Spirit as the source of Jesus'
power is "an eternal sin" (3:29). By contrast, to see God's power at work in Jesus
and to participate with Jesus in his activity is to "do the will of God" and thus
to belong to Jesus' true family.[98] The teaching and the powerful acts which
precede this passage give content to the "will of God."[99]

---

[89] Schlatter, *Markus,* 170.

[90] Bultmann, "πιστεύω," 206 n. 240; Hahn, "Verständnis," 55; Ebeling, "Jesus and
Faith," 235; Aune, "Magic," 1535.

[91] Robbins, *Jesus,* 113–19.

[92] Ibid., 117.

[93] Ibid., 119.

[94] Richard Glöckner, *Neutestamentliche Wundergeschichten und das Lob der Wundertaten Gottes in den Psalmen* (Mainz: Matthias-Grünewald, 1983) 16, 25, 49.

[95] Pesch, *Markusevangelium,* 1:143.

[96] Morton Smith, *Jesus the Magician* (New York: Harper and Row, 1978) 32–33.

[97] Fridrichsen, *Problem,* 108. Cf. 1:7, 1:12–13.

[98] Donahue, "Neglected Factor," 584.

[99] Pesch, *Markusevangelium,* 1:225.

Two further examples show how the Markan miracle stories are shaped in order to attribute Jesus' power to God. After exorcising the Gerasene demoniac, Jesus tells him, "Go home to your friends and tell them how much the Lord (ὁ κύριος) has done for you and how he has had mercy on you" (5:19). The man, however, reports what Jesus did for him (5:20). In this way, Mark makes it clear to the audience that what Jesus does is really done by God![100]

The onlookers' response to the healing of the deaf mute (7:37) functions in the same way. The acclamation, "He has done everything well" (καλῶς πάντα πεποίηκεν), echoes LXX Gen 1:31 on the activity of God in creation: εἶδεν ὁ θεὸς τὰ πάντα, ὅσα ἐποίησεν, καὶ ἰδοὺ καλὰ λίαν.[101] The second part of the acclamation alludes to Isaiah's vision of the new creation when God will cause the deaf to hear and the dumb to speak (Isa 35:5-6). Again, Jesus' power is the power of God![102]

When, in Mark 11, Peter calls attention to the miraculous withering of the fig tree, the response of the Markan Jesus, which simultaneously ends the fig tree pericope and introduces the prayer logia is, "Have faith in God." This clearly indicates that the power that withered the tree is the power of God, confirming that the power behind all of Jesus' miracles is God's power and therefore that all confidence in Jesus as miracle-worker is faith in God. When Jesus performs a mighty act, or when the community receives what it asks in prayer, no matter how impossible, the correct interpretation is that God has acted. To give another interpretation is to stand in danger of "blasphemy against the Holy Spirit" (3:28-30).

We have already seen the similarity between the function of the Epidaurus inscriptions and the function of the Markan miracle stories; in both cases the mighty acts of benevolence of the deity in the past are presented as encouragement to those who seek the god's aid in the present. Dieter Zeller[103] and Richard Glöckner[104] have argued that this function of the miracle stories in the early Christian communities is reminiscent of the cultic setting of the Psalms of thanksgiving, in which the recipient of divine aid rendered public testimony to the miraculous intervention of Yahweh and offered thanks. The miracle stories of the Jesus tradition, according to this view, would have served as instruction in and encouragement to prayer![105] Similarly, Ernest Best writes that in Mark the miracles emphasize "the care of Jesus for the community as it is exercised in the present, i.e., Mark's present . . ."[106]

---

[100] Ibid., 1:293-94.

[101] Cf. Eccl 3:11: τὰ πάντα ἐποίησεν καλὰ ἐν καιρῷ αὐτοῦ.

[102] Schmithals, *Markus,* 1:359-60; Glöckner, *Wundergeschichten,* 28.

[103] Dieter Zeller, "Wunder und Bekenntnis: zum Sitz im Leben urchristlicher Wundergeschichten," *BZ* 25 (1981) 204-22.

[104] Glöckner, *Wundergeschichten,* 16-17, 161-66 and passim.

[105] Ibid., 164-65.

[106] Best, *Mark,* 65.

This view of the miracle stories as part of the Markan prayer catechesis brings us back to the Markan miracle story in which prayer is emphasized: the story of the demon-possessed boy. Here the emphasis on God as the source of the power to perform miracles is brought into connection with the disciples as miracle-workers.

THE RELATIONSHIP BETWEEN PRAYER AND POWER

The author of Mark has a concern not only to emphasize Jesus' dependence on God's power, but also to remind his community that it has no power of its own. By connecting miracle working with prayer and by presenting Jesus as a person of prayer the evangelist makes the point that the power of the community to heal and exorcise depends entirely on believing prayer.

"Not by Anything but Prayer" (9:29)

The story about the disciples' inability to cast a demon out of a boy is found in all three synoptic accounts, but only Matthew and Mark include the private conversation in which the disciples question Jesus about their failure. According to Matt 17:20, Jesus' answer is, "Because of your little faith." The mountain-moving saying follows, as an example of the kind of power that would be theirs if they had faith. By contrast, the Markan Jesus responds, "This kind cannot be driven out by anything but prayer."[107]

Another interesting feature of the Markan version of the story is the conversation between Jesus and the father, which is lacking in Matthew and in Luke![108] It appears that whereas Matthew used the story only to emphasize the importance of faith on the part of miracle-workers, Mark had two agendas. He wanted to make a point about faith, as we have already seen, but he also wanted to emphasize the importance of prayer. In order to make both points, the evangelist deflected the charge of unbelief from the disciples and focused it on the father. The disciples still have blame in the Markan version, but their fault is not lack of faith, but prayerlessness![109]

---

[107] The variant "and fasting" is a later addition which reflects a development in the praxis of the church, according to Metzger (*Commentary,* 101) and Achtemeier ('Miracles," 476; see his examples in n. 18).

[108] The conversation between Jesus and the father stands at the center of the story. Lang ('Soteriologie," 322) provides the following outline of the pericope:

A	14–18	Focus on the failure of the disciples
B	19–20	Focus on the boy and the crowd
C	21–24	Conversation between Jesus and the father
B'	25–27	Focus on the boy and the crowd
A'	28–29	Focus on the failure of the disciples

[109] There are at least two schools of thought on the origin of the Markan story. Achtemeier ("Miracles," 471–91) and Bultmann (*History,* 211) argue that two originally independent stories have been combined and a postscript (9:28–29) added. W. Schenk

The narrative as it stands thus gives two reasons for the failed exorcism: The father lacked faith and the disciples neglected prayer. There is no attempt here to discredit the historical disciples or some particular group in Mark's church![110] Rather, the evangelist wants to instruct his community in the necessity of both prayer and faith![111] That the introduction of prayer in the epilogue betrays a Markan concern is evident because the private instruction scene "in the house" where the disciples ask for and receive additional clarification of the preceding scene is so typically Markan (4:10-12, 7:17-23, 10:10-11)![112]

("Tradition und Redaktion in der Epileptiker-Pericope Mk 9, 14-29," *ZNW* 63 [1972] 76-94) thinks that one original story has been expanded. This question may remain open, as we are concerned about the present form of the story.

The point of view from which the story is narrated is that of Jesus. The narrator stands at Jesus' side as it were, and views each scene from that perspective. It is necessary to keep this in mind in order to sort out the pronouns in 14-20, and to identify the addressees of Jesus' epithet ἄπιστος in verse 19. Schmithals (*Markus*, 2:415), Telford (*Barren*, 108), Schweizer (*Mark*, 188) and others assume that the disciples are included as members of the "faithless generation" which Jesus laments, but the narrative does not support this assumption, as Cook ("Text Linguistic Approach," 256) observes.

The pericope follows the transfiguration and so opens with Jesus, Peter, James, and John approaching the other disciples: ἐλθόντες πρὸς τοὺς μαθητὰς. Standing with Jesus and the three, the narrator says, "they saw a great crowd around *them* and scribes arguing with *them*." In both instances αὐτούς refers to the (nine) disciples. In verse 15, the crowd leaves the disciples and runs up to greet Jesus: προστρέχοντες ἠσπάζοντο αὐτόν. From this point on, the disciples are out of the picture altogether until the private scene in verse 28 "in the house." All the dialogue in 16-19 takes place between Jesus and the crowd, of which the boy's father and the scribes are members (Haenchen, *Weg*, 320).

It is to this composite group that Jesus addresses the question τί συζητεῖτε πρὸς αὐτούς. The group, which includes the scribes, is the subject of συζητεῖτε (cf. 14) and αὐτούς once again refers to the disciples. The father answers for the group: the topic of the argument was the disciples' failure to exorcise his son. Jesus' lament in response, which begins ὦ γενεὰ ἄπιστος refers to the crowd, the father and the scribes. In the synoptic tradition γενεά is used negatively to refer to the opponents of Jesus (Matt 12:39-45, 16:4, 23:36, Luke 11:29, 50, 16:8, 17:25). In Mark 8:38 the "adulterous and sinful generation" are those who reject Jesus. In Mark 8:12 the Pharisees who argue with Jesus (συζητεῖν) are meant: "this generation seeks a sign." Mark does not include the disciples in 'this generation" (Held, "Matthew," 191 n. 2; Lang, "Soteriologie," 325). Although the disciples receive their share of rebuke from the Markan Jesus, the criticism in 9:19 is directed to the crowd, including the scribes and the father. The conversation with the father in the center of the pericope focuses on him as the one who lacks faith.

[110] Malbon, "Fallible," 30.

[111] Reploh thinks that τοῦτο τὸ γένος is an indication that the Markan community was having difficulty with a particular kind of demon-possession (*Markus*, 217). It is clear, however, that Mark regarded prayer as an integral part of the community's involvement with miracle in general, as 11:23-24 shows.

[112] Achtemeier, "Miracles," 475-76.

Schmithals objects that although the Markan Jesus calls for prayer in connection with the disciples' failure to exorcise the boy, Jesus himself did not use prayer in the exorcism.[113] However, Jesus does pray at important points in the Markan narrative, and other scholars argue that Jesus is presented as a model of prayer by the evangelist.[114]

The Praying Jesus as a Model for the Community

Three times in the narrative the audience is informed that Jesus withdrew for solitary prayer. The first, 1:35–39, precedes the expansion of his ministry of teaching, healing and exorcism beyond Capernaum into "all Galilee" indicating that both the direction and the power of Jesus' ministry are given by God in prayer.[115] The second prayer scene, 6:46, follows the first feeding miracle and precedes the dramatic epiphany scene of 6:47–52. The third prayer scene takes place in Gethsemane (14:32–42).[116] Just as the first prayer scene ends with Jesus' summons to his disciples to accompany him in his ministry of preaching, healing and exorcism, the third prayer scene ends with Jesus' summons to his disciples to accompany him in his suffering: ἄγωμεν, 1:38, 14:42.[117]

The references to Jesus' blessing and giving thanks prior to the two Markan feeding miracles should also be taken as prayer.[118] In both cases the inability of the disciples to feed the crowd is contrasted with Jesus' ability to do so after he looks up to heaven (ἀναβλέψας εἰς τὸν οὐρανὸν, 6:41), blesses the food (εὐλογέω, 6:41, 8:6), and gives thanks (εὐχαριστέω, 8:6, cf. 14:22).[119] The "looking up to heaven" which precedes the healing of the deaf mute (ἀναβλέψας εἰς τὸν οὐρανὸν, 7:34) should be regarded as a prayer gesture as well.[120] The curse which Jesus pronounces on the fig tree is couched in the aorist optative (μηχέτι . . . μηδεὶς . . . φάγον, 11:14), the optative being typically used for oaths, prayers, and wishes.[121] The placement of the prayer logia immediately after the notice of the

---

[113] Schmithals, Markus, 2:424.

[114] Pesch, Markusevangelium, 2:97; Caba, Oración, 325.

[115] Schmithals, Markus, 1:135.

[116] See the discussion in chapter 8.

[117] R. H. Lightfoot, "A Consideration of Three Passages in St. Mark's Gospel," In Memoriam Ernst Lohmeyer (ed. W. Schmauch; Stuttgart: Evangelisches Verlagswerk, 1951) 114.

[118] Swete, Mark, 134; Taylor, Mark, 324.

[119] Since these prayers are thanksgivings, it is not strictly correct to regard the multiplication of the food as an "answer" to Jesus' prayer as Dietzel ("Erhörungsgewissheit," 99–100) does. Theissen (Miracle Stories, 65) observes, "There is nowhere any indication that the multiplication of the loaves results from this prayer." However, the inclusion of prayer in the portrait of Jesus the miracle-worker does serve to reinforce the idea that Jesus' power comes from God.

[120] Dietzel, "Erhörungsgewissheit," 101; Taylor, Mark, 355; Theissen, Miracle Stories, 65.

[121] Robertson, Grammar, 939.

effectiveness of Jesus' curse interprets the curse itself as a prayer and the withering as an act of God.[122] Unlike his modern interpreters, Mark is not concerned
about the moral and ecological implications of destroying trees. His concern is
to establish that the power to perform miracles belongs to God and can be prayed
for but not presumed upon.

The portrayal of the praying Jesus is intended by the evangelist to serve as
a model for his community.[123] If even Jesus found it necessary to pray, how much
more should they do so. Reploh believes that the author of Mark wants to blame
a neglect of prayer for a diminution in the spiritual power of his community. He
thinks that when the gospel was written successful healings and exorcisms were
becoming infrequent, and that in 9:29 the evangelist issues a renewed call to
prayer for power.[124] If this were the case, then the impatience of the disciples with
Jesus' early morning prayer outside Capernaum could be regarded as an early
warning in the narrative of the disciples' failure to exorcise the boy in 9:14-29.

In 1:36, Jesus' prayer is interrupted by "Simon and those with him" who
pursue Jesus (κατεδίωξεν αὐτὸν) and report that everyone is looking for him
(πάντες ζητοῦσίν σε, 1:37). Both of these verbs have negative nuances[125] and
indicate that Jesus is wanted for his healing power and that his withdrawing to
pray is regarded as inappropriate by Simon, the disciples and the crowds. Why
is he away praying when there are so many to be healed in Capernaum! This is
the first indication in the gospel of the disciples' failure to understand Jesus![126]

If Reploh is correct about the situation in the Markan community, then the
audience would be expected to make the connection between the disciples'
impatience with prayer and their bungled exorcism in 9:14-29. Jesus has to
remind them that power belongs to God and is received through prayer. Both of
the other Markan prayer scenes present the audience with vivid contrasts
between Jesus and the disciples. In 6:46-48 the audience is presented with the
picture of Jesus praying on the mountain and the disciples down in the water
rowing frantically against the wind. In Gethsemane, Jesus prays while the
disciples sleep. Again they have to be reminded to pray (14:38). These contrasts
may lend support to Reploh's thesis, but in fact his method does not give him
certain access to the situation of the Markan community, so his speculation can
be no more than that.[127] Whatever the situation in his community may have been,

---

[122] Swete, *Mark*, 259; Lohmeyer, *Markus*, 239.

[123] Walter Kirchschläger, "Jesu Gebetsverhalten als Paradigma zu Mk 1, 35," *Kairos* 20
(1978) 306.

[124] Reploh, *Markus*, 217-18.

[125] Pesch, *Markusevangelium*, 1:138; Gnilka, *Markus*, 1:88.

[126] Kelber, *Kingdom*, 45.

[127] It is equally possible and equally impossible to prove that it is the *success* of the
community's healers and exorcists which presents a problem for Mark. More than once
in the gospel he represents the demand of the crowds for healing as a problem for Jesus
and the disciples. In 1:37 the demand intrudes on Jesus' prayer. In 3:9 the crowds, "hearing
all that he did," threaten to crush Jesus. In 3:20 the demands of the crowd prevent Jesus

the evangelist emphasizes in 9:29 and in 11:22-25 that miraculous power resides not in healers and exorcists but in God and therefore members of the community do not, strictly speaking, *perform* miracles, but they may *pray* for miracles.

SUMMARY: PRAYER, FAITH, AND POWER

The meaning of faith in the logia collection of 11:22-23 cannot be understood except in the context of the gospel narrative which precedes it. That narrative presents the audience with a main character, Jesus, who as Son of God is dependent on God for his miraculous power. As the model for his followers he prays, preaches, exorcises and heals. The other characters in the narrative exemplify right and wrong responses to Jesus' modeling. The disciples preach, heal and exorcise, but they are impatient with prayer and respond to difficulties with anxiety instead of faith in God who does the impossible. Jesus calms the storm for them in spite of their unbelief and continues to involve them (e.g. in the feeding miracles), in spite of their failures. When they fail to exorcise a boy, he reminds them of the importance of prayer.

Members of the crowd serve as examples of faith in the power of God which works through Jesus. They believe because of the reports of his miracles and come to him with implicit or explicit requests for his help. Sometimes Jesus labels trust in his power "faith" and sometimes he does not. Faith is the world-view that attributes to God the power to do the impossible. Mere curiosity about miracles is not faith, but even the unbelief in Nazareth does not completely block God's power in Jesus.

Faith never questions God's power. When the father's discouragement over the unsuccessful exorcism evokes such a question from him, Jesus reminds him of the unlimited nature of the power available to faith. Unable to overcome his doubt, the father asks for help and receives it in the form of the desired miracle.

Thus, the audience which hears or reads the prayer teaching in 11:22-25 is prepared to understand that faith which prays for miracles is faith in God, not in a human healer who may fail, nor in a special amount of faith, since God is free to respond to a cry for help no matter how much faith is present. But the praying community is exhorted to hold on to its world-view in which everything is possible for God and not to give in to the doubts which challenge that world-view from every side. When what they ask is not given immediately they are to trust that their prayers were answered on the first request and to continue to pray.

Our observations about the Gospel of Mark support the thesis formulated by the sociology of religion: ". . . religious ideation is grounded in religious

---

and the disciples from eating, and in 6:30-33 they can neither eat nor rest. All of these instances occur in Markan summaries or transitions. It would be possible to argue that the healers in the Markan community are so pressed that they do not take time for prayer. The warning of 9:14-29 would then be that they will lose their power unless they change their ways. Again, the situation cannot be established with certainty.

activity, relating to it in a dialectical manner . . ."[128] Or, put another way, theology and pastoral praxis are interdependent. The Markan community holds to the world view that "everything is possible for God." This theological construct is supported by the earlier biblical tradition and by the miracle stories of the Jesus tradition which are told and retold in the community. The repetition of the formula of omnipotence, the miracle stories, and the prayer catechesis from the logia tradition encourage and keep alive the prayer practice of the community, which includes prayer for healing and exorcism. The experiences connected with the prayer practice give impetus to faith in the power and benevolence of the Lord of the community, strengthening their conviction that "everything is possible," and enabling them to endure delayed answers and failures. Faith leads to prayer, which leads to miracles, which leads to faith.

The final condition for effective prayer is given in 11:25. The community which experiences God's miraculous power must be a community of mutual forgiveness.

[128] Berger, *Canopy*, 40.

6
Prayer and Forgiveness

The last authentic logion in the Markan prayer teaching is 11:25: "And whenever you stand praying, forgive, if you have anything against anyone; so that your Father also who is in heaven may forgive you your trespasses." Commentators are divided over the question of whether this logion has been attached to 11:24 by the catch-word "prayer,"[1] or whether the evangelist thought that an attitude of forgiveness was a condition for effective petition.[2] Among scholars who take the latter position there are differences of opinion about the sense in which forgiveness is a condition for petitionary prayer. In this chapter we will explore the options and suggest an interpretation of the relationship between prayer and forgiveness. If an intrinsic connection can be found between forgiveness and effective petition, the presumption of this study, namely, that the author of Mark is not merely a collector of traditions, but a master of narrative theology, will be reinforced.

INTERPRETATIONS OF MARK 11:25

Forgiveness is mentioned in the context of prayers of petition not only in Mark but in Matthew and Luke as well.[3] In Luke, a saying on forgiveness (17:3b-4) immediately precedes the saying on faith that works miracles (17:5-6). The forgiveness sayings in Matt 6:14-15 are contained within the section of instruction on prayer and fasting in 6:5-18.[4] There seems to be a connection

---

[1] Cranfield, *Mark*, 361; Haenchen, *Weg*, 391; Schmithals, *Markus*, 2:503; Schmid, *Mark*, 212.

[2] Scholars who regard 11:25 as a condition for petition without explaining *how* forgiveness conditions prayer include Lagrange, *Marc*, 301; Marrion, "Petitionary Prayer," 44; Bacon, *Beginnings*, 163; Zmijewski, "Glaube," 90; Caba, *Oración*, 211.

[3] Quentin Quesnell, *The Mind of Mark* (Rome: Pontifical Biblical Institute, 1969) 151 n. 51.

[4] Caba (*Oración*, 322) regards the Johannine commandment to "love one another" as equivalent to the synoptic admonitions on mutual forgiveness. In John 15 there is a clear relationship between community relationships and answered prayer. If the community "abides," whatever they ask in prayer will be done (ὃ ἐὰν θέλητε αἰτήσασθε, καὶ γενήσεται ὑμῖν, 15:7). Abiding is contingent upon keeping Jesus' commandments (15:10). His commandment is that they "love one another" (15:12, 17). If they love one another, the Father will answer their prayers (15:16: ὅ τι ἂν αἰτήσητε τὸν πατέρα ἐν τῷ ὀνόματι μου δῷ ὑμῖν. Cf. 1 John

between forgiveness and petition in early Christianity, but what is the connection? Specifically, how does the author of Mark understand the connection?

Two suggestions have been made with regard to the relationship between 11:25 and the prayer teaching that precedes it. Some interpreters think that the author of Mark wanted to exclude imprecatory prayer and that the forgiveness logion has this function in its present context. Others argue that the Markan text reflects a belief that broken relationships within the community render the community's petitions impotent.

Forgiveness Excludes Imprecation

Schlatter, Grundmann, and Gnilka take the position that the forgiveness logion is attached to the prayer teaching in order to prevent Jesus' cursing of the fig tree from being taken too seriously as an example by the community.[5] In other words, the power of God is not to be exercised in anger for destructive purposes.

The acceptance of this view would require that we understand the evangelist to have held the opinion that the cursing of the fig tree was morally repugnant and needed correction, lest the community follow Jesus' example. However, it is not likely that the evangelist objected to the fig tree pericope, for two reasons. First, if he had found the story offensive he could simply have omitted it, as did the author of Luke. Second, given the expectations of biographical narrative in the first century, it is unthinkable that the evangelist would portray Jesus as acting in a way that could have been construed as contradicting his teaching. In the ancient mind, a teacher's actions had to be completely congruent with his teachings. In fact, teachers were thought to instruct as much through their actions as through their words.[6] The author of Mark would not have used a teaching of Jesus to correct an action of Jesus. It is more likely that he saw nothing objectionable about the withering of the fig tree. The author of Luke found it necessary to portray Jesus as rebuking those who would perform destructive miracles (9:52-56), but apparently the author of Mark was not faced with that particular problem.

Forgiveness and the Eschatological Community

According to Krister Stendahl, there was a belief in primitive Christianity that it was necessary to maintain unbroken relationships within the eschatological community if the powers of the new age were to be manifested.[7] Stendahl

---

3:22-24). In 1 John 4:10-11 the Father's love for the community is manifested in his forgiving their sins. They are then commanded to love one another. The implication is that their love for one another will also be manifested in forgiveness.

[5] Schlatter, *Markus*, 216; Walter Grundmann, *Das Evangelium nach Markus* (3d ed.; Berlin: Evangelische Verlagsanstalt, 1965) 234; Gnilka, *Markus*, 2:135.

[6] Talbert, *Literary Patterns*, 90-93; Talbert, *What Is a Gospel?*, 102-3.

[7] Stendahl, "Prayer," 75-86.

believes that this view of the relationship between petitionary prayer and mutual forgiveness is reflected in the Markan forgiveness logion, but soon thereafter was lost from the consciousness of the church.[8] This interpretation, which has a number of adherents,[9] would paraphrase Mark 11:25 as follows:

> When you stand and pray—especially if you expect your prayer to share in the power of the messianic age—forgive if you have something against somebody, in order that also your Father who is in heaven may forgive you your trespasses.[10]

The importance of unbroken fellowship within the community receives explicit attention in Matt 5:23-24, 6:14-15, and 18:10-35. In Matthew 6, the logia on forgiveness follow the Lord's Prayer, thus emphasizing, according to Stendahl, that "the very right to utter such a prayer depends upon a status of mutual forgiven-ness," as the precondition for their being the messianic community.[11] Although Mark 11:25 is similar in some ways to Matthew 6:14, it also resembles the saying on reconciliation in Matthew 5:23-24, where the worshiper who brings a gift to the altar is instructed to be reconciled with the brother who has something against him or her (ἔχει τι κατὰ σοῦ) before making the offering.[12] In Mark, the situation is stated in reverse: τι ἔχετε κατά τινος. The language "to have something against someone" appears again in Colossians 3:13: ἐάν τις πρός τινα ἔχῃ μομφήν (a complaint),[13] where, as in Matthew, the discussion is about relationships within the Christian community. These similarities in language and emphasis point to the likelihood that Mark 11:25 also refers to forgiveness within the community, despite the apparent generality of τινος.[14] Thus, the power promised to believing prayer in 11:23-24 is explicitly conditioned by forgiveness within the community: "The right to pray the prayer envisioned in verses 23-24

---

[8] Ibid., 77.

[9] Lane (*Mark*, 411) and Jerome Murphy-O'Connor ('Péché et Communauté dans le Nouveau Testament," *RB* 74 [1967] 177) cite Stendahl in agreement. Similar views are expressed by Carrington, (*Mark*, 245), Bultmann (*History*, 132), R. C. H. Lenski (*The Interpretation of St. Mark's Gospel* [Minneapolis: Augsburg, 1946] 496), and Hugh Anderson (*The Gospel of Mark* [London: Oliphants, 1976] 268). Schlatter, Grundmann, and Gnilka mention unbroken community relationships as a second point along with their interpretation of verse 25 as a warning against destructive miracles.

[10] Stendahl, "Prayer," 85.

[11] Ibid., 83.

[12] Carrington (*Mark*, 245) suggests that Mark 11:25 is a condensed form of Matt 5:23-24 for a Gentile congregation more familiar with prayer than with Jewish temple worship. Cf. Bultmann, *History*, 148.

[13] References from Swete, *Mark*, 261.

[14] Grundmann, *Markus*, 234; Lane, *Mark*, 411; Carrington, *Mark*, 245. In contrast, other commentators generalize 11:25 to include "enemies" (Bacon, *Beginnings*, 160) or "fellow men" (Gnilka, *Markus*, 2:135; Anderson, *Mark*, 268). Lenski (*Interpretation*, 497) says explicitly that the saying includes non-disciples.

belongs only to brothers who are mutually reconciled and united in a community of faith."[15] This interpretation is attractive and has much to recommend it, but it is only partially correct. The logion does not state that mutual forgiveness is a condition for effective petition, but rather that mutual forgiveness within the community is the condition for the community's receiving forgiveness from God for its trespasses against God![16] That the community must be forgiven by God before it can expect its prayers to be heard by God was an assumption that the Christians shared with their Jewish neighbors and, to a more limited extent, with adherents of other Hellenistic religions, as we shall see. This is the proper sense in which mutual forgiveness is a condition for effective petition![17] The meaning of Mark 11:25 in relation to the rest of the logia collection is that God responds favorably to the prayers of a community which stands in right relationship to God, that is, a community whose sins are forgiven; and God forgives the sins of the community in which mutual forgiveness is practiced![18]

SIN AS AN OBSTACLE TO PRAYER

Throughout the Hebrew scriptures it is understood that obedience to the commandments of Yahweh is a basic prerequisite for answered prayer![19] "The LORD is far from the wicked, but he hears the prayer of the righteous" (Prov 15:29, RSV).[20] This is the principle that lies behind John 9:31: "We know that God does not listen to sinners, but if anyone is a worshiper of God and does his

---

[15] Lane, *Mark*, 411.

[16] παράπτωμα: false step, transgression, sin. Usually, as here, it is found in the plural referring to offenses against God. It refers to offenses against other people only in Matt 6:14–15. Swete, *Mark*, 261; BAG, 627.

[17] Carrington (*Mark*, 244–45) and Lenski (*Interpretation*, 497) mention sin as a barrier to access to God, but do not discuss the concept further.

[18] Hellenistic Judaism knew this requirement. Sirach 28:1–5 (RSV) reads "He that takes vengeance will suffer vengeance from the Lord, and he will firmly establish his sins. Forgive your neighbor the wrong he has done, and then your sins will be pardoned when you pray. Does a man harbor anger against another, and yet seek for healing from the Lord? Does he have no mercy toward a man like himself, and yet pray for his own sins? If he himself, being flesh, maintains wrath, who will make expiation for his sins?" See Pesch, *Markusevangelium*, 2:207.

Similar ideas appear in rabbinic literature: "As often as you are merciful, the All-merciful will have mercy upon you" (*Tos. Baba Kumma* 9. 30). "He who is merciful to others, mercy is shown to him by heaven, while he who is not merciful to others, mercy is not shown to him by heaven" (*Shab* 151b, cited in Ernst Lohmeyer, *"Our Father": An Introduction to the Lord's Prayer* [trans. J. Bowden; New York: Harper and Row, 1965] 167).

[19] Dietzel, "Erhörungsgewissheit," 40.

[20] Cf. Prov 15:8, Ps 66:18. Johannes Döller, *Das Gebet im Alten Testament* (Hildesheim: Gerstenberg, 1974) 93.

will, God listens to him" (RSV).[21] The prophets stress Israel's sin as a barrier to answered prayer: "Behold, the LORD's hand is not shortened, that it cannot save, or his ear dull, that it cannot hear; but your iniquities have made a separation between you and your God, and your sins have hid his face from you so that he does not hear" (Isa 59:1-2, RSV; cf. Isa 1:15; Jer 7:16-17, 11:14-15, 14:11-12; Mic 3:4; Zech 7:13).[22]

The remedy for this situation is repentance and confession of sin, to which God responds by forgiving the sin, thus removing the barrier between God and the community.[23] The community recognized that God had forgiven its sin when it was protected against harm, or when its good fortune was restored after a difficult period.[24] Within this framework of thought, in which misfortune and even need are regarded as punishment for sin, petitionary prayer is often accompanied by repentance and prayer for forgiveness. Thus, the thoroughly Deuteronomic prayer attributed to Solomon on the occasion of the dedication of the temple (1 Kgs 8:22-53) includes the repetition of the formula, "hear thou in heaven and forgive the sin," with petitions for deliverance from enemies, for rain, for healing and for restoration from exile. Similarly, the prayers in Neh 1:4-11 and Dan 9:3-20 include confession of sin along with petitionary prayer. It is taken for granted that before the petitions can be granted, the sin must be forgiven: "O LORD, hear; O LORD, forgive; O LORD, give heed and act" (Dan 9:19, RSV).[25]

Hellenistic and rabbinic Judaism retained the connection between the need for forgiveness and the efficacy of petition. Confession of sin appears in the lengthy prayer in Baruch 1:15-3:8. In the Prayer of the Eighteen Benedictions, petitions for relief from affliction, for healing, for rain, and for national restoration are preceded by a prayer for an attitude of repentance (5) and a request for forgiveness (6).[26] The prayers for rain in Mishnah tractate Ta'anit are accompanied by fasting and repentance.[27] Both Philo and Josephus insists that unjust and sinful persons are not heard by God unless they repent, confess their sin, and ask God's forgiveness.[28] Of course, this is also the conception

[21] Dietzel, "Erhörungsgewissheit," 54.

[22] Ibid., 40-41; Döller, *Gebet,* 93.

[23] Döller, *Gebet,* 93.

[24] Eichrodt, *Theology,* 2:435.

[25] See Moses Hadas, *Hellenistic Culture* (Morningside Heights, NY: Columbia University Press, 1959) 200.

[26] English translations of the Palestinian and Babylonian versions of the Eighteen may be found in J. J. Petuchowski and Michael Brocke, eds., *The Lord's Prayer and Jewish Liturgy* (New York: Seabury, 1978) 27-35.

[27] Herbert Danby, trans., *The Mishnah* (Oxford: Oxford University Press, 1933) 194-201.

[28] *Som.* 2. 299; *Fug.* 80; *Cherub.* 94-96; *Det. Pot. Ins.* 95; *Deus Immut.* 8-9; *Mos.* 2. 107; *Virt.* 79; *A.J.* 8. 115 and 9. 173-76. See Dietzel, "Erhörungsgewissheit," 68-74, and Greeven, "εὔχομαι," 783.

of James 5:13-18, where confession of sin accompanies prayer for healing.[29]

The relationship between sin and ineffective petitionary prayer is also found, to a lesser extent, in Greek and Roman religion. Homer's Achilles knows that the gods listen to the prayers of those who obey them.[30] Aeschylus and Euripides insist that the gods do not grant the requests of immoral and unjust persons.[31] Xenophon's Socrates suggests to a young man that he ask the gods to forgive him for neglecting his mother; otherwise they will refuse to do good things for him because of his ingratitude.[32]

In general, the favor of the Greek and Roman gods was sought through the offering of sacrifices, or through vows that promised a sacrifice if the petition were answered favorably.[33] When the gods were offended, however, the promise of a handsome sacrifice might not be enough to persuade them to grant one's request. In such cases, the Greeks, and later the Romans, learned from the oriental cults that confession of sin and pleas for forgiveness could be added to petitionary prayer.[34] Juvenal attests penitential practices in the Isis religion in Rome during the first century C.E., the point of which was to avert the danger of fever.[35] Inscriptions from Phrygia and Lydia, which can be dated in the second and third centuries of the Common Era, explicitly connect the confession of sin with the expectation of miraculous intervention by the offended deity to rescue the petitioner from misfortune inflicted as punishment for sin.[36]

Like his Jewish and pagan contemporaries, the author of Mark knows that sin in the community can render its petitions impotent. The "Father who is in heaven" is prepared to forgive the sins of the community, but only if they are prepared to forgive each other. Therefore, "Whenever you stand praying, forgive, if you have anything against anyone; so that also your Father who is in heaven may forgive you your trespasses (so that he may then grant your requests)." If faith is understood as confidence in the power of God, then forgiveness, the letting go (ἀφίημι) of the right to avenge oneself, may be understood as an

---

[29] Stendahl, "Prayer," 84: "We are within a more general Jewish framework, as we would expect in the Epistle of James."

[30] *Iliad* 1. 218: ὅς κε θεοῖς ἐπιπείθηται, μάλα τ'ἔκλυον αὐτοῦ. Cf. Xenophon *Mem.* 4. 3. 17.

[31] *Agam.* 396; *Medea* 1391.

[32] *Mem.* 2. 2. 14.

[33] Using the correct epithets and terms of reverence was also important, as was determining to which god one should appeal. See Dietzel, "Erhörungsgewissheit," 9–15, 22–28.

[34] *Hippol.* 117; *Iph. Taur.* 1400. Confession of sin does not seem to have been indigenous to Greek or Roman religion, but it is found in texts and inscriptions that have been influenced by the worship of the Egyptian Isis, the Anatolian Great Mother, the Dea Syria or some other eastern deity. See Raffaele Pettazzoni, "Confession of Sins and the Classics," *HTR* 30 (1937) 1–14; Hadas, *Hellenistic Culture*, 210–11; Lohmeyer, "*Our Father*," 167–68.

[35] Pettazzoni, "Confession," 2, 5.

[36] Pettazzoni, "Confession," 3. See the very interesting anecdote that Pettazzoni relates on page 4, in which supernatural strength is granted to a female worshiper of the Magna Mater as proof of her purity of life.

expression of confidence in the justice and protection of God. According to the Gospel of Mark, both are necessary components of efficacious communal prayer.

SUMMARY: THE THEOLOGY OF THE MARKAN PRAYER LOGIA

Our study of the Markan prayer logia in 11:22-25 has confirmed the findings of recent studies of the miracle traditions. It is not the case, as proponents of "corrective christology" once claimed, that the evangelist is attempting to discredit a theology of divine presence and power and to replace it with a theology in which only weakness and suffering have positive value. On the contrary, Kee, Best and others are correct in asserting that the author of Mark expects the healings and exorcisms of the Jesus traditions to be repeated in the ministry of his community.[37] What we have in 11:22-25 is a series of instructions about how that ministry is to be understood and practiced.

It is through prayer that the inclusive community, the "house of prayer for all the nations," experiences the miracle-working power of God. The God to whom the community prays is not limited in power; rather, this God is one who can do the impossible, symbolized by the mountain-moving image in 11:23. Therefore, nothing the community asks in prayer is impossible for God; they are to regard everything they request as already received from the hand of God (11:24). But in the pluralistic setting of the early imperial period, there were many who would challenge the community's confidence in God's power. The evangelist calls for "faith in God," by which he means a stubborn adherence to the worldview by which the community lives and interprets its experience. Forgiveness within the community is also essential because the power invoked in Christian prayer is not an amoral force. As community members forgive each other they are forgiven by God, and this forgiveness removes the sin which could block the flow of divine power. In this context of faith and mutual forgiveness, the community is to pray for "anything" (πάντα ὅσα) and "it will be done" for them.

The theological function of prayer according to 11:22-25 is that prayer serves as the vehicle by means of which the God who can do the impossible meets the needs of the Christian community. It remains to be seen, however, how prayer functions when God chooses not to intervene. God's negative response to the prayer of Jesus in Gethsemane raises within the Markan text the problem of theodicy and the function of prayer when miracles are not forthcoming. It is to this problem that we must now direct our attention.

[37] Kee, *Community,* 27, 38; Best, "Miracles," 543.

PART III

PRAYER AND
THEODICY IN MARK

7

The Will of God in Mark

Taken together, the prayer teaching of 11:22–25 and the stories about Jesus' acts of power in response to requests for help present a thoroughly positive view of God's ability and willingness to respond to prayer. But the passion narrative, and especially the pivotal Gethsemane pericope, which focuses on the praying Jesus, appear to contradict the theology of the miracle and prayer traditions. In 14:36 the Markan Jesus expresses unwavering confidence in the omnipotence of God ("everything is possible for you") and makes a straightforward petition ("take this cup away from me!"). According to his own teaching in chapter 11, the result should be that whatever he asks be "done for him." But instead, what happens is the arrest, trial and crucifixion of Jesus, whose last prayer is, "My God, my God, why have you forsaken me?"

The author of the gospel explains the discrepancy between Jesus' teaching on prayer and the negative result of Jesus' own prayer in Gethsemane by his use of the concept "will of God." In 14:36 the Markan Jesus ends his prayer, "Not what I will, but what you will" (οὐ τί ἐγὼ θέλω ἀλλὰ τί σύ)![1] Since the Gethsemane scene is followed by the arrest, trial and crucifixion of Jesus, the audience is forced to conclude that the reason that Jesus' petition to be delivered from suffering was not answered was because the passion was the will of God. In fact, the evangelist makes it clear throughout the gospel that not only Jesus, but also his followers will be called upon to suffer.

SUFFERING AS THE WILL OF GOD IN MARK

During the last twenty years of Markan scholarship, the theological significance of the cross and of suffering as a mode of discipleship has received considerable attention. Indeed, as J. R. Donahue has pointed out, in some treatments of Mark, "suffering becomes almost equated with believing in the gospel."[2] It is certainly the case that the author of Mark places positive value both on Jesus' suffering and on the suffering of Jesus' followers.

---

[1] The translation, "May not what I will, but what you will, be done" is made improbable by the case of τί and the absence of a relative pronoun (e.g., ὃ τι) which could turn the whole phrase into the object of an implied verb. Besides, as Swete (*Mark,* 344) points out, in that case the negative particle should be μή rather than οὐ. He translates, "However, the question is not what is My will, etc."

[2] Donahue, "Neglected Factor," 586.

The Passion as the Will of God

The threat of suffering for Jesus is present almost from the beginning of the Markan text. As early as 2:6 there is the hint that the bridegroom will be taken away, and by 3:6 Jesus' enemies are already plotting to destroy him. That their plot will succeed is made clear by the three passion predictions, the first of which (8:31) emphasizes the divine will behind the passion by the use of δεῖ: "It is necessary for the Son of Man to suffer many things . . ."[3]

Then, within the passion narrative itself, the Markan Jesus quotes Zech 13:7b in support of his prediction that the disciples will desert him: "I will strike the shepherd and the sheep will be scattered" (14:27). Here the original imperative ("Strike the shepherd") has been changed to the indicative ("I will strike the shepherd") in order to emphasize the prophet's point that both the striking of the "shepherd" and the scattering of the "sheep" are God's doing.

Similarly, the Markan Jesus claims that "it is written of the Son of man, that he should suffer many things and be treated with contempt" (9:12) and "the Son of man goes as it is written of him" (14:21). Although the author does not specify where he found it "written" that Jesus must suffer and die, his use of the formula indicating an appeal to prophecy shows that he understands Jesus' suffering and death as the will of God.[4]

Suffering and Discipleship

In the central discipleship section of the Gospel of Mark, 8:22–10:52, the Markan Jesus includes his followers among those who must suffer. In 8:34–37 the disciples and the crowd are told that following Jesus entails denying self, taking up one's cross, and saving one's life by losing it for Jesus' sake and for the sake of the gospel. At 10:29–30 loss of family and persecution are part of the experience of discipleship. When James and John come with their request for places of honor, Jesus predicts that they, like Jesus himself, will have to "drink the cup" of suffering (10:39). In 13:9–13 Jesus predicts that disciples will be persecuted, betrayed and killed. This passage in the apocalyptic discourse echoes the interpretation of the parable of the soils, in which some who hear the word fall away because of "tribulation or persecution" (4:17).

It should be noted that the suffering that is identified in the Markan narrative as a part of following Jesus is always suffering or persecution related to one's identification as a Christian: "for my sake and the gospel's" (8:35, 10:29); "for my sake" (13:9); "on account of the word" (4:17). Thus, it is not suffering in general that has positive value for disciples, but readiness to

---

[3] Lane, *Mark*, 300–301; W. Grundmann, "δεῖ," *TDNT* 2 (1964) 21–25. See also W. J. Bennett, "The Role of (the Greek word) 'Dei' in the Markan Understanding of the Passion" (Ph.D. dissertation, Drew University, 1968).

[4] See Taylor, *Mark*, 541–42.

endure persecution for one's Christian confession.[5]

It is also important to realize that in the Markan narrative suffering and miracle-working are not opposed to one another as mutually exclusive ways of understanding Christian existence. In fact, the first notice of a plot to destroy Jesus (3:6) comes at the end of a cycle of controversy stories which begins and ends with healing miracles, suggesting that Jesus' suffering is, at least in part, a result of his being a miracle-worker.[6] Although Weeden identifies suffering and service as positive aspects of discipleship and opposes them to miracle-working, which he regards as self-serving, the Markan narrative itself resists this kind of interpretation.[7] In Mark most of the miracles performed by Jesus are directly related to alleviating suffering and meeting the needs of others, and when Jesus sends the disciples out to serve others, they do so by healing, exorcising and preaching (3:14–15; 6:12–13).[8] Thus, suffering servanthood in the Gospel of Mark does not exclude miracle-working, but includes it.

Scholars who emphasize suffering as the central and dominant feature of discipleship in Mark appeal to 8:34b–35:

> If anyone wants to come after me, let him deny himself and take up his cross and follow me. For whoever wants to save his life will lose it; and whoever loses his life for my sake and the gospel's will save it.[9]

J. R. Donahue has pointed out, however, that the ὃς ἂν sayings of 8:35 are members of a much larger group of gnomic sayings that characterize discipleship in Mark. Formerly called "legal sayings" by Bultmann and "sentences of holy

---

[5] David J. Lull ("Interpreting Mark's Story of Jesus' Death: Toward a Theology of Suffering," *SBL 1985 Seminar Papers* [ed. K. Richards; Atlanta: Scholars, 1985] 4) and Joel Marcus (*The Mystery of the Kingdom of God* [SBLDS 90; Atlanta: Scholars, 1986] 70) think that the community for which the Gospel of Mark was written was being persecuted. J. R. Donahue ("Preaching '85: The Gospel of Mark," *Church* Charter Issue [1985] 13) wonders whether Mark's portrayal of the disciples is intended "to encourage those in Mark's community who have failed in the face of persecution." See also Donald W. Riddle, "The Martyr Motif in the Gospel According to Mark," *JR* 4 (1924) 397–410. I am inclined to think that these and other scholars who read the gospel this way are correct. However, I am not persuaded that our sources and methods enable us to be certain about the situation of the community behind the gospel.

[6] See Kolenkow, "Beyond Miracles," 158, 189; Schierling, "Woman," 172.

[7] T. J. Weeden, "The Cross as Power in Weakness (Mark 15:20b–41)," *The Passion in Mark* (ed. W. H. Kelber; Philadelphia: Fortress, 1976) 117, 132–33.

[8] Schierling, "Woman," 43.

[9] On the background of this idea in Greek literature see William A. Beardslee, "Saving One's Life By Losing It," *JAAR* 47 (1979) 57–72 and Vernon K. Robbins, "Interpreting the Gospel of Mark as a Jewish Document in a Graeco-Roman World," (FS Henry A. Fischel, forthcoming).

law" by Käsemann, these sayings have been shown by Klaus Berger to have a parenetic function![10]

Donahue argues persuasively that of all such gnomic sayings in Mark, the most important is not 8:35 but 3:35: "Whoever does the will of God is my brother, and sister, and mother." He writes:

> The summons of Jesus in 1:15 is to believe in the gospel and 3:35 states the fundamental condition of that belief, doing the will of God. The other gnomic sayings then provide concrete instances of such doing the will of God. This involves respect for God's creative intent in marriage (10:11); losing one's life "for the gospel" (8:35); forsaking riches (10:20); enduring persecution (13:13); welcoming the powerless children (9:36–37); living a life of service (10:43–44); performing the duties of hospitality (9:41); and trust in the power of prayer (11:23)![11]

Thus, discipleship cannot be reduced to suffering. "The essence of responding to the gospel is doing the will of God and the Marcan Jesus is one who summons people to such obedience rather than to literal imitation of his own life."[12] According to Donahue, the will of God in Mark is not limited to suffering, though it may include suffering for Christians, as it did for Jesus![13]

MIRACLES AS THE WILL OF GOD IN MARK

Donahue's observation that the concept "will of God" includes more than suffering and martyrdom is supported by the evidence examined in chapter 5 that the author of Mark is careful to attribute Jesus' miraculous power to God. The miracle traditions and the prayer teaching of 11:22–25 taken together show that, for the evangelist, an important aspect of the will of God is God's intervention on behalf of the community in response to petitionary prayer.

This is explicitly the case as early as the first chapter of the gospel. In 1:35 Jesus is seen at prayer. Following his prayer, Jesus announces to his disciples that his mission is not limited to Capernaum, and he proceeds to travel "throughout all Galilee" preaching and exorcising. The following pericope, the healing of a leper (1:40–45), provides a specific example of Jesus' activity in "all Galilee." In this pericope, the connection between miracle and the will of God is made explicit.

"If You Will, You Can . . ." (Mark 1:40–45)

In 1:40 the leper is portrayed in an attitude of petition: he is imploring Jesus (παρακαλῶν αὐτὸν) to heal him![14] Here we have an example of a miracle story

---

[10] See Donahue's discussion, with references, in "Neglected Factor," 584–85.

[11] Ibid., 585.

[12] Ibid., 586.

[13] Ibid., 585–87.

[14] The reference to kneeling is possible, but textually uncertain. See Metzger, *Commentary*, 76.

serving as an encouragement to prayer, the function which Glöckner suggests for most of the miracle traditions.[15] Like the praying Jesus in Gethsemane (πάντα δυνατά σοι), the leper includes in his prayer an expression of confidence in the power of the one to whom he appeals: ἐὰν θέλῃς δύνασαί με καθαρίσαι. The two expressions are equivalent; that everything is possible for God means that God is able to do whatever God wills.

These expressions are found in both pagan and Jewish writers in the Hellenistic period. Dio Chrysostom writes that it is characteristic of a god to be able "to make possible that which seems impossible, if it should be his will": τὰ ἀδύνατα δοκοῦντα ποιῆσαι δυνατά, εἰ βούλοιτο.[16] The insistence of Hellenistic Judaism on the omnipotence of God[17] carried with it the corollary that for God to will is to be able to act: ὅταν θέλῃς, τὸ δύνασθαι (Wis 12:18). This emphasis was already present in the Psalms: "the Lord does whatever he wills" (πάντα, ὅσα ἠθέλησεν ὁ κύριος, ἐποίησεν, LXX Ps 124:6). "Our God is in the heavens; he does whatever he wills" (πάντα, ὅσα ἠθέλησεν, ἐποίησεν, LXX Ps 113:11).

The leper is portrayed as praying with the confidence in divine power which Mark elsewhere calls πίστις. as we have seen.[18] He is contrasted with the father in 9:22, whose prayer begins εἴ τι δύνῃ [19] and is immediately corrected by Jesus' πάντα δυνατὰ τῷ πιστεύοντι. Since it was understood that no one could heal leprosy except God, the fact that Jesus is able to heal the leper with a touch makes it clear to the audience of the gospel that it is God's power which is at work through Jesus.[20] Jesus exercises God's power to do whatever God wills, and his response to the leper (θέλω, καθαρίσθητι) shows that in this case, God's will is to heal. By healing the leper, Jesus is doing the will of God.

It is essential for Mark to show that Jesus' miracles, and by extension, the miracles which take place in the Christian community, are done by God and conform to the will of God. This focus on the will and agency of God is the means by which the author of Mark differentiates Christian miracle-workers from the magicians so familiar to Hellenistic audiences. Since Christians are commissioned to preach, heal and exorcise (3:14–15; 6:7–13) and since Christian prayer receives God's power to do the impossible (11:22–25), the evangelist has to protect against the possibility that Christian miracle-workers may be tempted to try to exercise the divine power to do their own will. There was also the possibility that the Jesus traditions and the healing and exorcism practices of the Markan community could be interpreted as magic by outsiders. By focusing on the will of God the author of Mark eliminates magic as a possible misinterpretation of Christian miracle-working practice by either outsiders or insiders. A brief

[15] Glöckner, *Wundergeschichten,* 164–65.
[16] *Oration* 3. 30.
[17] See "Omnipotence in Hellenistic Judaism," chapter 4.
[18] See chapter 5.
[19] So, e.g., Schmithals, *Markus,* 1:141.
[20] Pesch, *Markusevangelium,* 1:143.

survey of the ancient literature on magic shows how pervasive were the twin themes of will and compulsion.

Will and Compulsion in Hellenistic Magic

That the magician, sorcerer or witch is able to accomplish whatever he or she wills to do is a commonplace in ancient descriptions of magic. Propertius (*Elegies* 4. 5) writes of a witch, "Should she will it (*illa velit*) the magnet will refuse to draw the steel, and the bird prove a stepmother to her nestlings . . . She dared put spells upon the moon to do her bidding (*audax cantatae leges imponere lunae*), and to disguise her shape . . ." Ovid's Medea addresses the gods as follows: "With your help when I have willed it (*cum volui*) the streams have run back to their fountainheads . . . I move the forests, I bid the mountains shake . . ." (*Met.* 7. 199–205). Tibullus (1. 2. 42, 47) describes as *magico* a witch's spells: "at will (*cum libet*) she chases the clouds from the frowning heavens; at will she musters the snow in the summer skies."

Virgil's Dido describes a Massylian priestess: "She with her charms can free what hearts she will (*quas velit*), . . . stay the rivers' flow; turn back the stars and wake the ghosts of night" (*Aeneid* 4. 488). A few lines later these practices are called *magicas* (4. 493).[21] Similarly, Xenophon writes (*Mem.* 2. 6. 10): "There are spells (ἐπῳδάς), they say, wherewith those who know them charm whom they will (ἂν βούλωνται) and make friends of them, and drugs which those who know give to whom they will (ἂν βούλωνται) and win their love."

According to Apuleius, it was commonly believed that, "a magician (*magum*) is properly a person who, from communication and discourse with the immortal gods, is able, by a certain incredible power centered in his incantations, to do everything he wills" (*omnia quae velit, Apologia* 26). Similarly, the author of the pseudo-Clementine *Recognitions* (2. 9) has Simon Magus boast, "I can make myself invisible to those who would seize me, and again, if I will to be seen (*volens videri*), I can appear before them . . . whatever I will to do I shall be able to do" (*quidquid voluero facere, potero*).[22] In one of the Berlin magical papyri, the functions of a familiar spirit (δαίμων πάρεδρος) are described: "He changes you into the form of any animal that you wish . . . He will quickly freeze the rivers and the sea so that you can run upon them as many furlongs as you wish . . ."[23] A magician whose claims are recorded in a second- century papyrus boasts: ". . . if I command the moon, it will come down; and if I will (θελήσω) to delay the day, the night stays for me . . . And if I will (θελήσω) to sail the sea, I do not need a ship; and if I will to go through the air I shall be made light . . ."[24]

---

[21] See further examples in Pease, *Aeneidos* IV, 401.

[22] Translated by Campbell Bonner, "A Papyrus Describing Magical Powers," *Trans. American Philological Association* 52 (1921) 116–17.

[23] Ibid., 115.

[24] Ibid., 112, 114.

In these examples we see the deity's ability to perform the impossible transferred to the magician and linked with the concept of will. The magician is able to do whatever he or she wills, including (especially) the impossible.[25]

Moreover, the techniques employed by a magician are designed to impose the operator's will upon the god or demon whose power is needed to perform the "impossible" task. In the first book against Rufinus, Claudian's witch defines "the gift of magic" (*magicae*): "I have learned the incantations wherewith Thessalian witches pull down the bright moon, I know the meaning of the wise Egyptians' runes, the art whereby the Chaldeans impose their will upon the subject gods (*qua gens Chaldea vocatis imperet arte deis*) . . ." (*In Rufin.* 1. 145–49). This is followed by the traditional list of ἀδύνατα (1. 155–63).

The magicians whose recipes are recorded in the magical papyri are explicit about their intention to compel the gods to do their will. J. M. Hull translates one spell: "Come to me, such-and-such a god, be revealed to me in this present hour and do not startle my eyes. Come to me . . . be heard by me, for thus wills and commands Achchor Achchor Achachach."[26] A magician using a formula to compel the moon says, "You have to do it, whether you want to or not" (τὸ δεῖνα πράξεις κἂν θέλῃς κἂν μὴ θέλῃς).[27]

One of the most chilling passages in the literature on magic comes to us from a contemporary of the author of Mark, the Roman poet Lucan.[28] Here, in the account of Sextus Pompey's dealings with the witch Erichtho (*Pharsalia* 6. 413–830), Lucan informs the reader that, "Thessaly produces the poisonous plants and magical stones used for incantatory purposes by witches who wish to make the gods subservient . . . Moreover, the impious spells which these infamous women utter do, in fact, force the reluctant gods to pay heed . . ." (6. 438–44). There follows a long passage laced with ἀδύνατα: witches turn day to night, arrest a waterfall, reduce the height of mountains and restrain the tide (461–91). Erichtho, the most wicked of all witches, did not invoke the gods with a hymn as was usual for suppliants nor did she offer propitiatory sacrifices (523–25), but "no sooner had she stated her demands than the gods granted them, for fear of being subjected to a second spell" (*omne nefas superi prima iam voce precantis concedunt carmenque timent audire secundum*). However, the gods do prove themselves slow to resuscitate the corpse that Erichtho has

---

[25] ". . . the accomplishment of the otherwise impossible is the business of magic." Canter, "ADYNATON," 32 n. 1. See Grant, *Miracle*, 61–62.

[26] John M. Hull, *Hellenistic Magic and the Synoptic Tradition* (London: SCM, 1974) 27, citing *PGM* 4. 239ff.

[27] Text: Th. Hopfner, "Mageia," PW 14/1 (1930) 344, citing C. Wessely, *Griech Zauberpapyrus von Paris und London*, no. 2242. Translation: W. W. Tarn, *Hellenistic Civilization* (3d ed.; Cleveland/NY: World, 1961) 352.

[28] A. D. Nock asserts that the practices described in the later papyri are similar to those described by Lucan. See Nock's *Essays on Religion and the Ancient World* (2 vols.; ed. Zeph Stewart; Cambridge, MA: Harvard University Press, 1972) 1:185–87.

selected to prophesy the outcome of the battle. Erichtho breaks into angry threats which run for twenty lines (6. 730–49), eventually forcing the deities to do her will.

However overdrawn Lucan's portrait of Erichtho may be, it serves as a literary example, written a decade or less prior to the Gospel of Mark, of the widespread opinion that magic served to impose human will on deity. The explicit contrast between prayers of supplication and the spells of magicians in 6. 523–28 is significant, as we shall see.

This claim of the magicians to impose their will on the gods was attacked by some ancient writers as impious. In the fifth century B.C.E. the author of the Hippocratic treatise "On the Sacred Disease" raised objections against such claims.[29] The magicians claim to be able to do all sorts of impossible things, the writer tells us (4. 1–4), but this only reveals their arrogance, since divine power (τοῦ θείου ἡ δύναμις) can obviously not be "overcome and enslaved by the cunning of man" (ὑπὸ ἀνθρώπου γνώμης κρατεῖται καὶ δεδούλωται, 4. 15–16).

Eusebius, writing in the early fourth century of our era, takes a strikingly similar view in *Praep. Ev.* 5. 9. 197b:

> How can they deserve to be admired and honoured with divine worship who are enslaved by γόησι of the most abandoned character, and compelled (ἀναγκαζόμενοι) to perform what is neither honourable nor expedient contrary to their judgment, and are led and dragged down, not because they approve of men's morality, nor to promote virtue or any branch of philosophy, but by forbidden practices of γοήτων.

In support of his view that the gods are compelled to do the will of the γόης, Eusebius quotes Porphyry's *Of the Philosophy to be derived from Oracles* (third century), who quotes one Pythagoras of Rhodes whose dates are unknown.[30] Pythagoras puts the following remark in the mouth of a god who has been invoked for the purpose of prophecy: "Hear the unwilling voice thy power constrains" (κλῦθι μὲν οὐκ ἐθέλοντος, ἐπεί μ' ἐπέδησας ἀνάγκῃ, *Praep. Ev.* 5. 8. 194b). It is not possible to tell whether Pythagoras opposes the notion of compulsion, but Porphyry clearly does oppose it. Eusebius quotes from Porphyry's *Epistle to Anebo:*

> But what utterly perplexes me is, how, though invoked as superiors, they receive orders as inferiors . . . But much more absurd than this is the notion that a man . . . should employ threats . . . to the royal Sun himself, or the Moon, or any of the deities in heaven . . ." (*Praep. Ev.* 5. 10. 197d–98a).

These objections in Porphyry's *Epistle to Anebo* were addressed by Iamblichus in his ten books *On the Mysteries.* However, as Morton Smith points out, Iamblichus' denial that divination and magic compel the deities (*De Mysteriis* 3. 18) merely proves that the opinion that compulsion was precisely the

---

[29] Nock (*Essays,* 1:309) dates this treatise in the 5th century B.C.E.
[30] Konrat Ziegler, "Pythagoras von Rhodos," PW 24/1 (1963) 304–5.

point of magic was widespread.[31] And indeed in *De Mysteriis* 4. 2 Iamblichus is forced to admit that some spirits *are* commanded by the theurgist.

The Stoics were also among those who objected to any claim to be able to compel the gods. Submission to the will of the gods was one of the most basic emphases of Stoicism, and one which the Stoics derived from Socrates' "if so it is pleasing to the gods, so let it be" (εἰ ταύτῃ τοῖς θεοῖς φίλον, ταύτῃ γενέσθω).[32] Since, for the Stoic, the will of God was equivalent to destiny or fate, resistance was useless.[33] The wise person prays with Cleanthes:

> Lead thou me on, O Zeus, and Destiny,
> To that goal long ago to me assigned.
> I'll follow and not falter; if my will
> Prove weak and craven, still I'll follow on.
>   (Epictetus, *Enchiridion* 53. 1)

Seneca (*Epistle* 107. 11) adds a fifth line which expresses the Stoics' best argument for embracing the will of God: "The willing are led by fate; the unwilling dragged."

Stoic submission to the will of God is not, however, synonymous with suffering. Epictetus makes it clear in *Diss.* 2. 16. 42 that such submission accepts the power of office or a private life, riches or poverty, a life of comfort or a life in exile, as God wills. This general principle is followed by a specific example in 2. 16. 44. Epictetus praises Hercules for his single-minded devotion to God (οὐδὲν φίλτερον τοῦ θεοῦ) in that he "went about clearing away wickedness and lawlessness" in obedience (πειθόμενος) to God. It is on that account that Hercules "was believed to be a son of God, and was" (διὰ τοῦτο ἐπιστεύθη Διὸς υἱὸς εἶναι καὶ ἦν). In this passage, Hercules' status as son of God is attributed to his obedience to the will of God. The specific expression of that obedience is the performing of powerful acts (καθαίρων ἀδικίαν καὶ ἀνομίαν).

In the following section of the same book, Epictetus contrasts the stance of the Stoic sage toward the will of God with that of Medea, the most infamous of all practitioners of magic. His discussion clearly presupposes the claims which, as we have seen, were made by and attributed to magicians: (1) to be able to do whatever they will to do and (2) to be able to compel the gods to do the magician's will. Epictetus denies both claims and shows that only of the Stoic sage can it be said that everything he wills happens.

First, following Euripides' plot, Epictetus shows that Medea was not able to cause to happen those things which she willed to happen, and was therefore driven to the desperate act of killing her own children (*Diss.* 2. 17. 20-21). "For she did not know," Epictetus explains, "where the power lies to do what we will" (ποῦ κεῖται τὸ ποιεῖν ἃ θέλομεν, 2. 17. 21). The solution is simple: "Give up willing

---

[31] Morton Smith, *Clement of Alexandria and a Secret Gospel of Mark* (Cambridge, MA: Harvard University Press, 1973) 222 n. 8.

[32] Epictetus, *Enchiridion* 53. 3; a modified version of Plato, *Crito* 43 D.

[33] Sevenster, *Seneca*, 42-43.

anything but what God wills (ἃ ὁ θεὸς θέλει). And who will prevent you, who will compel (ἀναγχάσει) you? No one, any more than anyone prevents or compels Zeus!" (2. 17. 22).

Thus, magicians are not able to do whatever they will, because Medea was not. Magicians are not able to compel the gods, because no one can. But the Stoic sage has whatever he wants because, unlike Medea, he has aligned his will (συνθέλης, 2. 17. 22) with the will of Zeus. Everything happens as the sage wills, since the sage wills only what God wills, and whatever happens is the will of God. Thus, only of the sage can it be said: μηδὲν ἔσται τοῦ μὴ θέλοντος, θέλοντος μηδὲν οὐκ ἔσται (2. 17. 28).

Taken together, these two passages from Epictetus yield useful information about how a Stoic teacher could use the concept "will of God" in the formation of disciples.[34] The first passage shows that doing the will of God does not look the same in every case; either suffering or extraordinary power may be the experience of one who does the will of God. The powerful hero Hercules is an example of one who did the will of God and was therefore "son of God." The second passage uses the claims of magicians as a foil to emphasize the attitude appropriate for the true Stoic. Compelling the gods and seeking to do one's own will is contrasted with choosing the will of God.[35]

In descriptions of magic written before the Gospel of Mark, contemporary with the gospel and in the second, third, and fourth centuries of our era, certain features are constant: (1) magicians claim to be able to do whatever they will, that is, to be able to do the impossible, (2) magicians claim to be able to compel the gods, (3) people who oppose magic regard these claims as impious or false or both. It is not surprising, then, to discover that when an ancient biographer or apologist wants to defend a miracle-worker against the charge of being a magician it is necessary to show that the miracle-worker is a pious worshiper of the gods, and does not attempt to compel them with spells, but rather petitions them for assistance and does only what they will.

Petition vs. Compulsion in Miracle Apologetics

In his biography of Apollonius of Tyana, Philostratus takes pains to portray Apollonius as a person who worships the gods and gives them the credit for the

---

[34] Both passages, like most of the discourses, are cast in the form of advice, using the second person: "do you think . . .? Why are you troubled?" etc.

[35] Of course, for the Stoic the only choice is between willing the will of God or making oneself miserable by willing something else. The point of Cleanthes' hymn is that everyone finally does the will of God whether willingly or reluctantly. Thus, the Stoic teacher does not couple submission to the will of God with confidence in the efficacy of petitionary prayer, but with inward serenity in the face of circumstance. In his study of Roman prayer, Georg Appel links expressions of submission to the will of God with scepticism about the efficacy of petitionary prayer. See *De Romanorum Precantionibus*, 217-18 and Dietzel, "Erhörungsgewissheit," 17-29.

miracles which his enemies call magic. In his *apologia* before Domitian, Apollonius appeals to the high esteem in which he had been held by the emperor Vespasian, Domitian's father (8. 7. 2). Apollonius insists that Vespasian would never have trusted a person whom he regarded as a γόης:

> He did not come and say such things as this to me: Compel the Fates or compel Zeus to appoint me tyrant, or to work miracles and portents in my behalf, and show me the sun rising in the west and setting at the point where he rises.

Here the ability to perform the impossible and the ability to compel the gods are both attributes of a γόης. Later in the same passage, Apollonius asserts that, unlike a γόης, he does not "compel the gods," but rather teaches "how the gods ought to be worshiped." Thus, Apollonius insists, he is engaged in "the direct opposite" of magic (οἷς πᾶσιν ἐναντίον χρῆμα οἱ γόητες) and if his ideals were realized, magic would come to an end (οὐκ ἔσται ἡ τέχνη).

Besides the insistence that he cannot be a γόης, because he does not compel the gods, but rather worships them, Apollonius offers another defense in 8. 7. 9 which is similar to the Markan portrait of Jesus. In this passage Apollonius argues that he cannot be considered a γόης because he does not pretend to do remarkable deeds by his own power, but rather prays to the gods and gives them the credit for the salvific actions with which they respond to his prayers. It was by praying (εὔχομαι) to Hercules that Apollonius exorcised a spirit of disease from Ephesus, and Apollonius promptly gave Hercules the credit by erecting a temple to him. "Who then," Apollonius asks, "being ambitious to be considered a γόης, would dedicate his achievement to a god? . . . And who would pray to Hercules if he were a γόης?" This argument coincides with the opinion that Philostratus expresses in the *Lives of the Sophists* 494, where he writes of the Persian magi, "though they involve the gods in their secret rites, they avoid any public profession of belief in a deity because they do not wish it to be thought that their own powers are derived from that source." For Philostratus, a magician is one who claims to have power to compel the gods to do his will, whereas Apollonius prays to the gods and attributes his power to them.[36]

A similar argument is used by Irenaeus and Origen to differentiate Christian miracle-workers and exorcists from magicians. Irenaeus (*Adv. Haer.* 3. 32. 5) argues that the church "does nothing through invocations of angels or incantations or out of any other perverse inquisitiveness; rather, addressing prayers in a pure, chaste, and open manner to the Lord, who made all things, and invoking the name of our Lord Jesus Christ, it has worked miracles, not to lead people astray but for their benefit." Origen (*C. Cels.* 7. 4) writes that Christians perform exorcisms "not by use of anything curious and magical, or any potion, but by

---

[36] See the discussion by A. B. Kolenkow, "A Problem of Power: How Miracle Doers Counter Charges of Magic in the Hellenistic World," *SBL 1976 Seminar Papers* (ed. George MacRae; Missoula: Scholars, 1976) 105–110.

prayer alone and the simplest adjurations" (οὐδενὶ περιέργῳ καὶ μαγικῷ ἢ φαρμακευτικῷ πράγματι ἀλλὰ μόνῃ εὐχῇ καὶ ὁρκώσεσιν ἀπλουστέραις).[37]

In these arguments by Philostratus, Irenaeus and Origen there is no attempt to deny that Apollonius or the Christians performed miracles or exorcisms, nor is there any indication that such activity was considered inappropriate. The concern of the authors is to legitimate the miracle-workers and their activity by showing that they are not magicians because their power is given by the deity in response to petitionary prayer.

Because the ancient sources use the issue of compulsion to distinguish magic from religion,[38] modern scholars of religion have often adopted the distinction. Thus, A. A. Barb could write that "the magician forces the supernatural powers to accomplish what he desires and avert what he fears," whereas the religious man submits to the will of the deity.[39] H. C. Kee makes use of a similar distinction, which he concedes is not universally accepted by anthropologists.[40] It has recently become fashionable to insist that there is no justification for distinguishing magic from religion. This was the position of A. D. Nock,[41] and has been argued by Morton Smith,[42] Judah Goldin,[43] John M. Hull[44] and Harold Remus[45] among others. In his article, "Magic in Early Christianity," David Aune surveys the status of the magic/religion debate and concludes that magic is "a constant, if subordinate, feature of all religious traditions."[46]

It is not within the scope of this study to enter into the debate about whether or not ancient writers were correct when they distinguished magic from religion by arguing that whereas a magician harnesses divine power to do his own will, the religious person prays for divine power in order to do the will of the deity, or submits to the will of the gods in the absence of their intervention on his or her behalf. This study will not defend this ancient distinction between magic and religion, but will be satisfied to observe that such a distinction *was made* in antiquity. The fact that the word for prayer (εὐχή) can be found in the magical papyri and that the word for spell (ἐπῳδή) can have a non-pejorative sense,[47] or the fact

---

[37] Remus, *Conflict*, 245 n. 89.

[38] J. Z. Smith, *Map*, 188.

[39] A. A. Barb, "The Survival of Magic Arts," *The Conflict Between Paganism and Christianity in the Fourth Century* (ed. A. Momigliano; Oxford: Clarendon, 1963) 101.

[40] Kee, *Miracle*, 62–63.

[41] "Paul and the Magus," *Essays*, 1:313–15.

[42] *Magician*, 69, 132 and passim.

[43] "The Magic of Magic and Superstition," *Aspects of Religious Propaganda in Judaism and Early Christianity* (ed. E. S. Fiorenza; Notre Dame: University of Notre Dame Press, 1976) 122.

[44] *Hellenistic Magic*, 45–72.

[45] *Conflict*, 47–72.

[46] "Magic," 1557.

[47] Remus, *Conflict*, 64–67, citing Nock, Pfister and others.

that magicians sometimes prayed[48] did not prevent ancient writers on magical practice and ancient apologists for wonder-workers from using the categories compulsion, petition and submission to distinguish magicians from other wonder-workers. I will argue that these are the categories employed by the author of the Gospel of Mark. I will not enter into the debate about whether or not the evangelist was correct in his assessment.[49]

It is certainly clear, as scholars like Smith, Remus and Goldin point out, that in the final analysis the determinative factor is group consciousness. "Our" practices are religious and pious, but "theirs" are magical. "We" know this because "our" authorities define what is magic and what is not. Since the author of the Gospel of Mark is one such religious authority, we would expect him to use the familiar arguments to justify the practices of his community and its founder. This is in fact precisely what we find in Mark's only passage of anti-magic apologetic: 3:20-35.

Jesus' Miracles as "Will of God" (Mark 3:20-35)

Mark 3:20-35 is an example of the technique of "intercalation," discussed above in connection with Mark 11.[50] In this passage, the accusation of the scribes

---

[48] Smith, *Magician*, 130-32. Smith cites one example of a prayer which he regards as submission to the will of the deity. The reference is *PGM* xii. 189 (i.e., vol. 2, section 12, line 189): δός μ[οι εὐμεν]ῶς, ὃ ἔαν βούλῃ. The context is a spell which may be recited to pacify someone (a deity?) who is angry with the practitioner. After the spell a prayer is recited in which the deity is addressed in flattering terms. This prayer is followed by more magical syllables and the closing request, "give me whatever you wish." If this is submission, it is combined with overtly manipulative flattery.

[49] It is interesting to note that the denial that magic can be distinguished from religion is not exclusively a modern argument. On the contrary, it was commonly employed by magicians in their own defense. Apuleius, defending himself against the charge of practicing magic, argues that a *magus* in Persia was an honorable priest and that *mageia* is the worship of the gods (*Apology*, 25. See Remus, *Conflict*, 68-69). That this argument was often used by magicians to justify their practices is attested by John Chrysostom in a sermon on Colossians (*In epist. ad. Col. Cap.* III, *Homily* 8. 5 = Migne *PG* 62. 358. The translation is found in *NPNF*, First Series, 13:298).

Chrysostom is arguing against idolatry and extolling the faithfulness of the Christian mother who would rather see her sick child or husband die than to attempt a cure by the use of magical amulets (περίαπτα). The magicians who profit from the sale of such charms argue as follows, "We call upon God and do nothing unusual" (τὸν θεὸν καλοῦμεν, καὶ οὐδὲν πλέον ποιοῦμεν) and, "The old woman is a Christian and faithful" (Χριστιανή ἐστιν ἡ γραῦς καὶ πιστή), and therefore does nothing wrong, if she uses a little magic on the side. Nevertheless, Chrysostom thunders, "The thing is idolatry!" (εἰδωλολατρεία τὸ πρᾶγμά ἐστι). When David was in the same situation, agonizing over a sick child, "he brought neither soothsayers nor chanters of spells . . . but rather made supplication to God" (οὔτε δὲ μάντεις ἤγαγεν, οὔτε ἐπῳδοὺς . . . ἀλλὰ τὸν θεὸν ἱκέτευε). Here, in a text from the fourth century C.E., the claim that magic is a sub-category of religion is recognized as a favorite ploy of magicians themselves and is explicitly denied.

[50] Donahue, *Discipleship*, 33.

and Jesus' refutation (3:22–30) are framed by negative encounters between Jesus and his family. In 3:20–21 his family members (οἱ παρ' αὐτοῦ)[51] try to seize him because, they say, "He is beside himself," which is equivalent to the scribes' accusation that he is possessed by a demon.[52] In 3:31–35 Jesus contrasts his mother and his brothers, who are "outside" waiting to see him, with the crowd seated around him and says, "Whoever does the will of God is my brother, and sister, and mother."

Vernon Robbins has recently pointed out that 3:20–35 is organized in a chiastic pattern which states three charges against Jesus and answers them in reverse order:[53]

A - Family: "He is beside himself" - 3:21
B - Scribes: "He has Beelzebul" - 3:22
C - Scribes: "He casts out demons by the ruler of demons" - 3:22[54]
C' - Refutation: Satan does not cast out Satan - 3:23-27
B' - Refutation: Jesus "has" the Holy Spirit - 3:28-30
A' - Refutation: Jesus and his true family do the will of God - 3:31-35

An examination of these arguments yields interesting results.

The third charge, that Jesus is using demonic power to defeat demonic power, is countered by the argument about a "divided house." Jesus says that if he were in league with demons, he could not cast them out.[55] On the contrary,

[51] The controversy over whether or not Jesus' family is meant here is discussed in full by Ernest Best in "Mark III. 20, 21, 31–35," NTS 22 (1975/76) 309–19. Best concludes that the best interpretation is the majority view which understands οἱ παρ' αὐτοῦ as Jesus' family and sees 20–21 and 31–35 as framing 22–30.

[52] Best, "Mark III," 316; M. Smith, Magician, 32.

[53] Burton L. Mack and Vernon K. Robbins, Patterns of Persuasion in the Gospels (Sonoma, CA: Polebridge Press, forthcoming) chapter VII, "Rhetorical Composition and the Beelzebul Controversy." J. Lambrecht found a chiastic pattern in this passage, but he combined the scribes' two accusations into one, so his outline is slightly different from Robbins'. See J. Lambrecht, 'Ware verwantschap en eeuwige zonde. Ontstaan en structuur van Mc. 3, 20–35 (III)," Bijdragen 29 (1968) 369–93 or English abstract by the author in NTA 13 (1969) 327–28.

[54] Morton Smith also finds two separate charges in 3:22 (Magician, 32–33).

[55] Robbins (Mack and Robbins, Patterns, ms. 11) notes the ironic emphasis of Jesus' statement about the weakness of "a house divided against itself:" he implies that Satan is, in fact, "coming to an end." Hendrikus Boers ("Four Times Mark," 12) suggests that this may be "a cryptic reference to the fact that the chief priests, the scribes and elders are divided against what should be their allies, the demons and impure spirits, and therefore contribute to the downfall of their kingdom." That is, by having Jesus crucified, the religious leaders guarantee the defeat of the demons. This interpretation of the cross, which is found in 1 Cor 2:6-8 and Col 2:15, is not, however, explicit elsewhere in Mark and, if present here in the "house divided" remark is at most cryptic.

he is able to cast out demons because he has bound "the strong man," who corresponds to "the ruler of demons," or "Satan" (3:23).[56] Mark has already informed his audience that Jesus is "the stronger one" (ἰσχυρότερος) in 1:7.[57] Later, in the encounter with the Gerasene demoniac, Jesus is able to subdue the powers that no one else is strong enough to control (οὐδεὶς ἴσχυεν αὐτὸν δαμάσαι, 5:4).

The second charge, that Jesus is possessed by Beelzebul (3:22), an "unclean spirit" (3:30), is forthrightly called blasphemy (3:28-29). Jesus' power does not come from an unclean spirit, but from the Holy Spirit (3:29),[58] as the audience knows because they witnessed Jesus' baptism (1:9-11). In the baptism scene, the heavenly voice established Jesus' identity as Son of God and sanctioned his activity as pleasing to God (1:11). After this introductory scene, the audience understands that the preaching, healing and exorcisms which follow are the work of the Holy Spirit that descended on Jesus at his baptism and that Jesus' ministry is pleasing to God. This is explicitly claimed in the anti-magic apologetic here in chapter 3.

Implicit in the Markan Jesus' definition of his true family as "whoever does the will of God" is the claim that Jesus himself does the will of God. This is his response to the charge by his relatives that he is "beside himself," i.e., demon-possessed. On the contrary, the Markan Jesus says, his mind and his activities are directed toward the will of God.[59] In this context, doing the will of God means performing the exorcisms which are the topic of controversy. More broadly, the will of God includes all Jesus' preaching, healing and exorcism since his reception of the Holy Spirit at baptism.[60] Here in 3:35 the audience learns that Jesus' "I will; be cleansed," of 1:41 expresses not merely his will, but the will of God, by whose Spirit Jesus heals and casts out demons (3:29).

There is no evidence that the author of Mark wants to deny that these phenomena were part of the ministry of Jesus, nor that he wants to eliminate miracles from the practice of his church. However, it is clear that the evangelist wants to control the interpretation of these phenomena. In the Beelzebul pericope he makes three points by which he distinguishes the practices of Jesus

---

[56] So Smith, *Magician*, 33.

[57] Donahue, *Dicipleship*, 33.

[58] Smith, *Magician*, 33.

[59] That the saying on Jesus' true family is part of the rhetorical defense of Jesus by Mark is Robbins' observation (*Patterns*, ms. 13). Morton Smith (*Magician*, 32) writes: "From this it seems that Jesus' exorcisms were accompanied by abnormal behavior on his part. Magicians who want to make demons obey often scream their spells, gesticulate, and match the mad in fury." However, Smith does not cite his sources for this knowledge of magical exorcism, so it is impossible to know whether ἐξέστη here necessarily implies abnormal behavior.

[60] Fridrichsen, *Problem*, 103. Pesch (*Markusevangelium*, 1:225) thinks the will of God here refers to Jesus' activity in 2:1-3:6, but, like Fridrichsen, I see no reason to exclude the "day in Capernaum" material of Mark 1:21-45.

(and of the Markan community) from magical practices: (1) Jesus (and his followers) have the Holy Spirit, not an unclean spirit; (2) therefore, God is the power behind the miracles performed by Jesus (and Christians), not Satan or demons; (3) Jesus and his true family (the Christian community) are not magicians, because they do the will of God. The portrayal of Jesus at prayer (1:35–38, 6:45–46, 14:32–42) and the teaching material which links miracle-working to prayer (9:28–29, 11:22–25) add the further emphasis that Jesus and his followers do not impose their will on God by magical spells and manipulations, but rather petition God who alone has the power to do the impossible. As we have seen, these are the very themes which a Hellenistic audience would have expected in an apologetic for miracle workers.

Thus, John Hull completely misses the point when he writes that the Gospel of Mark incorporates magical elements in a naive and unself-conscious manner with no attempt to protect Jesus and the Christian community from the charge of magic.[61] He takes this position because he correctly observes that the author of Mark allows to stand in the miracle stories magical details that Matthew eliminates.[62] Because the author of Mark does not use the same arguments that Justin and Origen used to defend the miracle traditions about Jesus, Hull fails to recognize the argument which the evangelist does employ effectively.[63]

The author of Mark may have been well aware that the healing and exorcistic practices of his community differed little, if at all, from those of outsiders. Why should they? In a period of pluralism and syncretism like the first century, religious paraphernalia become common property. Since pagans, Jews, and Christians all prayed standing with hands uplifted, it should not be surprising that pagan, Jewish, and Christian healing and exorcistic practices were also similar.[64] As Grant puts it, "The contexts are different; the phenomena are

---

[61] Hull, *Hellenistic Magic*, 144.

[62] These are familiar to most students of the miracle traditions. See Hull, *Hellenistic Magic*, chapters 5, 7 and pages 142–45, and M. Smith, *Secret Gospel*, 224–27. Kee (*Miracle*, 169–70) acknowledges these elements, but since he has no explanation for their presence, he asserts that Mark is not obliged to be consistent.

[63] Aune ("Magic," 1543) criticizes Hull for failing to see that in Mark anti-magic apologetic is present side-by-side with magical traditions. In note 150, Aune refers specifically to the Beelzebul pericope. It is interesting to note that Hull regards the focus on compelling the deity to do one's will as "the most central characteristic of magic" (27), and that he recognizes that "the records of magic contain nothing like the self-sacrifice of the Gethsemane Christ" (145). Still, he fails to see that the issue of will is where Mark has chosen to focus his defense, and that the Gethsemane pericope is a part of that defense.

[64] Judah Goldin ("The Magic of Magic and Superstition," 121–22, citing the *Peskita de Rav Kahana* 74f) provides an example of the issue of magic vs. religion in Jewish apologetic. When confronted with great similarity in detail between Jewish ritual and pagan witchcraft, Yohanan ben Zakkai responds by saying that the difference is that the Jewish ritual has been commanded by God. Therefore, the Jewish ritual is done in obedience to the will of God, however much it may resemble magic in practice. The Markan position is similar in that the evangelist does not attempt to differentiate Christian

somewhat similar."[65] Our evangelist, like other Hellenistic authors, distinguished the practices of his community and its founder from the practices of magicians by insisting that his group relied on petition rather than spells and did not seek to impose their will on God. On the contrary, he argues, miracles which happen in the Christian community are done by God, for whom all things are possible. They represent the will of God.

The presence of this kind of apologetic in the Gospel of Mark is not to be interpreted as evidence that the purpose of the gospel is primarily polemical. As Jonathan Z. Smith has observed, a defense against the charge of magic is necessarily a part of "every major religious biography (and associated autobiographical materials) of the Greco-Roman period." Moreover, Smith points out, this defense is directed not only to outsiders but also to the members of the religious community whose identity is formed by the text in question.[66] This double focus of the defense against a magical view of miracle protects the Christian miracle-workers from accusation by outsiders and controls their interpretation of the phenomena in which they participate. How they think of themselves is just as important to the evangelist as their reputation among outsiders. They are to see themselves as asking for God's help, not as controlling God. They are reminded of the identity of the power at work among them (the Holy Spirit) lest they resort to invoking other names when their petitions go unanswered. Magicians always had alternative names and alternative spells if the first one failed to work. The Markan community has but one source of power. Their only alternative when they get no response is to "keep on believing" and to continue to pray (11:24).

SUMMARY: THE WILL OF GOD IN MARK

In the Gospel of Mark, the essence of discipleship is following Jesus in doing the will of God. Recent interpreters of the gospel have correctly noted the evangelist's insistence that being a disciple involves the willingness to follow Jesus "on the way" to suffering and death. However, Donahue's work has called attention to the fact that the obedient acceptance of suffering and persecution, is but one facet of doing the will of God. Disciples are not people who follow Jesus by suffering, but people who follow Jesus in doing the will of God, whatever that may involve (3:35). In the Markan narrative, Jesus' doing the will of God is manifested in his healing, preaching, casting out demons, suffering and dying. But the author of Mark is not so naive as to think that this way of

---

practice from magic on the level of details of operation, but on the level of the stance of the practitioner in relationship to the will of God.

[65] Grant, *Miracle,* 173.

[66] J. Z. Smith, "Good News is No News: Aretalogy and Gospel" *Christianity, Judaism and Other Greco-Roman Cults.* Studies for Morton Smith at Sixty, Part 1: *New Testament* (SJLA 12; Leiden: Brill, 1975) 25.

understanding discipleship is easily grasped or easily lived out. In Gethsemane the audience of the Markan narrative comes to grips with what is involved in following Jesus and doing the will of God.

8
Gethsemane and
the Problem of Theodicy

We saw in chapter 1 that Markan scholars are becoming increasingly dissatisfied with the reading of Mark which understands the gospel as an attempt to reject the theology behind the miracle traditions and replace it with a theology of the cross that excludes divine presence and power from Christian self-understanding. Our study of the prayer logia has contributed to the re-evaluation of Mark's attitude toward miracles by demonstrating that the evangelist views prayer as the means by which the community participates in God's unlimited salvific power. In the last chapter we saw that an important part of Mark's interpretation of the miracle and prayer traditions is his use of the category "will of God."

It is the will of God to heal, raise the dead, cast out demons, feed multitudes, and rescue disciples from danger. It is the will of God for Jesus to suffer, die, and rise again. Those who would follow Jesus are confronted by the author of Mark with the necessity of participating in both power and suffering, and this sets up a tension within the text. In this chapter we will examine the prayer scene in the Gethsemane pericope in an attempt to discover the function of prayer with respect to this tension between the power available to Jesus and to the community of faith and the suffering that is also a part of their obedience to God.

GETHSEMANE: MARK 14:32-42

A great deal of work has been done on the question of sources and redaction in this passage.[1] This study will be limited to an attempt to interpret the passage in its present form, with a specific focus on the way in which the audience of the gospel is confronted with the tension between power and suffering.

Within the Markan passion narrative, the pericopae comprising the section 14:26-52 are unified by a common dramatic location: the Mount of Olives. Within this section there are four pericopae of varying length: 14:26-31 (prediction of the disciples' failure and of Peter's denial), 14:32-42 (Gethsemane),

---

[1] For this bibliography see Kelber, "Hour," 41 n. 1.

151

14:43-50 (arrest of Jesus and flight of the disciples) and 14:51-52 (flight of the young man). The Gethsemane pericope, 14:32-42, is rounded off on both ends by references to the movements of Jesus and the disciples. In 14:32 the evangelist writes, "And they went (ἔρχονται) to a place named Gethsemane." In 14:42 he has Jesus say, "Rise—let us be going" (ἄγωμεν). That 14:43 begins a new literary unit is made evident by the introduction of additional characters: "And immediately, while he was still speaking, Judas came . . ." The same narrative device is used at 5:35 to mark the end of the story of the hemorrhaging woman and the resumption of the narrative about Jairus' daughter: "While he was still speaking, they came from the ruler's house . . ."

The Gethsemane pericope is constructed of two sections, each having three parts.[2] In the first section, 14:32-36, there are three reports of movements, each followed by a report of Jesus' speech:

1) 32   and *they came* to a place called Gethsemane
          and *he said* to his disciples . . .
2) 33   and *he took along* Peter and James and John . . .
    34   and *he said* to them . . .
3) 35   and *going ahead* a little, he fell down . . .
    36   and *he said* . . .

In the second section, 14:37-42, the narrator reports that Jesus returned from prayer three times and found the disciples sleeping:

    37   and *he came* and found them *sleeping*
    40   and, *coming again,* he found them *sleeping*
    41   and *he came the third time* and said to them, "*Sleep,* then . . ."

Jesus' prayer stands at the center of the pericope and is presented first in indirect discourse (14:35b), then in direct discourse (14:36).[3]

At the beginning of the pericope the narrator lets his audience know that something important is about to happen. The last time in the narrative that Jesus separated himself from the disciples in order to pray, they next met him walking on the sea (6:45-52). Leaving the larger group behind, Jesus selects Peter, James and John and takes them with him (33a). One of the reasons Jesus appointed the disciples was to be "with him," (3:14) but in this scene Jesus will ultimately be alone. These were the three who saw Jesus defeat death in the case of Jairus' daughter (5:35-43) and who were present at the epiphanic transfiguration scene (9:2-8).[4] Jesus' choice of them here is a signal of the significance of what is to

[2] Ibid., 47.
[3] Harrington, *Mark,* 223.
[4] Pesch, *Markusevangelium,* 2:389.

happen,[5] and not an attempt to discredit the Jerusalem church by stressing their failure. The same device is used in the Old Testament to emphasize the solemnity of an event. In Genesis 22:5 Abraham and Isaac leave the servants behind with instructions as they go ahead to the mountain. In Exodus 24:14 Moses takes Aaron up on the mountain into the presence of God and leaves the elders behind to attend to the affairs of the people.[6]

The verbs used in 33b to describe Jesus' emotional state (ἤρξατο ἐκθαμβεῖσθαι καὶ ἀδημονεῖν) express deep anguish.[7] Reports of Jesus' emotions are rare in the Markan narrative,[8] and never up to this point has the audience had any indication that Jesus felt distress about his own situation. Previously the Markan Jesus has reacted in anger, compassion or amazement to the actions or conditions of other characters. Here he is described as being in agony over his own situation and the picture is immediately reinforced by direct discourse: "My grief is enough to kill me" (14:34a).[9]

This sudden shift in the characterization of Jesus has important consequences for the impact that the Gethsemane pericope has on the audience of the gospel. The audience is completely unprepared for Jesus' extreme distress and for his request that God intervene to prevent his death (14:36).

Up to this point in the narrative, the Markan Jesus had talked about the passion with seriousness but with detachment. All three of the passion predictions are cast in the third person: "The Son of Man must suffer many things . . ." (8:31, cf. 9:31, 10:32–34). The third person is also employed at 10:45 (The Son of Man came to serve and to give his life). Predicting Judas' betrayal, Jesus says, "One of you will betray me, one who is eating with me," but it is the disciples who are then described as "sorrowful," not Jesus (14:19). In the prediction of Peter's denial Jesus says, "You will deny me," (14:30), but the prediction of the disciples' "falling away" is impersonal: "You will all fall away" (14:27; Matt adds ἐν ἐμοί)![10]

---

[5] Kelber, "Hour," 47.

[6] Taylor, *Mark*, 552.

[7] Boomershine, "Storyteller," 145, and see also note 66. Translators struggle with this phrase: "He . . . began to be greatly distressed and troubled" (RSV); "And a sudden fear came over him, and great distress" (JB); "Distress and anguish came over him" (TEV); "He . . . began to be horror-stricken and desperately depressed" (Phillips).

[8] Prior to 14:33b they are: 1:41, σπλαγχνισθείς (being filled with compassion) or ὀργισθείς (being angry); 3:5, μετ' ὀργῆς, συλλυπούμενος (with anger, being grieved [by their hardness of heart]); 6:6, ἐθαύμαζεν (he was amazed [at their unbelief]); 6:34, ἐσπλαγχνίσθη (he had compassion on them); 8:2, σπλαγχνίζομαι (I have compassion); 10:14, ἠγανάκτησεν (he was angry); 10:21, ἠγάπησεν (he loved him). This list is Boomershine's ("Storyteller," 145).

[9] Boomershine, "Storyteller," 147. Swete (*Mark*, 342) writes, "His words recall Ps. xli. (xlii) 6, 12, xlii (xliii) 5 . . . But His sorrow exceeds the Psalmist's; it is ἕως θανάτου, a sorrow which well-nigh kills."

[10] Harrington (*Mark*, 223) observes, "The Jesus who had, up to now, almost casually contemplated his fate, is [in Gethsemane] brought rudely face to face with the harsh

Jesus' emotional detachment from the announcements of his impending suffering is the narrative device by means of which the author has avoided a direct collision between the two conflicting themes of power and suffering up to this point. The audience is aware that there is a problem, because they have witnessed the dramatic encounter between Jesus and Peter in 8:31-33. There, Peter had tried to eliminate the tension between power and suffering by denying the necessity of Jesus' suffering. For this attempt, Peter was rebuked as "Satan"—one who thinks humanly and does not see things from God's perspective.

By the time they arrive at Gethsemane with Jesus and the disciples, the members of the audience have realized that Peter and the other disciples are not going to be able to "think the things of God." Instead, they are going to "fall away," like the people in the parable of the soils. The disciples' impending failure and disgrace is experienced by the audience of the gospel as the final blow in a series of disappointments. They have been encouraged to identify with the disciples who now are proving to be unreliable models.

Robert Tannehill has called attention to the way in which the Markan narrative influences its audience.[11] He observes that at the beginning of the gospel the evangelist leads his audience to assume that Jesus and the disciples are embarked on the same course. The disciples follow Jesus and share in his work of preaching and exorcism. As Tannehill puts it, the author "emphasizes the parallel between Jesus' commission and the disciples' commission."[12] The initially positive portrayal of the disciples in the narrative encourages the audience to identify with them.[13] They, too, see themselves as followers of Jesus. However, the disciples' anxious self-concern causes tension in the narrative between them and Jesus,[14] which puts the audience in conflict. "The implied criticism of the disciples threatens to become criticism of the reader."[15] Will the audience continue to identify with the blind and fearful disciples, or will they switch their allegiance to Jesus?

---

reality." Jerry H. Stone ("The Gospel of Mark and *Oedipus the King:* Two Tragic Visions," *Soundings* 67 [1984] 60) asserts that the Markan Jesus, like Oedipus, both knows and does not know his true identity and that the third-person form of the passion predictions reflect Jesus' uncertainty about "identifying himself as the one to whom this must happen." It seems to me, however, that the function of the characterization of Jesus in the gospel is not to portray Jesus as uncertain of his identity but, as Tannehill argues, to affect the self-understanding of the audience.

[11] "The Disciples in Mark: The Function of a Narrative Role," *JR* 57 (1977) 386-405 and "The Gospel of Mark as Narrative Christology," *Semeia* 16 (1979) 57-95.

[12] Tannehill, "Christology," 65.

[13] Ibid., 70.

[14] Tannehill, "Disciples," and "Christology," 70.

[15] Tannehill, "Christology," 70.

On the way to Gethsemane Jesus predicts that all the disciples will abandon him and the audience is inclined to believe Jesus in spite of the protests of Peter and the other disciples. After all, Jesus is the character within the narrative who is consistently portrayed as reliable,[16] and two of his most recent predictions have been proven accurate (11:1-6, 14:12-16). Surely Jesus can be relied upon to provide a satisfactory resolution of the tensions that have built up in the narrative. But it is just at this point, when the audience is ready to abandon the disciples and to identify with Jesus, that the author confronts them with the Gethsemane scene, where even Jesus' resolution seems to falter.[17]

Arriving at Gethsemane, Jesus leaves most of the disciples behind and takes with him Peter, James, John, and the audience. Then he leaves the three with the admonition to keep alert and goes on a little further alone — except for the audience who have no choice but to follow. By this time Jesus himself is overcome with horror and anguish and the audience realizes that they are the ones who have been betrayed because the conflict between power and suffering has not been settled in advance and the evangelist has closed off all possible avenues of escape.[18] There is no escape through docetism; Mark's language for Jesus' emotional state makes it clear that the suffering is real. There is no escape through determinism, which says that God does not intervene and the wise man accepts his appointed lot without complaint; instead, "everything is possible for God." There is no escape through avoidance; the disciples sleep, and later they will flee, but the narrator forces the audience to witness Jesus' struggle with the God who is at the same moment wielder of unlimited power, trusted *abba,* and the source of Jesus' assignment to experience unspeakable suffering.

Just as Jesus' anguish was described first in indirect discourse and then in a direct quotation, so his prayer, which stands at the center of the pericope, is also given in indirect, then direct, discourse. The indirect presentation of Jesus' prayer states a condition first, then a petition: "if it were possible, the hour might pass from him." The direct form is significantly different, in that it has four parts:[19]

1. Address: Abba, Father[20]

---

[16] Tannehill, "Disciples," 391.

[17] Tannehill, "Christology," 85.

[18] E. S. Gerstenberger and W. Schrage, *Suffering* (trans. J. Steely; Nashville: Abingdon, 1980) 174.

[19] D. Daube ("A Prayer Pattern in Judaism," *Studia Evangelica* (ed. Kurt Aland, et al.; Berlin: Akademie, 1959) 539–45) proposes a three-part arrangement based on a present-day Jewish death-bed prayer, but he is not able to trace this prayer to the time of Mark.

[20] One of the most recent contributions to the discussion of *abba* is that of Joseph Grassi, "Abba, Father (Mark 14:36): Another Approach," *JAAR* 50 (1982) 449–58. Grassi thinks the use of the term in Targum Onkelos and Ps. Jonathan on Genesis 22 indicates that the Gethsemane tradition portrays Jesus as the obedient son like Isaac. The term is also discussed by Georg Strecker, "Vaterunser und Glaube," *Glaube im Neuen Testament*

2. Formula of omnipotence: Everything is possible for you.
3. Petition: Take this cup away from me![21]
4. Submission: But the issue is not what I will, but what
you will.[22]

The first and fourth parts of the prayer express trust in the benevolence of God,[23] while the second and third parts express confidence in the power of God. The issue of possibility changes from a condition in 14:35b to a statement of fact in 14:36: πάντα δυνατά σοι. The condition imposed in 35b is met.[24] Everything is possible for God.

The power of the Gethsemane pericope depends upon the fact that even at this point in the narrative, deliverance from the cross is a real possibility.[25] The

---

(FS Hermann Binder; ed. F. Hahn and H. Klein; Neukirchen-Vluyn: Neukirchener, 1982) 11–28. This study will not discuss the issue of the continuity or discontinuity with Judaism of the use of *abba* as an address to God, nor the issue of whether we have here the genuine usage of Jesus. For Mark, *abba* was an expression of intimacy and trust in relationship to God. I think it is likely that Mark's community used the Aramaic expression in prayer as other Gentile churches did (Rom 8:15, Gal 4:6). Majority view: J. Jeremias, *The Prayers of Jesus* (Naperville: Allenson, 1967); R. Baumann, "Abba, Lieber Vater. Zum biblischen Gottesbild," *BK* 22 (1967) 73–78; W. Marchel, "Abba, Pater. Oratio Christi et christianorum," *VD* 39 (1961) 240–47; R. Kittel, "ἀββᾶ," *TDNT* 1 (1964) 5–6. Challenges to the consensus: S. V. McCasland, "Abba, Father," *JBL* 72 (1953) 79–91; D. Zeller, "God as Father in the Proclamation and in the Prayer of Jesus," *Standing Before God* (FS J. Oesterreicher; ed. A. Finkel and L. Frizzell; New York: Ktav, 1981) 117–29; A. Finkel, "The Prayer of Jesus in Matthew," *Standing Before God*, 131–70; J. Oesterreicher, "Abba Father: On the Humanity of Jesus," *The Lord's Prayer and the Jewish Liturgy* (ed. J. J. Petuchowski and M. Brocke; London: Burns and Oates, 1978) 119–38.

[21] The "cup" is a metaphor for suffering and death; so E. Schweizer (*Mark*, 313) and M. Black ("The Cup Metaphor in Mark xiv 36," *Exp Tim* 59 [1947–48] 195), who warns against interpreting every New Testament passage with the full weight of the Old Testament citation. But see Cranfield, "The Cup Metaphor in Mark xiv 36 and Parallels," *Exp Tim* 59 (1947–48) 137–38 and *Mark*, 433; also Taylor, *Mark*, 554.

[22] See the discussion of the translation in chapter 7, note 1.

[23] Harrington (*Mark*, 223) writes, "The utterance of this trustful *Abba* already contains 'thy will be done.' "

[24] Boomershine, "Storyteller," 149.

[25] Tannehill, "Christology," 85–86. Lull ("Jesus' Death," 5) puts it slightly differently: "Mark's Gethsemane story implies that Jesus really could have played the coward and refused to obey; although Mark does not say this outright, without that assumption the story is inexplicable." I prefer Tannehill's interpretation, which sees the option as miraculous rescue because it seems to me that at this point in the passion narrative playing the coward would not have done Jesus much good, as the plot of Mark already has Judas on the way to Gethsemane with a small army. The use of the formula of omnipotence in Jesus' prayer suggests that the evangelist wants to say that God might still intervene, not that Jesus might still run away.

use of the omnipotence formula recalls 10:27 and 9:23. At 10:27 the same formula was used in the context of God's sovereign reversal of soteriological principles. Although the Deuteronomic tradition equated prosperity with righteousness, the Markan Jesus declared that it was impossible for a rich man to enter the kingdom. Then in a second reversal Jesus had said that God was able to accomplish even this impossible feat. That which is impossible for humans is possible for God. The principle had been applied to prayer in 9:14–29 and 11:22–25. God will do the impossible in response to the prayers of the community which has confidence in his power. In 13:18 the prayers of the community may even be directed toward altering the timing of the events of the eschaton: "Pray that it may not happen in winter."[26]

So when the Markan Jesus repeats the omnipotence formula in his prayer and follows it with a request that the δεῖ of 8:31 be reversed, the audience understands this prayer as one which meets all the criteria for efficacious petition which have preceded it. The narrative up to this point has emphasized God's power and willingness to eliminate suffering no less than the necessity for Jesus' suffering and death. It is the real possibility of divine rescue at this point in the narrative that makes the scene in Gethsemane so terrible. The fact that the audience already knows that Jesus will die does not diminish the narrative tension, any more than the familiarity of Greek audiences with the mythological traditions prevented their experiencing the catharsis that the tragedies evoked.

It is important to recognize that in his prayer at the center of the Gethsemane pericope, the Markan Jesus does not reject miraculous rescue and choose to suffer. Rather, he rejects his own will, that is, he "denies himself" as he advocated in 8:34, and chooses the will of God. If, as we have argued, the praying Jesus is to be understood as a model for the community, then what the evangelist holds up as a model is not Stoic resignation but its contrary. The Markan Jesus prays for deliverance from suffering even in the face of overwhelming evidence that God wills *not* to intervene. Not only that, but the petition for rescue is repeated even after the initial submission to the will of God (καὶ πάλιν ἀπελθὼν προσηύξατο τὸν αὐτὸν λόγον εἰπών, 14:39). The prayer of submission does not replace the prayer for divine intervention; it accompanies it.

This tension between the expectation of God's powerful intervention and the willingness to fulfill God's commission to take up the cross is not relaxed even after the pivotal Gethsemane scene. Throughout the passion narrative, as Tannehill observes, the narrator continues to suggest that there may yet be a reversal.[27] In 14:47 there is a short-lived attempt at armed resistance to Jesus' arrest before the disciples flee (14:50). At Jesus' trial the witnesses do not agree, suggesting that Jesus may have to be acquitted. But Jesus himself provides the damning confession. Pilate tries to release Jesus, but is not successful. Even as Jesus hangs on the cross, bystanders half expect Elijah to come to his rescue (15:36). In his final words in the gospel, the Markan Jesus prays, not in passive resignation but in a cry of protest at God's inaction: "My God, my God, why have you forsaken me?"[28]

While Donahue rejects the equation of suffering with discipleship in the Gospel of Mark, he nevertheless insists that suffering does have an important theological function in the gospel. He writes:

> Therefore the problem of suffering for Mark is one of *theodicy;* the cross becomes the stumbling block because it cannot be reconciled with the way one thinks of God. ... Jesus is not simply a model to be followed on the way of suffering, but a model of one who in the midst of suffering can address God as *abba,* and who can see in suffering the will of God, even with the awareness that this will could be otherwise (14:34–36).[29]

The power of the scene in Gethsemane is to be attributed to the evangelist's refusal to compromise the power of God in the face of suffering. The scene is terrible, not because Jesus must suffer, but because his suffering is the will of the God who is powerful enough to prevent it, and who has eliminated so much suffering in the narrative prior to this scene. What makes discipleship in the Markan community so difficult is not that it involves suffering, but that it involves suffering by those who participate in God's power to do the impossible. The God who wills to move the mountain does not always will to take away the cup. Those who belong to Jesus' true family do the will of God, whether it involves miracles or suffering.

The disciples and the audience were only too happy to do the will of God when that involved preaching, healing and exorcism. Just before Gethsemane the audience learns that the disciples are not yet ready to do the will of God when that involves suffering. Jesus predicts that they will all be scandalized. Then, in Gethsemane, the disciples fail to watch and pray, which is the proper response to suffering, according to Mark 13. The audience is confronted with the decision whether, like the disciples, they will sleep and finally flee, or whether, like Jesus, they will watch and pray, and do the will of God.

PRAYER AND THEODICY IN MARK

If, as Donahue thinks, suffering must be seen as a part of the larger question of theodicy in the Gospel of Mark, and not as part of some polemic against miracle-workers, how does the evangelist resolve the problem?[30] It is clear that

---

[28] Lull ("Jesus' Death," 10) correctly insists that the cry of dereliction is a protest at God's inaction. All attempts to read the whole of Psalm 22 into this one line falter on its glaring absence from Luke and John, indicating that the line was understood, "not as the beginning of a psalm of victory, but as a lament" (Lull, "Jesus' Death," 6).

[29] Donahue, "Neglected Factor," 587.

[30] Lull ("Jesus' Death,") interprets the passion narrative as an attempt to cope with theodicy. Theodicy is also behind the treatment of Markan christology by M. Eugene

he understands the problem in the same way that it was understood by his contemporaries, because he uses the same categories to express the polarities: the category of will and the category of power. Those are the categories used in the classical statement of the problem of theodicy, attributed to Epicurus by Lactantius (*De Ira Dei* 13. 19):

> God either wills (*vult*) to take away evils and is not able (*non potest*), or he is able and does not will to do so, or he is neither willing nor able, or he is both willing and able.

The Epicurean statement goes on to argue that to deny either omnipotence or benevolence is to be left with a deity who is not worthy of the designation, but to affirm both, "which alone is suitable for God," is to be unable to account for either the origin or the continued existence of evil in the world. Lactantius says that the Epicureans avoid this dilemma by asserting "that God takes no interest in anything," and Lactantius is correct, as we have seen.[31] The Epicurean solution to the problem of theodicy eliminates both superstition and prayer by denying any divine agency to events in the world. The gods cannot be held responsible for suffering because they cannot be held responsible for anything.

The Stoic position, although it is in one sense precisely the opposite of the Epicurean position, has exactly the same effect on the practice of prayer. For the Stoic, the deity is not aloof from events in the world, but in complete control of them. But when Zeus is identified with destiny, as in the hymn of Cleanthes quoted above,[32] the only appropriate prayers are prayers in praise of the wisdom and benevolence of the all-controlling deity and prayers of submission to the inexorable will of deity. Everyone does the will of God whether gladly or reluctantly. A Stoic wise man would never pray, "Take this cup away from me."

Platonism solved the problem by denying the omnipotence of deity. As Galen says, some things are impossible by nature. Thus, "it would not have been possible for [the demiurge] to make a man out of stone in an instant, by simply willing (ἐθελήσειεν) to do so." (*De usu partium* 11. 14). The demiurge is not to blame for imperfections within the created order which result in suffering because the demiurge is limited in power by the intransigence of matter.[33]

The author of the Gospel of Mark affirms that God is both able and willing to eliminate suffering. He takes this position, not just because it is a given in the traditions which he has received, but also because healing, exorcism and other manifestations of divine power are a part of the life of his community. Few scholars would now deny this; recent controversies in Markan scholarship have

---

Boring (*Truly Human/Truly Divine* [St. Louis, MO: CBP Press, 1984] 43 and passim). Neither author cites Donahue's article.

[31] See the discussion of Epicureanism in chapter 4.

[32] "Will and Compulsion in Hellenistic Magic," chapter 7.

[33] E.g., *Timaeus* 47E–48A.

focused on whether the evangelist favors or opposes miracle-working as a component of discipleship.

The Markan community also knows about suffering. Without attempting to describe their situation more precisely than the gospel permits, we can say that persecution is either experienced or expected by the community (4:17; 8:34-35; 10:30, 39; 13:9-13).[34] Suffering and death at the hands of enemies was not only a part of the tradition about Jesus, but was also a present or anticipated reality for this community of his followers in the second generation.

Since the evangelist is unwilling, indeed unable, to qualify either God's power to eliminate suffering or God's willingness to do so, and since the cross and its implications for discipleship stand at the heart of the story he must tell, he can offer *no* solution to the problem of theodicy. In fact, several potential solutions are explicitly rejected in the narrative.

The solution which denies that suffering can be part of a commission from God is called "thinking the things of humans" by the Markan Jesus (8:33) and is eliminated by the way in which the evangelist constructs the central discipleship section and the passion narrative.[35] On the other hand, Jesus rebukes as unbelief the suggestion that God's power to eliminate suffering may be limited (εἴ τι δύνῃ, 9:22),[36] and the anxious self-concern which result from such lack of confidence in God's power and provision (4:35-41, cf. 6:50, 8:14-21).[37] It must

---

[34] See "Suffering and Discipleship," chapter 7.

[35] See Donahue, "Neglected Factor," 586-87.

[36] Lull ("Jesus' Death," 7) argues that the view that "all power is God's" is not found in Mark, since other beings in the narrative have power. He has to concede that the phrase "everything is possible for God" means, "that God has so much power that God can accomplish anything God chooses, that is, that no other power can successfully resist God's." His use of a process hermeneutic necessarily entails a limitation on God's power as a solution to the problem of theodicy: "Can we really believe that this is how God would have had Jesus' life turn out if God were in total control? Instead, it is possible that God could not prevent Jesus' crucifixion." (8). For some of the relevant literature on process theodicies, see "Jesus' Death," page 7, note 16.

I do not believe that the author of Mark entertained the notion of a limitation on God's power. That is why he can offer no solution to the problem of theodicy. He does not give his audience a defense of God, but a way to relate to God. Lull correctly recognizes the cry of dereliction (15:34) as a protest against God's failure to intervene. Such a protest is meaningful only if God is understood as able to intervene; if God cannot prevent Jesus' death, then the cry is mere petulance. Lull ("Jesus' Death," 10) indicates that Mark and his audience would have shared the concept that God was omnipotent in the sense that God can do whatever God decides to do. Thus, Lull's solution would not have been a possible one for the evangelist.

[37] The phrase "anxious self-concern" is Tannehill's ("Christology," 70), and it is his suggestion that all three boat scenes should be taken together as images of inadequate responses by the disciples to their commission as followers of Jesus.

not be forgotten that the gospel ends with the telling of a miracle story. The women, who arrive at the tomb expecting nothing except to struggle with a stone and then to anoint a corpse, are struck dumb by the news that God has overcome even death, and that Jesus is already on his way to fulfill his promise to those who have not kept their promises to him. But this God who raises the dead is also the one whose inaction Jesus protested a few lines earlier. No solution which qualifies either the power of God or the reality of suffering is permitted by the narrative.

Another possible solution, namely the idea that suffering can be attributed to a lack of faith, is also eliminated by the narrative. Jesus twice comes to the rescue of the disciples even when they are fearful and faithless (4:35-41, 6:47-52).[38] Jesus restores the demon-possessed boy in spite of his father's inability to believe (9:14-29). In other healings and exorcisms faith may or may not be mentioned.[39] In the Gethsemane prayer scene, the use of the formula of omnipotence is an explicit statement of Jesus' faith. Jesus has the same kind of faith which is advocated in 11:22-24. Yet his petition is the only one in the gospel which does *not* result in God's powerful deliverance. Jesus, although he believes, does not receive everything he asks in prayer.

If the author of Mark rejects the solution which blames suffering on the victim's lack of faith, he is equally disdainful of the Deuteronomistic equation of suffering with disobedience to God. This is the understanding which lies behind the disciples' astonishment in 10:23-31 at the notion that prosperity is not an indicator of righteousness. Entry into the kingdom is not earned but given by the God who does that which is impossible for humans.

The Markan narrative demands at every point that the power and willingness of God to eliminate human suffering be held in dialectical tension with the persecution, suffering, and death of God's beloved son and of those who follow him.[40] Narrative is a particularly apt medium for the maintenance of this kind of tension because the scenes of the narrative are presented to the audience

[38] H. Fleddermann ("And He Wanted to Pass by Them [Mark 6:48c]," *CBQ* 45 [1983] 392) translates the strange καὶ ἤθελεν παρελθεῖν αὐτούς, "and he wanted to save them," based on a comparison with LXX Amos 7:8, 8:2. If his argument stands, it provides yet another example of Mark's insistence that God is not only able to save but willing (θέλω) to save. In any case, the story represents the saving help as purely gracious, since the disciples neither believe nor pray. In the other sea-rescue story, 4:35-41 they pray, but in unbelief: "Teacher, do you not care if we perish?"

[39] "Faith and power in the Markan miracle stories," chapter 5. There are no stories in which people who come to Jesus for help are refused. The miracle stories appear to have the function of encouraging prayer for healing and exorcism. "Unanswered" prayer is not explicitly dealt with in the healing stories. Nowhere in Mark does one find a parallel to James 1:6-8 where unsuccessful prayer is explicitly blamed on doubt. Tannehill ("Christology," 71) points out that the miracle stories emphasize God's grace and power.

[40] Gnilka, *Markus,* 1:224.

sequentially, so that the audience becomes increasingly uneasy without necessarily becoming aware that their discomfort is due to the fact that they are being forced to entertain conflicting propositions simultaneously.[41] Before they realize what is happening to them, the Markan audience has left the disciples behind as unworthy models and followed Jesus into Gethsemane, where theodicy leaves the realm of speculation and becomes a prayer of wrenching proportions.

The author of Mark does not offer his community a solution to the problem of theodicy, but he does offer them a way of coping with the tension that pervades their existence as empowered sufferers. That tension, which may not be relaxed, is to be integrated into the community's prayers. Like Jesus in Gethsemane, they are to combine affirmations of God's omnipotence and requests for God's powerful help with expressions of trust and intimacy and to confess that whether they heal and exorcise or whether they suffer and die, it is God's will, not their own, that they do. However much they may have to suffer, they are not to retreat from their world-view; they are not to stop expecting God to intervene on their behalf. They are not to flee from suffering, but they are to expect God's help. Even at the moment of death they are permitted the cry of protest against suffering that is modeled by Jesus in 15:39. And finally, they are promised that suffering that is the will of God is redemptive suffering. Whoever loses his or her life for Jesus' sake and for the sake of the gospel will ultimately save it.

---

[41] Boring (*Human/Divine*, 107) writes: "Conflicting pictures can be held together more readily than conflicting propositions." His focus is on christology, but the observation holds true for theodicy, with which christology is closely tied in the gospel.

9

The Theological Function
of Prayer in Mark

A widespread interpretation of the Gospel of Mark has seen the gospel as a polemic against the theology of the miracle traditions. According to this view, the author of Mark wanted to discourage the members of his community from seeing themselves as miracle-workers because such a self-understanding led to a devaluation of the cross and an unwillingness to suffer for the sake of the gospel. The Gethsemane scene has been read as settling the question once and for all: miracles are rejected and replaced by suffering, which is identical with the will of God.

This negative view of miracles is also reflected by the commentators on the Markan prayer teaching, whether or not they subscribe to the view of the gospel as polemic. The promises of God's powerful response to petitionary prayer in 11:22–25 are characterized as "very dangerous,"[1] "an encouragement to fanaticism,"[2] and perilously close to magic.[3] Protection against these dangers is often found in an appeal to the Gethsemane prayer scene. Schmithals, for example, uses 14:36 to qualify 11:24 and observes that "the greatest work of faith is the surrender of one's own will to God."[4] Schweizer uses the same approach: "Of course, a person with this kind of faith always prays that the will of God be done, not his own."[5] This emphasis on prayer for the will of God, in contrast to "egotistical prayer" leads Schreiber to write that "the prayer of faith does not look for its own salvation," in plain contradiction of Mark 14:36: "take this cup away from me."[6] Similar remarks are made by other scholars.[7]

As we saw in chapter 1, changes are taking place in the way the evangelist's attitude toward the miracle stories is understood. Many scholars are now inclined toward the view that the author of Mark places positive value on the miracle

---

[1] Haenchen, *Weg,* 391.
[2] Bacon, *Beginnings,* 163.
[3] Schmithals, *Markus,* 2:501.
[4] Ibid., 2:502.
[5] Schweizer, *Mark,* 234.
[6] Johannes Schreiber, *Theologie des Vertrauens* (Hamburg: Furche-Verlag, 1967) 241.
[7] Gnilka, *Markus,* 2:135; Nineham, *Mark,* 300.

traditions as well as on the passion traditions. Our study of Mark 11:22–25 and of its relationship to other passages in the gospel which deal with faith and prayer has confirmed the new direction in Markan studies. At the same time, we have discovered that the evangelist does not share his interpreters' disapproval of the prayer teaching in Mark 11. Rather, the prayer logia make explicit the views of God's power and the community's access to that power that were implicit in the miracle stories prior to Mark 11.

The Markan community shares with Hellenistic Judaism the world-view that "everything is possible for God." To live within that world-view is to "believe" or to have "faith." That faith is expressed in prayer for miraculous intervention, such as healing and exorcism, and the phenomena which are interpreted as God's response to such prayers reinforce the community's faith. The thaumaturgical phenomena in the Markan community are not to be understood as magic, according to the evangelist. Miracles are done by God, not by unclean spirits; prayer for these phenomena is communal, not private like the magician- client relationship. Those who pray for miracles are merely asking that God's will to heal and exorcise be done; they are not imposing their will on God, as magicians do. The community that receives miraculous answers to prayer must be a community where mutual forgiveness is practiced, because for prayer to be effective, the sins of those praying must be forgiven by God, and God forgives those who forgive each other.

The evangelist is aware that both miracles and prayer can be misused. He warns against false Christs and false prophets who may show "signs and wonders" in order to lead the community astray (13:22), and against "scribes" who "for a pretense make long prayers" (12:40). However, it does not occur to the evangelist that because these practices are vulnerable to abuse, they should be eliminated. Rather, he structures his narrative in such a way as to control the interpretation and practice of these phenomena in the community.

But prayer in the Markan community is not understood one-dimensionally as a vehicle for power with no other purpose. Persecution and suffering are also present or anticipated experiences of the community. These experiences also are to be brought before the trusted *abba* in prayer. Like Jesus, those who are persecuted are to pray for divine deliverance; like Jesus they are to be prepared to lose their lives if that should be God's will. At such times they may, like Jesus, feel deserted by God, but the evangelist assures them that to lose one's life in this way is really to save it. Even those who flee persecution may, like the disciples, yet see the risen Lord (16:7).

Prayer in the Markan narrative and in the Markan community functions as the practice in which the tension between power and suffering is faithfully maintained. Prayer is the context for the community's experiences of power, and prayer is the context for the community's experiences of suffering and martyrdom. The community that follows Jesus does the will of God, whatever that may be. By substituting the practice of prayer for a rational solution to the problem of theodicy, the evangelist is able to take seriously all the material in his religious tradition and all the experience of his community without being guilty of reductionism. At the same time, his approach serves the pastoral function of continually bringing the community back to the presence of God who is the source of their power and the only value worth dying for. The "danger" of the Markan approach to prayer is not that it will be taken too seriously, but that the formative document of a community that experienced both divine power and devastating persecution will be trivialized by a church that experiences neither.

Bibliography

I. ANCIENT TEXTS AND TRANSLATIONS

A. Editions and Collections

Aland, Kurt et al., eds. *Novum Testamentum Graece*. 26th ed. Stuttgart: Deutsche Bibelstiftung, 1979.

Arnim, Hans Friedrich August von, ed. *Stoicorum Veterum Fragmenta*. 4 vols. Leipzig: Teubner, 1903-24.

Braude, William G., trans. *The Midrash on Psalms*. 2 vols. New Haven: Yale University Press, 1959.

Danby, Herbert, trans. *The Mishnah*. Oxford: Oxford University Press, 1933.

Edelstein, E. J. and Edelstein, L. *Asclepius: A Collection and Interpretation of the Testimonies*. 2 vols. Baltimore: Johns Hopkins, 1945.

Elliger, K. and Rudolph, W., eds. *Biblia Hebraica Stuttgartensia*. Stuttgart: Deutsche Bibelstiftung, 1977.

Epstein, Isidore, ed. *The Babylonian Talmud*. 17 vols. London: Soncino, 1961.

Freedman, H. and Simon, M., trans. *The Midrash*. 10 vols. London: Soncino, 1939.

Goold, G. P., ed. *The Loeb Classical Library*. 471 vols. Cambridge: Harvard University Press, 1912-1982; London: William Heinemann, 1912-1982.

Grenfell, B. P.; Hunt, A. S. et al., eds. and trans. *The Oxyrhynchus Papyri*. 52 vols. London: Egypt Exploration Fund, 1898-1984.

Hennecke, Edgar and Schneemelcher, Wilhelm, eds. *New Testament Apocrypha*. 2 vols. Translated by E. Best et al. Translation edited by R. McL. Wilson. Philadelphia: Westminster, 1963-65.

Lake, Kirsopp, trans. *The Apostolic Fathers*. 2 vols. LCL. Cambridge: Harvard University Press, 1912-13.

Migne, Jacques Paul, ed. *Patrologiae Cursus Completus Series Graeca*. 161 vols. Paris: Migne, 1866; reprint ed., Turnhout: Brepols, 1977.

Preisendanz, Karl, ed. and trans. *Papyri Graecae Magicae: Die griechischen Zauberpapyri*. 3 vols. Leipzig and Berlin: Teubner, 1928-42.

Rahlfs, Alfred, ed. *Septuaginta*. Stuttgart: Deutsche Bibelstiftung, 1935.

Roberts, Alexander and Donaldson, James, eds. *The Ante-Nicene Fathers.* 10 vols. Buffalo and New York: Christian Literature Publishing Company, 1886–1897.

Schaff, Philip, ed. *A Select Library of the Nicene and Post-Nicene Fathers of the Christian Church.* First Series. 14 vols. Buffalo and New York: Christian Literature Publishing Company, 1886–90.

Usener, Herman K., ed. *Epicurea.* Stuttgart: Teubner, 1966.

B. Individual Authors and Works

Aeschylus. *Agamemnon. Aeschylus* 2, LCL. Translated by Herbert Weir Smyth.

Apuleius. *Apologia. Apulei Apologia.* Introduction and commentary by H. E. Butler and A. S. Owen. Hildesheim: Georg Olms, 1967.

——. *Metamorphoses. L. Apulei Opera Omnia.* 2 vols. Edited by G. F. Hildebrand. Hildesheim: Georg Olms, 1968.

——. *The Works of Apuleius.* London: George Bell, 1881.

Aristotle. *Ethica Nicomachea. Aristotle* 19, LCL. Translated by H. Rackham.

——. *De Incessu Animalium. Aristotle* 12, LCL. Translated by E. S. Forster.

——. *Categoriae. De Interpretatione. Physica. The Basic Works of Aristotle.* Edited by Richard McKeon. New York: Random House, 1941.

Cicero. *De Natura Deorum. Academica. Cicero* 19, LCL. Translated by H. Rackham.

——. *De Divinatione. Cicero* 20, LCL. Translated by W. A. Falconer.

Claudian. *In Rufinum. Claudian* 1, LCL. Translated by Maurice Platnauer.

Clement of Alexandria. *Stromateis. Clemens Alexandrinus. Bd. 2. Stromata Buch I–VI.* Edited by O. Stählin and L. Früchtel. Berlin: Akademie, 1960.

——. *The Stromata, or Miscellanies.* ANF 2:299–556.

Dio Chrysostom. *Dio Chrysostom* 1, LCL. Translated by J. W. Cohoon.

Epictetus. *Discourses. Enchiridion. Epictetus* 1–2, LCL. Translated by W. A. Oldfather.

Euripides. *Hippolytus, Medea. Euripides* 4, LCL. Translated by A. S. Way.

——. *Iphigeneia in Taurica. Euripides* 2, LCL. Translated by A. S. Way.

Eusebius of Caesarea. *Praeparatio Evangelica. Eusèbe de Césarée: La Preparation Evangelique, Livres IV–V, 1–17.* Introduced, translated and annotated by Odile Zink. Greek text revised by E. des Places. Paris: Cerf, 1979.

——. Eusebius: *Preparation for the Gospel, Part 1, Books 1–9.* Translated by E. H. Gifford. Oxford: Clarendon, 1903; reprint ed. Grand Rapids: Baker, 1981.

Galen. *De Usu Partium. Galen on Jews and Christians.* By R. Walzer. London: Oxford University Press, 1944.

Greek Anthology 1–5, LCL. Translated by W. R. Paton.

Herodotus. *Herodotus* 1-4, LCL. Translated by A. D. Godley.

Hippocrates. *De Morbo Sacro. Hippocrates* 2, LCL. Translated by W. H. S. Jones.

Homer. *Iliad. Iliad* 1-2, LCL. Translated by A. T. Murray.

——. *Odyssey. Odyssey* 1-2, LCL. Translated by A. T. Murray.

Iamblichus. *De Mysteriis. Jamblique: Les Mystères d'Egypte.* Edited by E. des Places. Paris: Société d'Edition "Les Belles Lettres," 1966.

——. *Iamblichus: On the Mysteries.* Translated by Thomas Taylor. San Diego, CA: Wizards Bookshelf, 1984.

——. *De Vita Pythagorica. Iamblichi de Vita Pythagorica liber.* Edited by L. Deubner. Stuttgart: Teubner, 1975.

——. *Iamblichus' Life of Pythagoras.* Translated by Thomas Taylor. London: A. J. Valpy, 1818.

Josephus. *Antiquitates Judaicae. Josephus* 4-10, LCL. Translated by H. St. J. Thackeray, R. Marcus, A. Wikgren and L. H. Feldman.

——. *Bellum Judaicum. Josephus* 2-3, LCL. Translated by H. St. J. Thackeray.

John Chrysostom. *Homilia in Epistolam ad Colossenses 8 (Col 3:5-7).* Migne, PG 62:351-60.

——. *Homily 8 on Colossians.* NPNF 13:293-300. Translated by J. A. Broadus.

Lactantius. *De Ira Dei. A Treatise on the Anger of God.* ANF 7:259-280.

Lucan. *Bellum Civile. Lucain: La Guerre Civile.* 2 vols. Edited by A. Bourgery and M. Ponchont. Paris: Société d'Edition "Les Belles Lettres," 1974.

——. *Lucan: Pharsalia.* Translated by Robert Graves. Baltimore: Penguin Books, 1957.

Lucian. *Demonax. Verae Historiae. Lucian* 1, LCL. Translated by A. M. Harmon.

——. *Icaromenippus. Juppiter Tragoedus. Lucian* 2, LCL. Translated by A. M. Harmon.

——. *Philopseudes. Lucian* 3, LCL. Translated by A. M. Harmon.

Lucretius. *De Rerum Natura. Lucretius,* LCL. Translated by W. H. D. Rouse.

Ovid. *Metamorphoses. Ovid* 3-4, LCL. Translated by F. J. Miller.

Philo of Alexandria. *Philo* 1-10, LCL. Translated by F. H. Colson, G. H. Whitaker, and R. Marcus.

Philostratus. *Vita Apollonii. Life of Apollonius of Tyana* 1-2, LCL. Translated by F. C. Conybeare.

Pindar. *The Odes of Pindar,* LCL. Translated by J. Sandys.

Plato. *Timaeus. Plato's Cosmology: The Timaeus of Plato.* Translation and commentary by F. M. Cornford.

Pliny the Elder. *Historia Naturalis. Pliny: Natural History* 1, LCL. Translated by H. Rackham.

Plutarch. *Consolatio ad Apollonium. De Superstitione.* Moralia 2, LCL. Translated by F. C. Babbit.

——. *Coriolanus. Plutarch's Lives* 4, LCL. Translated by Bernadotte Perrin.

——. *Non posse suaviter vivi secundum Epicurum. Moralia* 14, LCL. Translated by Benedict Einarson and Phillip H. Delacy.

——. *Pericles. Plutarch's Lives* 3, LCL. Translated by Bernadotte Perrin.

Propertius. *Propertius,* LCL. Translated by H. E. Butler.

Pseudo-Clement. *Recognitionum, Liber Secundus.* Migne, PG 1:1247-82.

——. *Recognitions of Clement.* ANF 8:97-117.

Rufinus. [Anecdote about Gregory Thaumaturgus and the mountain]. *Eusebius.* Bd. 2, T. 2. GCS. Edited by Eduard Schwartz. Leipzig: J. C. Hinrichs, 1908.

Seneca. *Ad Lucilium Epistulae Morales. Seneca* 4-6, LCL. Translated by R. M. Gummere.

——. *Moral Essays. Seneca* 1-3, LCL. Translated by J. W. Basore.

——. *Naturales Quaestiones. Seneca* 7, 10, LCL. Translated by T. H. Corcoran.

Strabo. *The Geography of Strabo* 1-8, LCL. Translated by H. L. Jones.

Tibullus. *Catullus, Tibullus Pervigilium Veneris,* LCL. Translated by F. W. Cornish, J. P. Postgate and J. W. Mackail.

Virgil. *Aeneid. The Aeneid of Virgil.* 2 vols. Translated by Charles J. Billson. London: Edward Arnold, 1906.

Xenophon. *Memorabilia. Xenophon* 4, LCL. Translated by E. C. Marchant.

II. WORKS OF MODERN SCHOLARSHIP

A. Reference Works

Bauer, Walter. *A Greek-English Lexicon of the New Testament and Other Early Christian Literature.* 4th ed. Translated and adapted by W. F. Arndt and F. W. Gingrich. Chicago: University of Chicago Press, 1957.

Blass, F. and Debrunner, A. *A Greek Grammar of the New Testament and Other Early Christian Literature.* Revised by A. Debrunner. Translated and edited by Robert W. Funk. Chicago: University of Chicago Press, 1961.

Dana, H. E. and Mantey, J. R. *A Manual Grammar of the Greek New Testament.* New York: Macmillan, 1927.

Galling, Kurt et al., eds. *Die Religion in Geschichte und Gegenwart.* 7 vols. 3d ed. Tübingen: J. C. B. Mohr (Paul Siebeck) 1957-65.

Glare, P. G. W., ed. *Oxford Latin Dictionary.* Oxford: Clarendon, 1982.

Hammond, N. G. L. and Scullard, H. H., eds. *The Oxford Classical Dictionary.* 2d ed. Oxford: Clarendon, 1970.

Jaques Cattel Press, ed. *Directory of American Scholars.* 8th ed. 4 vols. New York: Bowker, 1982.

Kittel, Gerhard and Friedrich, Gerhard, eds. *Theological Dictionary of the New Testament.* 10 vols. Translated by Geoffrey W. Bromiley. Grand Rapids: Eerdmans, 1964-76.

Klauser, Theodor, et al., eds. *Reallexikon für Antike und Christentum.* 12 vols. Stuttgart: Heisemann, 1950-81.

Liddell, H. G. and Scott, R. *A Greek-English Lexicon.* 9th ed. Revised and augmented by H. S. Jones. Oxford: Clarendon, 1968.

Metzger, Bruce M. *A Textual Commentary on the Greek New Testament.* Stuttgart: United Bible Societies, 1971.

Robertson, A. T. *A Grammar of the Greek New Testament in the Light of Historical Research.* Nashville: Broadman, 1934.

Quasten, Johannes. *Patrology.* 3 vols. Utrecht: Spectrum, 1962-66.

Wissowa, Georg, ed. *Paulys Real-encyclopädie der classischen Altertumswissenschaft.* 49 vols. Stuttgart: J. B. Metzler; München: Alfred Drukenmüller, 1893-1978.

B. Articles, Commentaries, and Studies

Achtemeier, Paul J. " 'And He Followed Him': Miracles and Discipleship in Mark 10:46-52." *Semeia* 11 (1978) 115-45.

———. " 'He Taught Them Many Things': Reflections on Marcan Christology." *CBQ* 42 (1980) 465-81.

———. "An Imperfect Union: Reflections on Gerd Theissen, *Urchristliche Wundergeschichten.*" *Semeia* 11 (1978) 49-68.

———. "Jesus and the Disciples as Miracle Workers in the Apocryphal New Testament." *Aspects of Religious Propaganda in Judaism and Early Christianity,* 149-86. Edited by E. S. Fiorenza. Notre Dame: University of Notre Dame Press, 1976.

———. *Mark.* Proclamation Commentaries. Philadelphia: Fortress, 1975.

———. "Miracles and the Historical Jesus: A Study of Mark 9:14-29." *CBQ* 37 (1975) 471-91.

———. "The Origin and Function of the Pre-Marcan Miracle Catenae." *JBL* 91 (1972) 198-221.

———. "Person and Deed: Jesus and the Storm-Tossed Sea." *Int* 16 (1962) 169-76.

———. Review of *Die Bedeutung der Wundererzählungen für die Christologie des Markusevangeliums,* by D.-A. Koch. *JBL* 95 (1976) 666-67.

———. "Toward the Isolation of Pre-Markan Miracle Catenae." *JBL* 89 (1970) 265-91.

Ambrozic, A. M. "New Teaching with Power (Mk 1:27)." *Word and Spirit,* 113–49. Essays in honor of David Michael Stanley, S.J. on his 60th birthday. Edited by J. Plevnik. Willowdale, ON: Regis College, 1975.

Anderson, Bernard W. *Out of the Depths.* Rev. ed. Philadelphia: Westminster, 1983.

Anderson, Hugh. *The Gospel of Mark.* London: Oliphants, 1976.

Appel, Georg. *De Romanorum Precantionibus.* Giessen: Töpelmann, 1909; reprint ed., New York: Arno Press, 1975.

Arnold, E. V. *Roman Stoicism.* New York: Humanities Press, 1958.

Attridge, Harold W. *First-Century Cynicism in the Epistles of Heraclitus.* HTS 29. Missoula: Scholars, 1976.

———. *The Interpretation of Biblical History in the Antiquities Judaicae of Flavius Josephus.* HDR 7. Missoula: Scholars, 1976.

Aune, D. E. "Magic in Early Christianity." *ANRW* 2.23.2. *Religion. vorkonstantinisches Christentum: Verhältnis zu römischem Staat und heidnischer Religion,* 1507–57. Edited by W. Haase. Berlin: Walter de Gruyter, 1980.

Ausfeld, Carolus. *De Graecorum Precantionibus Quaestiones.* Leipzig: Teubner, 1903.

Bacon, B. W. *The Beginnings of Gospel Story.* New Haven: Yale University Press, 1904.

Barb, A. A. "The Survival of Magic Arts." *The Conflict Between Paganism and Christianity in the Fourth Century,* 100–125. Edited by A. Momigliano. Oxford: Clarendon, 1963.

Barth, Gerhard. "Glaube und Zweifel in der synoptischen Evangelien." *ZTK* 72 (1975) 269–92.

Baumann, R. "Abba, lieber Vater. Zum biblischen Gottesbild." *BK* 22 (1967) 73–78.

Beardslee, William A. *Literary Criticism of the New Testament.* Philadelphia: Fortress, 1970.

———. "Saving One's Life by Losing It." *JAAR* 47 (1979) 57–72.

Bennett, W. J. "The Role of (the Greek word) 'Dei' in the Markan Understanding of the Passion." Ph.D. dissertation, Drew University, 1968.

Berchman, R. M. *From Philo to Origen.* Chico: Scholars, 1984.

Berger, Peter. *The Sacred Canopy.* Garden City, NY: Doubleday, Anchor, 1967.

Best, Ernest. *Following Jesus. Discipleship in the Gospel of Mark.* JSNTSup 4. Sheffield: JSOT, 1981.

———. *Mark: The Gospel as Story.* Edinburgh: T & T Clark, 1983.

———. "Mark's Preservation of the Tradition." *The Interpretation of Mark,* 119–33. Edited by W. R. Telford. Philadelphia: Fortress, 1985.

———. "Mark III. 20, 21, 31–35." *NTS* 22 (1975) 309–19.

——. "The Miracles in Mark." *RevExp* 75 (1978) 539-54.

Betz, Hans Dieter. *Lukian von Samosata und das Neue Testament.* Berlin: Akademie, 1961.

Biguzzi, G. "Mc 11, 23-25 e il Pater." *RivB* 27 (1979) 57-68.

Black, Matthew. "The Cup Metaphor in Mark xiv 36." *ExpTim* 59 (1947-48) 195.

Boers, Hendrikus W. "Four Times the Gospel of Mark." (Mimeographed).

——. "Polarities at the Roots of New Testament Thought: Methodological Considerations." *PRS* 11 (1984) 55-75.

——. "Where Christology is Real: A Survey of Recent Research on New Testament Christology." *Int* 26 (1972) 300-327.

Bokser, Baruch M. "The Wall Separating God and Israel." *JQR* 73 (1983) 349-74.

Boomershine, Thomas E. "Mark 16:8 and the Apostolic Commission." *JBL* 100 (1981) 225-39.

——. "Mark, the Storyteller: A Rhetorical-Critical Investigation of Mark's Passion and Resurrection Narrative." Ph.D. dissertation, Union Theological Seminary, New York, 1974.

Bonner, Campbell. "A Papyrus Describing Magical Powers." *Transactions of the American Philological Association* 52 (1921) 111-18.

Boring, M. Eugene. *Truly Human/Truly Divine.* St. Louis, MO: CBP Press, 1984.

Brenk, Frederick E. *In Mist Appareled: Religious Themes in Plutarch's Moralia and Lives.* Leiden: Brill, 1977.

Broadhead, Edwin K. "Which Mountain Is 'This Mountain'? A Critical Note on Mark 11:22-25." *Paradigms* 2 (1986) 33-38.

Brown, Schuyler. *The Origins of Christianity.* Oxford and New York: Oxford University Press, 1984.

Büchsel, Friedrich, "διακρίνω." *TDNT* 3 (1965) 946-49.

Bultmann, Rudolf. *The History of the Synoptic Tradition.* Translated by John Marsh. New York: Harper and Row, 1963.

——. "πιστεύω." *TDNT* 6 (1968) 174-82, 197-228.

Burkill, T. A. "Anti-Semitism in St. Mark's Gospel." *NovT* 3 (1959) 34-53.

——. "Mark 3:7-12 and the Alleged Dualism in the Evangelist's Miracle Material." *JBL* 87 (1968) 409-17.

——. "The Notion of Miracle with Special Reference to St. Mark's Gospel." *ZNW* 50 (1959) 33-48.

Busemann, Rolf. *Die Jungergemeinde nach Markus 10.* Bonn: Peter Hanstein, 1983.

Butterworth, E. A. S. *The Tree at the Navel of the Earth.* Berlin: Walter de Gruyter, 1970.

Caba, José. *La oración de petición. Estudio exegético sobre los evangelios sinópticos y los escritos joaneos.* AnBib 62. Rome: Biblical Institute Press, 1974.

Canter, H. V. "The Figure ADYNATON in Greek and Latin Poetry." *AJP* 51 (1930) 32–41.

Carrington, Philip. *According to Mark. A Running Commentary on the Oldest Gospel.* Cambridge: Cambridge University Press, 1960.

Chadwick, Henry. "Origen, Celsus, and the Resurrection of the Body." *HTR* 41 (1948) 83–102.

Clark, Kenneth W. "Worship in the Jerusalem Temple After A.D. 70." *NTS* 6 (1960) 269–80.

Clements, R. E. *God and Temple.* Philadelphia: Fortress, 1965.

Cook, John. "A Text Linguistic Approach to the Gospel of Mark." Ph.D. dissertation, Emory University, 1985.

Copleston, Frederick. *A History of Philosophy.* Vol. 1: *Greece and Rome.* Part 2. New revised ed. Garden City, NY: Doubleday, Image Books, 1962.

Corrington, Gail Paterson. "The Divine Man in Hellenistic Popular Religion." Ph.D. dissertation, Drew University, 1983.

Countryman, L. William. "How Many Baskets Full? Mark 8:14–21 and the Value of Miracles in Mark." *CBQ* 47 (1985) 643–55.

Cranfield, C. E. B. "The Cup Metaphor in Mark xiv.36 and Parallels." *ExpTim* 59 (1947–48) 137–38.

———. *The Gospel According to Saint Mark.* Cambridge: Cambridge University Press, 1959.

Daube, David. "A Prayer Pattern in Judaism." *Studia Evangelica,* 539–45. Edited by Kurt Aland et al. Berlin: Akademie, 1959.

Delling, G. "Josephus und das Wunderbare." *NovT* 2 (1958) 291–309.

———. "λαμβάνω." *TDNT* 4 (1967) 5–15.

De Vogel, C. J. *Pythagoras and Early Pythagoreanism.* Assen: Van Gorcum, 1966.

Dibelius, Martin. *James.* Revised by H. Greeven. Translated by M. A. Williams. Hermeneia. Philadelphia: Fortress, 1976.

Dieterich, Albrecht. *Abraxas: Studien zur Religionsgeschichte der spätern Altertums.* Leipzig: Teubner, 1981.

Dietzel, Armin. "Die Gründe der Erhörungsgewissheit nach den Schriften des Neuen Testamentes." Inaugural Dissertation, Johannes Gutenberg Universität, Mainz, 1955.

Dobschütz, Ernst von. "Zur Erzählungskunst des Markus." *ZNW* 27 (1928) 193–98.

Dodd, C. H. *The Parables of the Kingdom.* London: Nisbet, 1935.

Döller, Johannes. *Das Gebet im Alten Testament.* Hildesheim: Gerstenberg, 1974.

Donahue, John R. *Are You the Christ? The Trial Narrative in the Gospel of Mark.* SBLDS 10. Missoula: SBL, 1973.

———. "Introduction: From Passion Traditions to Passion Narrative." *The Passion in Mark,* 1–20. Edited by W. H. Kelber. Philadelphia: Fortress, 1976.

———. "A Neglected Factor in the Theology of Mark." *JBL* 101 (1982) 563–94.

———. "Preaching '85: The Gospel of Mark." *Church* Charter Issue (1985) 10–16.

———. "Temple, Trial, and Royal Christology (Mark 14:53–65)." *The Passion in Mark,* 61–79. Edited by W. H. Kelber. Philadelphia: Fortress, 1976.

———. *The Theology and Setting of Discipleship in the Gospel of Mark.* 1983 Pere Marquette Theology Lecture. Milwaukee, WI: Marquette University Press, 1983.

Dowda, R. E. "The Cleansing of the Temple in the Synoptic Gospels." Ph.D. dissertation, Duke University, 1972.

Dutoit, Ernest. *Le Thème de L'Adynaton dans la Poésie Antique.* Paris: Société d'Edition "Les Belles Lettres," 1936.

Ebeling, Gerhard. "Jesus and Faith." *Word and Faith,* 201–46. Translated by James W. Leitch. Philadelphia: Fortress, 1963.

Eichrodt, Walther. *Theology of the Old Testament.* 2 vols. Translated by J. A. Baker. Philadelphia: Westminster, 1961–67.

Eliade, Mircea. *Patterns in Comparative Religion.* Translated by Rosemary Sheed. Cleveland and New York: World, Meridan, 1963.

Farah, Charles, Jr. "A Critical Analysis: The 'Roots and Fruits' of Faith-Formula Theology." *Pneuma* 3 (1981) 3–21.

Fee, Gordon. "The Gospel of Prosperity—an Alien Gospel." *The Pentecostal Evangel,* June 24, 1979, 4–8.

Finkel, A. "The Prayer of Jesus in Matthew." *Standing Before God.* 131–70. Festschrift for J. Oesterreicher. Edited by A. Finkel and L. Frizzell. New York: Ktav, 1981.

Fiorenza, Elizabeth Schüssler. "Miracles, Mission and Apologetics: An Introduction." *Aspects of Religious Propaganda in Judaism and Early Christianity,* 1–25. Edited by E. S. Fiorenza. Notre Dame: University of Notre Dame Press, 1976.

Fleddermann, H. "And He Wanted to Pass by Them (Mark 6:48c)." *CBQ* 45 (1983) 389–95.

Fridrichsen, Anton. *The Problem of Miracle in Primitive Christianity.* Translated by R. A. Harrisville and J. S. Hanson. Minneapolis: Augsburg, 1972.

Gärtner, Bertil. *The Areopagus Speech and Natural Revelation.* Translated by C. H. King. Uppsala: Gleerup, 1955.

————. *The Temple and the Community in Qumran and the New Testament.* Cambridge: Cambridge University Press, 1965.

Gaston, Lloyd. *No Stone on Another. Studies in the Significance of the Fall of Jerusalem in the Synoptic Gospels.* Leiden: Brill, 1970.

Georgi, Dieter. *Die Gegner des Paulus im 2. Korintherbrief.* WMANT 11. Neukirchen-Vluyn: Neukirchener, 1964.

————. "Socioeconomic Reasons for the 'Divine Man' as a Propagandistic Pattern." *Aspects of Religious Propaganda in Judaism and Early Christianity,* 27–42. Edited by E. S. Fiorenza. Notre Dame: University of Notre Dame Press, 1976.

Gereboff, Joel. *Rabbi Tarfon.* BJS 7. Missoula: Scholars, 1979.

Gerleman, Gillis. *Studies in the Septuagint Book of Job.* Lund: C. W. K. Gleerup, 1946.

Gerstenberger, E. S. and Schrage, W. *Suffering.* Translated by John Steely. Nashville: Abingdon, 1980.

Giesen, H. "Der verdorrte Feigenbaum—Eine symbolische Aussage? Zu Mk 11, 12–14.20f." *BZ* (1976) 95–111.

Glasswell, M. E. "The Use of Miracles in the Markan Gospel." *Miracles,* 149–62. Edited by C. F. D. Moule. London: Mowbray, 1965.

Glöckner, Richard. *Neutestamentliche Wundergeschichten und das Lob der Wundertaten Gottes in den Psalmen.* Mainz: Matthias-Grünewald, 1983.

Gnilka, Joachim. *Das Evangelium nach Markus.* 2 vols. EKKNT 2. Zürich: Benziger, 1978–79.

Goldin, Judah. "The Magic of Magic and Superstition." *Aspects of Religious Propaganda in Judaism and Early Christianity,* 115–47. Edited by E. S. Fiorenza. Notre Dame, University of Notre Dame Press, 1976.

Goulder, M. D. "The Composition of the Lord's Prayer." *JTS* 14 (1963) 32–45.

Grant, Robert M. "The Coming of the Kingdom." *JBL* 67 (1948) 297–303.

————. "Miracle and Mythology." *ZRGG* 4 (1952) 123–33.

————. *Miracle and Natural Law in Graeco-Roman and Early Christian Thought.* Amsterdam: North-Holland, 1952.

Grassi, Joseph. "Abba, Father (Mark 14:36): Another Approach." *JAAR* 50 (1982) 449–58.

Greeven, Heinrich. "εὔχομαι." *TDNT* 2 (1964) 775–84, 801–8.

Grundmann, Walter. "δεῖ." *TDNT* 2 (1964) 21–25.

————. "δύναμαι." *TDNT* 2 (1964) 284–317.

————. *Das Evangelium nach Markus.* 3d ed. Berlin: Evangelische Verlaganstalt, 1965.

Gunkel, Hermann, and Begrich, Joachim. *Einleitung in die Psalmen.* 2d ed. Göttingen: Vandenhoek & Ruprecht, 1966.

Hadas, Moses. *Hellenistic Culture*. Morningside Heights, NY: Columbia University Press, 1959.

Haenchen, Ernst. *The Acts of the Apostles*. Translated by B. Noble, G. Shinn, and H. Anderson. Revised by R. McL. Wilson. Philadelphia: Westminster, 1971.

———. *Der Weg Jesu. Eine Erklärung des Markus-Evangeliums und der kanonischen Parallelen*. Berlin: Alfred Töpelmann, 1966.

Hahn, Ferdinand. "Das Verständnis des Glaubens im Markusevangelium." *Glaube im Neuen Testament*, 43–67. Festschrift für Hermann Binder. Edited by F. Hahn and H. Klein. Neukirchen-Vluyn: Neukirchener, 1972.

Hamman, Adalbert. "La prière crétienne et la prière païenne, formes et différences." *ANRW* 2.23.2 (1980) 1190–1247.

Harrington, Wilfrid. *Mark*. Wilmington, DE: Michael Glazier, 1979.

Harris, O. G. "Prayer in Luke-Acts." Ph.D. dissertation, Vanderbilt University, 1966.

Hayes, John H. *Understanding the Psalms*. Valley Forge: Judson, 1976.

Hays, Richard B. *The Faith of Jesus Christ*. SBLDS 56. Chico: Scholars, 1983.

Heiler, Friedrich. *Prayer*. Translated and edited by Samuel McComb. London: Oxford, 1932.

Heinemann, Joseph. *Prayer in the Talmud*. Berlin: Walter de Gruyter, 1977.

Held, Heinz Joachim. "Matthew as Interpreter of the Miracle Stories." *Tradition and Interpretation in Matthew*, 165–299. By G. Bornkamm, G. Barth, and H. J. Held. Translated by P. Scott. Philadelphia: Westminster, 1963.

Hengel, Martin. *Studies in the Gospel of Mark*. Philadelphia: Fortress, 1985.

Heninger, S. K. *Touches of Sweet Harmony*. San Marino, CA: Huntington Library, 1974.

Herzog, R. *Die Wunderheilungen von Epidauros*. Leipzig: Dieterich, 1931.

Holladay, Carl R. *Theios Anēr in Hellenistic Judaism: A Critique of the Use of This Category in New Testament Christology*. SBLDS 40. Missoula: Scholars, 1977.

Hopfner, T. "Mageia." PW 14/1 (1930) 301–93.

Hull, John M. *Hellenistic Magic and the Synoptic Tradition*. London: SCM, 1974.

James, E. O. *The Tree of Life*. Leiden: Brill, 1966.

Jeremias, J. *The Prayers of Jesus*. Naperville, IL: Allenson, 1967.

Jervell, Jacob. "Der schwache Charismatiker." *Rechtfertigung*, 183–98. Festschrift für Ernst Käsemann zum 70. Geburtstag. Edited by J. Friedrich, W. Pöhlmann and P. Stuhlmacher. Tübingen: Mohr, 1976.

Johnson, Norman B. *Prayer in the Apocrypha and Pseudepigrapha*. Philadelphia: SBL, 1948.

Juel, Donald. *Messiah and Temple. The Trial of Jesus in the Gospel of Mark.* SBLDS 31. Missoula: Scholars, 1977.

Kealy, Sean P. *Mark's Gospel: A History of Its Interpretation.* New York: Paulist, 1982.

Keck, L. E. "Mark 3, 7–12 and Mark's Christology." *JBL* 84 (1965) 341–58.

Kee, Howard Clark. *Community of the New Age.* Philadelphia: Westminster, 1977.

———. *Miracle in the Early Christian World.* New Haven: Yale University Press, 1983.

———. "Self-Definition in the Asclepius Cult." *Self-Definition in the Greco-Roman World,* 118–36. Ed. B. F. Meyer and E. P. Sanders. Philadelphia: Fortress, 1982.

Kelber, Werner H. "The Hour of the Son of Man and the Temptation of the Disciples (Mark 14:32–42)." *The Passion in Mark.* Edited by W. H. Kelber. Philadelphia: Fortress, 1976.

———. *The Kingdom in Mark. A New Place and a New Time.* Philadelphia: Fortress, 1974.

———. *Mark's Story of Jesus.* Philadelphia: Fortress, 1979.

———. *The Oral and the Written Gospel.* Philadelphia: Fortress, 1983.

———. "Redaction Criticism: On the Nature and Exposition of the Gospels." *PRS* 6 (1979) 4–16.

Kennedy, George A. *New Testament Interpretation Through Rhetorical Criticism.* Chapel Hill, NC: University of North Carolina Press, 1984.

Kertelge, Karl. *Die Wunder Jesu im Markusevangelium.* SANT 23. Munich: Kösel, 1970.

Kingsbury, Jack Dean. *The Christology of Mark's Gospel.* Philadelphia: Fortress, 1983.

———. "The 'Divine Man' as the Key to Mark's Christology—The End of an Era?" *Int* 35 (1981) 243–57.

Kio, Stephen Hre. "A Prayer Framework in Mark 11." *BT* 37 (1986) 323–28. See note 1, chapter 2.

Kirchschläger, Walter. "Jesu Gebetsverhalten als Paradigma zu Mk 1, 35." *Kairos* 20 (1978) 303–10.

Kittel, R. "ἀββᾶ." *TDNT* 1 (1964) 5–6.

Klauck, Hans-Joseph. "Die erzählerische Rolle der Junger im Markusevangelium." *NovT* 24 (1982) 1–26.

Koch, Dietrich-Alex. *Die Bedeutung der Wundererzählungen für die Christologie des Markusevangeliums.* BZNW 42. Berlin: Walter de Gruyter, 1975.

Koester, Helmut. "GNOMAI DIAPHOROI: The Origin and Nature of Diversification in the History of Early Christianity." *HTR* 58 (1965) 279–318.

———. "Häretiker im Urchristentum" *RGG* 3 (1959) 17-21.

———. "One Jesus and Four Primitive Gospels." *HTR* 61 (1968) 203-47.

———. "The Structure and Criteria of Early Christian Beliefs." *Trajectories through Early Christianity,* 205-231. By J. M. Robinson and H. Koester. Philadelphia: Fortress, 1971.

Kolenkow, Anitra Bingham. "Beyond Miracles, Suffering and Eschatology." *SBL 1973 Seminar Papers,* 155-202. 2 vols. Edited by G. MacRae. Cambridge, Mass.: SBL, 1973.

———. "A Problem of Power: How Miracle Doers Counter Charges of Magic in the Hellenistic World." *SBL 1976 Seminar Papers,* 105-110. Edited by G. MacRae. Missoula: Scholars, 1976.

Kon, Abraham. *Prayer.* London: Soncino, 1971.

Kuhn, Heinz-Wolfgang. *Ältere Sammlungen im Markusevangelium.* SUNT 8. Göttingen: Vandenhoeck & Ruprecht, 1971.

Kümmel, W. G. *The New Testament: The History of the Investigation of Its Problems.* Translated by S. M. Gilmour and H. C. Kee. Nashville/New York: Abingdon, 1972.

Lagrange, M.-J. *Evangile selon Saint Marc.* Paris: Gabalda, 1966.

Lamarche, Paul. "Les Miracles de Jésus selon Marc." *Les Miracles de Jésus selon le Nouveau Testament,* 213-26. Edited by Xavier Léon-Dufour. Paris: Editions du Seuil, 1977.

Lambrecht, J. "Ware verwantschap en eeuwige zonde. Ontstaan en structuur van Mc.3, 20-35 (III)." *Bijdragen* 29 (1968) 369-93. English abstract: *NTA* 13 (1969) 327-28.

Lane, William L. *The Gospel According to Mark.* Grand Rapids: Eerdmans, 1974.

Lang, F. G. "Sola Gratia im Markusevangelium: Die Soteriologie des Markus nach 9, 14-29 und 10, 17-31." *Rechtfertigung,* 321-337. Festschrift für Ernst Käsemann zum 70. Geburtstag. Edited by J. Friedrich, W. Pöhlmann and P. Stuhlmacher. Tübingen: Mohr, 1976.

Légasse, Simon. "L'Historien en quête de l'événement." *Les Miracles de Jésus selon le Nouveau Testament,* 109-45. Edited by Xavier Léon-Dufour. Paris: Editions du Seuil, 1977.

Lemcio, Eugene E. "The Intention of the Evangelist, Mark." *NTS* 32 (1986) 187-206.

Lenski, R. C. H. *The Interpretation of St. Mark's Gospel.* Minneapolis: Augsburg, 1946.

Lightfoot, R. H. "A Consideration of Three Passages in St. Mark's Gospel." *In Memoriam Ernst Lohmeyer,* 110-15. Edited by Werner Schmauch. Stuttgart: Evangelisches Verlagswerk, 1951.

Lohmeyer, Ernst. *Das Evangelium des Markus.* Göttingen: Vandenhoeck & Ruprecht, 1957.

———. "Our Father": An Introduction to the Lord's Prayer. Translated by John Bowden. New York: Harper and Row, 1965.

Lohse, Eduard. "χειροποίητος." *TDNT* 9 (1974) 436-37.

Long, A. A. *Hellenistic Philosophy.* London: Duckworth, 1974.

Lührmann, Dieter. "Glaube." *RAC* 11 (1981) 47-122.

———. *Glaube im frühen Christentum.* Gütersloh: Mohn, 1976.

Lull, David J. "Interpreting Mark's Story of Jesus' Death: Toward a Theology of Suffering." *SBL 1985 Seminar Papers,* 1-12. Edited by K. Richards. Atlanta: Scholars, 1985.

Luz, Ulrich. "Markusforschung in der Sackgasse." *TLZ* 105 (1980) 641-55.

McCasland, S. V. "Abba, Father," *JBL* 72 (1953) 79-91.

Mack, B. L. and Robbins, V. K. *Patterns of Persuasion in the Gospels.* Sonoma, CA: Polebridge Press, forthcoming.

Mackay, B. S. "Plutarch and the Miraculous." *Miracles,* 93-111. Edited by C. F. D. Moule. London: Mowbray, 1965.

McKelvey, R. J. *The New Temple.* London: Oxford, 1969.

MacRae, George. "Miracle in the Antiquities of Josephus." *Miracles,* 127-47. Edited by C. F. D. Moule. London: Mowbray, 1965.

McVann, Mark E. "Dwelling Among the Tombs: Discourse, Discipleship, and the Gospel of Mark 4:35-5:43." Ph.D. dissertation, Emory University, 1984.

Malbon, Elizabeth Struthers. "Disciples/Crowds/Whoever: Markan Characters and Readers." *NovT* 28 (1986) 104-30.

———. "Fallible Followers: Women and Men in the Gospel of Mark." *Semeia* 28 (1983) 29-48.

———. *Narrative Space and Mythic Meaning in Mark.* San Francisco: Harper and Row, 1986.

———. "ΤΗ ΟΙΚΙΑ ΑΥΤΟΥ: Mark 2.15 in Context." *NTS* 31 (1985) 282-92.

Marchel, W. "Abba, Pater. Oratio Christi et christianorum." *VD* 39 (1961) 240-47.

Marcus, Joel. *The Mystery of the Kingdom of God.* SBLDS 90. Atlanta: Scholars, 1986.

Marrion, Malachy. "Petitionary Prayer in Mark and in the Q Material." S.T.D. dissertation, Catholic University of America, 1974.

Martin, Ralph P. *Mark: Evangelist and Theologian.* Exeter: Paternoster Press, 1972.

Martitz, P. W. von. "υἱός." *TDNT* 8 (1972) 334-40.

Marxsen, Willi. *Der Evangelist Markus.* FRLANT 67. Göttingen: Vandenhoeck & Ruprecht, 1956. ET: *Mark the Evangelist.* Translated by J. Boyce, D. Juel, W. Poehlmann and R. A. Harrisville. Nashville and New York: Abingdon, 1969.

Matera, F. J. "Interpreting Mark—Some Recent Theories of Redaction Criticism." *LS* 2 (1968) 113-31.

Meagher, J. C. *Clumsy Construction in Mark's Gospel.* New York and Toronto: Edwin Mellen, 1979.

Moule, C. F. D. *The Gospel According to Mark.* Cambridge: Cambridge University Press, 1965.

Münderlein, Gerhard. "Die Verfluchung des Feigenbaumes." *NTS* 10 (1963-64) 89-104.

Murphy-O'Connor, Jerome. "Péché et Communauté dans le Nouveau Testament." *RB* 74 (1967) 161-93.

Murray, Gilbert. *Five Stages of Greek Religion.* 3d ed. Garden City, NY: Doubleday, Anchor, 1951.

Neusner, Jacob. "Judaism in a Time of Crisis: Four Responses to the Destruction of the Second Temple." *Judaism* 21 (1972) 313-27.

———. "Map Without Territory: Mishnah's System of Sacrifice and Sanctuary." *HR* 19 (1979) 103-27.

Nineham, D. E. *The Gospel of Saint Mark.* Baltimore: Penguin Books, 1963.

Nock, A. D. *Essays on Religion and the Ancient World.* 2 vols. Edited by Zeph Stewart. Cambridge: Harvard University Press, 1972.

O'Brien, P. T. "Prayer in Luke-Acts." *TynBul* 24 (1973) 111-27.

O'Connor, Edward D. *Faith in the Synoptic Gospels.* Notre Dame: University of Notre Dame Press, 1961.

Oesterreicher, J. "Abba Father! On the Humanity of Jesus." *The Lord's Prayer and the Jewish Liturgy,* 119-38. Edited by J. J. Petuchowski and M. Brocke. London: Burns and Oates, 1978.

Ott, Wilhelm. *Gebet und Heil.* SANT 12. Munich: Kösel, 1965.

Oxford Classical Dictionary, 2d ed. S.v. "Neopythagoreanism." by E. R. Dodds.

Patten, Bebe Rebecca. "The Thaumaturgical Element in the Gospel of Mark." Ph.D. dissertation, Drew University, 1976.

Pease, A. S. M. *Tulli Ciceronis De Divinatione.* Darmstadt: Wissenschaftliche Buchgesellschaft, 1973.

———. *M. Tulli Ciceronis De Natura Deorum.* 2 vols. Darmstadt: Wissenschaftliche Buchgesellschaft, 1968.

———. *Publi Vergili Maronis Aeneidos IV.* Darmstadt: Wissenschaftliche Buchgesellschaft, 1967.

Perrin, Norman. "The Christology of Mark: A Study in Methodology." *JR* 51 (1971) 173-87.

——. "The Creative Use of the Son of Man Traditions by Mark." *USQR* 23 (1967-68) 357-65.

——. *A Modern Pilgrimage in New Testament Christology.* Philadelphia: Fortress, 1974.

——. "The Son of Man in the Synoptic Tradition." *BR* 13 (1968) 3-25.

——. *What Is Redaction Criticism?* Philadelphia: Fortress, 1969.

Pesch, Rudolf. *Das Markusevangelium.* 2 vols. HTKNT 2. Frieburg: Herder, 1976-77.

Pesch, Rudolf, ed. *Das Markus-Evangelium.* Darmstadt: Wissenschaftliche Buchgesellschaft, 1979.

Pettazzoni, Raffaele. "Confession of Sins and the Classics." *HTR* 30 (1937) 1-14.

Quesnell, Quentin. *The Mind of Mark.* Rome: Pontifical Biblical Institute, 1979.

Ramsay, W. M. *The Cities and Bishoprics of Phrygia.* 2 vols. Oxford: Clarendon, 1895.

Remus, Harold. *Pagan-Christian Conflict Over Miracle in the Second Century.* Cambridge, MA: Philadelphia Patristic Foundation, 1983.

Reploh, Karl-Georg. *Markus—Lehrer der Gemeinde.* SBM 9. Stuttgart: Katholische Bibelwerk, 1969.

Rhoads, David. "Narrative Criticism and the Gospel of Mark." *JAAR* 50 (1982) 411- 34.

Rhoads, David and Michie, Donald. *Mark as Story.* Philadelphia: Fortress, 1982.

Riddle, Donald W. "The Martyr Motif in the Gospel According to Mark." *JR* 4 (1924) 397-410.

Robbins, Vernon K. "*Dynamis* and *Sēmeia* in Mark." *BR* 18 (1973) 5-20.

——. "The Healing of Blind Bartimaeus (10:46-52) in the Marcan Theology." *JBL* 92 (1973) 224-43.

——. "Interpreting the Gospel of Mark as a Jewish Document in a Graeco-Roman World." Festschrift for Henry A. Fischel, forthcoming.

——. *Jesus the Teacher. A Socio-Rhetorical Interpretation of Mark.* Philadelphia: Fortress, 1984.

——. "Last Meal: Preparation, Betrayal, and Absence (Mark 14:12-25)." *The Passion in Mark,* 21-40. Edited by W. H. Kelber. Philadelphia: Fortress, 1976.

——. "The Woman Who Touched Jesus' Garment: Socio-Rhetorical Analysis of the Synoptic Accounts." *NTS* 33 (1987) 502-15.

Robinson, D. W. B. " 'Faith of Jesus Christ'—a New Testament Debate." *RTR* 29 (1970) 71-81.

Robinson, James M. "Introduction: The Dismantling and Reassembling of the Categories of New Testament Scholarship." *Trajectories through Early Christianity,* 1–19. By J. M. Robinson and H. Koester. Philadelphia: Fortress, 1971.

———. "Kerygma and History in the New Testament." *The Bible in Modern Scholarship,* 114–50. Edited by J. Philip Hyatt. Nashville: Abingdon, 1965.

Schenk, W. "Tradition und Redaction in der Epileptiker-Perikope Mk 9, 14–29." *ZNW* 63 (1972) 76–94.

Schenke, Ludgar. *Die Wundererzählungen des Markusevangeliums.* Stuttgart: Katholisches Bibelwerk, 1974.

Schierling, Marla J. Selvidge. "Woman, Cult and Miracle Recital: Mark 5:24–34." Ph.D. dissertation, St. Louis University, 1980.

Schlatter, Adolf. *Der Glaube im neuen Testament.* 5th ed. Stuttgart: Calwer, 1963.

———. *Markus, der Evangelist für die Griechen.* Stuttgart: Calwer, 1935.

Schmid, Josef. *The Gospel According to Mark.* RNT. Edited by A. Wikenhauser and O. Kuss. Translated by K. Condon. Staten Island, NY: Mercier Press, 1968.

Schmithals, Walter. *Das Evangelium nach Markus.* 2 vols. Gütersloh: Gütersloher Verlaghaus Mohn, 1979.

———. *Wunder und Glaube. Eine Auslegung von Markus 4,35–6,6a.* BibS(N) 59. Neukirchen-Vluyn: Neukirchener, 1970.

Schoedel, William R. and Malina, Bruce J. "Miracle or Magic?" *RelSRev* 12 (1986) 31–39.

Schreiber, Johannes. "Die Christologie des Markusevangeliums." *ZTK* 58 (1961) 154–83.

———. *Theologie des Vertrauens.* Hamburg: Furche-Verlag, 1967.

Schrenk, Gottlob. "ἱερός." *TDNT* 3 (1965) 221–83.

Schulz, Siegfried. "Die Decke des Moses." *ZNW* 49 (1958) 1–30.

———. *Die Stunde der Botschaft.* Hamburg: Furche-Verlag, 1967.

Schweizer, Eduard. "Anmerkungen zur Theologie des Markus." *Neotestamentica,* 93–104. By E. Schweizer. Zurich and Stuttgart: Zwingli, 1963.

———. *The Good News According to Mark.* Translated by D. Madvig. Atlanta: John Knox, 1970.

———. "Die Kirche als Leib Christi in den paulinischen Antilegomena." *Neotestamentica,* 293–316. By E. Schweizer. Zurich and Stuttgart: Zwingli, 1963.

———. "The Portrayal of the Life of Faith in the Gospel of Mark." *Interpreting the Gospels,* 168–82. Edited by J. L. Mays. Philadelphia: Fortress, 1981.

——. "Die theologische Leistung des Markus." *EvT* 24 (1964) 337–55.

Sevenster, J. N. *Paul and Seneca.* Leiden: Brill, 1961.

Smith, Jonathan Z. "Good News is No News: Aretalogy and Gospel." *Christianity, Judaism and Other Greco-Roman Cults.* Studies for Morton Smith at Sixty. Part 1. *New Testament,* 21–38. Edited by Jacob Neusner. SJLA 12. Leiden: Brill, 1975.

——. *Map Is Not Territory. Studies in the History of Religions.* SJLA 36. Leiden: Brill, 1978.

Smith, Morton. *Clement of Alexandria and a Secret Gospel of Mark.* Cambridge: Harvard University Press, 1973.

——. *Jesus the Magician.* New York: Harper and Row, 1978.

——. "Prolegomena to a Discussion of Aretalogies, Divine Men, the Gospels and Jesus." *JBL* 90 (1971) 174–99.

Stauffer, Ethelbert. *New Testament Theology.* Translated by John Marsh. New York: Macmillan, 1955.

Stein, R. H. "What is *Redaktionsgeschichte?*" *JBL* 88 (1969) 45–56.

Stendahl, Krister. "Prayer and Forgiveness." *SEÅ* 22–23 (1957–58) 75–86.

Stone, Jerry H. "The Gospel of Mark and *Oedipus the King:* Two Tragic Visions." *Soundings* 67 (1984) 55–69.

Strecker, Georg. "Vaterunser und Glaube." *Glaube im Neuen Testament,* 11–28. Festschrift für Hermann Binder. Edited by F. Hahn and H. Klein. Neukirchen-Vluyn: Neukirchener, 1982.

Swete, Henry Barclay. *The Gospel According to St. Mark.* 3d ed. Grand Rapids: Eerdmans, 1956.

——. *An Introduction to the Old Testament in Greek.* 2d ed. Cambridge: Cambridge University Press, 1914.

Tagawa, Kenzo. *Miracles et Evangile.* EHPR 62. Paris: Presses Universitaires de France. 1966.

Talbert, Charles H. "Ancient biography." *Anchor Bible Dictionary.* Edited by D. N. Freedman. Garden City, NY: Doubleday, forthcoming.

——. *Literary Patterns, Theological Themes and the Genre of Luke-Acts.* SBLMS 20. Missoula: Scholars, 1974.

——. "Luke-Acts: A Defense Against Gnosticism." Ph.D. dissertation, Vanderbilt University, 1963.

——. *What Is a Gospel? The Genre of the Canonical Gospels.* Philadelphia: Fortress, 1977.

Tannehill, Robert C. "The Disciples in Mark: The Function of a Narrative Role." *JR* 57 (1977) 386–405.

——. "The Gospel of Mark as Narrative Christology." *Semeia* 16 (1980) 57–95.

Tarn, W. W. *Hellenistic Civilization.* 3d ed. Cleveland: World, 1952.

Taylor, Vincent. *The Gospel According to St. Mark.* London: Macmillan, 1952.

Telford, W. R. *The Barren Temple and the Withered Tree. A Redactioncritical Analysis of the Cursing of the Fig Tree Pericope in Mark's Gospel and its Relation to the Cleansing of the Temple Tradition.* JSNTSup 1. Sheffield: JSOT Press, 1980.

Terrien, Samuel. *The Elusive Presence.* San Francisco: Harper and Row, 1978.

———. "The Omphalos Myth and Hebrew Religion." *VT* 20 (1970) 315-38.

Theissen, Gerd. *The Miracle Stories of the Early Christian Tradition.* Translated by Francis McDonagh. Edited by John Riches. Philadelphia: Fortress, 1983.

Thesleff, Holger. *An Introduction to the Pythagorean Writings of the Hellenistic Period.* Åbo: Åbo Akademie, 1961.

Thomas, Owen C., ed. *God's Activity in the World: The Contemporary Problem.* Chico: Scholars, 1983.

Tiede, David. *The Charismatic Figure as Miracle Worker.* SBLDS 1. Missoula: Scholars, 1972.

Trites, A. A. "The Prayer Motif in Luke-Acts." *Perspectives on Luke-Acts,* 168-86. Edited by Charles H. Talbert. Danville, VA: Baptist Professors of Religion, 1968.

Tyson, Joseph B. "The Blindness of the Disciples in Mark." *JBL* 80 (1961) 261-68.

Urbach, Ephraim E. *The Sages: Their Concepts and Beliefs.* 2 vols. Translated by Israel Abrahams. Jerusalem: Magnes Press, 1975.

van Unnik, Willem Cornelis. " 'Alles is dir Möglich' (Mk 14, 36)." *Verborum Veritas,* 27-36. Festschrift für Gustav Stählin. Edited by O. Böcher and K. Haacker. Wuppertal: Theologischer Verlag Rolf Brockhaus, 1970.

Vriezen, T. C. *An Outline of Old Testament Theology.* Translated by S. Neuijen. Newton, MA: Charles T. Branford, 1958.

Walzer, R. *Galen on Jews and Christians.* London: Oxford University Press, 1949.

Waybright, Gregory. "Discipleship and Possessions in the Gospel of Mark: A Narrative Study." Ph.D. dissertation, Marquette University, 1984.

Weeden, T. J. "The Cross as Power in Weakness (Mark 15:20b-41)." *The Passion in Mark,* 115-34. Edited by W. H. Kelber. Philadelphia: Fortress, 1976.

———. "The Heresy That Necessitated Mark's Gospel." Ph.D. dissertation, Claremont Graduate School, 1964.

———. "The Heresy That Necessitated Mark's Gospel." *ZNW* 59 (1968) 145-58.

———. Letter to Sharyn Dowd. 6 December 1984.

———. *Mark—Traditions in Conflict.* Philadelphia: Fortress, 1971.

Weinrich, Otto. *Gebet und Wunder.* Darmstadt: Wissenschaftliche Buchgesellschaft, 1968.

Wheeler, Samuel Billings. "Prayer and Temple in the Dedication Speech of Solomon, I Kings 8:14–61." Ph.D. dissertation, Columbia University, 1977.

Wilder, Amos Niven. *The Language of the Gospel: Early Christian Rhetoric.* New York: Harper and Row, 1964.

Wrede, William. *Das Messiasgeheimnis in den Evangelien.* 3rd ed. Göttingen: Vandenhoeck & Ruprecht, 1963.

Zeitlin, Solomon. "The Temple and Worship," *JQR* 51 (1961) 209–41.

Zeller, Dieter. "God as Father in the Proclamation and in the Prayer of Jesus." *Standing Before God,* 117–29. Festschrift for J. Oesterreicher. Edited by A. Finkel and L. Frizzell. New York: Ktav, 1981.

———. "Jesus als Mittler des Glaubens nach dem Markusevangelium." *BibLeb* 9 (1968) 278–86.

———. "Wunder und Bekenntnis: zum Sitz im Leben urchristlicher Wundergeschichten." *BZ* 25 (1981) 204–22.

Ziegler, Konrat. "Pythagoras von Rhodos." PW 24/1 (1963) 304–5.

Zmijewski, Joseph. "Der Glaube und seine Macht." *Begenung mit dem Wort,* 81–103. Festschrift für Heinrich Zimmermann. BBB 53. Edited by J. Zmijewski and E. Nellessen. Bonn: Peter Hanstein, 1980.